THE [illegible]

OF

A STONE BIRD

INDENTURE
A JOURNEY OF HOPE

A D MOODLEY

notionpress.com

INDIA • SINGAPORE • MALAYSIA

Notion Press

Old No. 38, New No. 6
McNichols Road, Chetpet
Chennai - 600 031

First Published by Notion Press 2020

ISBN 978-1-64805-728-1

Dedication

This book is dedicated to my grandparents and many like them who settled in foreign countries, resurrecting their lives, religion and the values of an ancient culture.

PREFACE

Since the time the first Indian immigrants arrived in Port Natal to the present day, much has been written or documented about their thoughts, dreams and achievements. Century-old photographs reflect languid faces, but deep in their hearts burnt desires so strong that the great obstacles they faced were simply challenges to overcome. They carved a niche so that their children and the generations that followed could enshrine their legacy, threaded together from fragments of indenture, mythology, disillusionment and dispossession, betrayal and heroism.

Despite starvation, ill-treatment, racial discrimination and a multitude of impediments, our grandparents built a foundation which enabled their descendants to proudly call South Africa 'home'. The immigrants drew their metaphors from nature and dressed their ideas with the richness of their experiences and culture.

The Flight of a Stone Bird is a compilation of the fireside or bedtime tales which were told by our grandfather, Venkatchella Konar. It would be difficult to put into words his feelings in a strange new country, but his comments and actions captured the character of the immigrants and their dedication to their responsibilities. The achievements of the men have used our grandfather's anecdotes to do so – his story being one of the many thousands of threads that have shaped the fabric of our lives.

The period that shaped the lives of the immigrants and their descendants was between the late 1920s and the early 1960s. It was a time when the Indians were wedged between a rock and a hard place. Misconceptions and ill-conceived viewpoints characterised popular sentiment. It was also a time when families shared the experiences etched in their memories, stored up and waiting to be told and each memory possessing lessons unique and powerful, to chart the way forward in their search for an identity.

It was also a time when the stifling rule of law prohibited growth and development. Segregated and grouped, they endured punishing restrictions. Overcoming illiteracy, the immigrants established schools and colleges, developed educationists and fought the lack of employment opportunities by developing businesses. These businesses, in turn, supported community projects, including welfare institutions, religious associations and countless others to secure a better life for all. It was not a miraculous solution, but simply the result of logical decisions taken to overcome adversity.

Notes

In combining the experiences of Venkatchella Konar and other indentured Indians, resemblance to actual events, localities, organisations, or persons, living or dead, is entirely coincidental and beyond the intent of both the author and the publisher. Venkatchella's or any other person's understanding of religious rituals and beliefs is not intended to contradict present-day practices, beliefs or customs.

The location of towns, landmarks, timelines, dates, places and people's names as remembered by Venkatchella Konar, cannot be taken as being entirely correct, as boyhood memories faded over time. In some cases, the actual experiences of other indentured Indians were used to enhance the manuscript.

There are hundreds, or even thousands, of stories about the heart-wrenching experiences of immigrants who left Madras and Calcutta, but I have chosen to tell a story that is very close to my heart. My grandfather undertook a journey and lived his life as it unfolded before him; fortified by faith and nature's plan, he stepped into the unknown. The choices he made and the changes he sought epitomised the character he instilled in his children and their children.

Today the legacies of many like him have left an indelible footprint on South African society. Venkatchella Konar, the young boy who braved the elements, would be proud to know that his descendants excel in the fields of commerce and industry, education, science, the judiciary, medicine, government, finance and entertainment, contributing to a great new democracy.

The Flight of a Stonebird is not meant to cast aspersions on the British people but colonialism itself, as indicted by Florence Nightingale – New York Times 1878.

"There is little to show in the British rule of India that the Government has had any higher idea than that of great returns for small outlays from that distant section of the Empire ... human slavery ... and also whose only result is to make English rule in India a disgrace to civilisation."

VENKATCHELLA KONAR

Acknowledgment

My sincerest gratitude to my wife, Padma, and my children, Evelyn, Donavan, Lyndon and Brandon, who helped me through difficult years.

INTRODUCTION

India is a land of myths and gods. Steeped in history and legends spanning thousands of years and cradled in her history are a million tales to fill an infinite number of pages.

Since the time when the Greco-Romans traded with ancient Southern India, with the seafaring kingdoms of Chola, Pandyan and the Chera dynasties, trading settlements were established which remained long after the fall of the Western Roman Empire and nation after nation enriched themselves with the pickings of an anointed land.

Ships ploughed the rough seas, laden with silk, cotton, figured linens and fine clothing, topaz, glassware, silver and gold plate, spices, wheat, rice and sesame oil, heading northwards to Rome and Gaul. Camel trains passed through the Khyber to Central Asia and others crossed into Persia, Mesopotamia, The Kingdom of Solomon, North Africa and ancient trading posts in the Middle East, China and realms beyond imagination. They also carried with them the essences of language, mathematics, astrology, astronomy and religious beliefs. India's hallowed contribution to antiquity and the modern world resonates within the foundations of many nations.

How much do we know of the history of India? How much do we know of the history of those who left India and stepped onto the shores of remote British colonies? As historians reflect on the India that was, we can reflect on the people we have become.

Driven by circumstance and opportunity, we all try to fulfil the dreams we harbour. So did our forefathers; forced by insurmountable challenges and filled with hope, undaunted and supported by faith, they undertook journeys and set the stage that we are part of today. All were figures in the dawn of a system that would change the character of the colonies of the British Empire.

This story took place during a period of brutality and violence, when indenture (sometimes referred to as 'girmit') prevailed. It was a time of poverty and degradation, of moral disintegration and cultural and social chaos – altogether a dark period, perhaps better left to fade into the more obscure pages of history.

Old beliefs and practices that had fallen away during migration and indenture were later restored in ways which incorporated both the old and the new. This process of retrieval and reconstruction was vital for the immigrant community in Africa, as a tool of survival as well as an instrument of resistance. The world of the indentured labourer was complex, full of turmoil, tension and uncertainty, benevolence, greed and curiosity. Old habits had to be discarded, and unfamiliar challenges faced. New experiences posed problems requiring creative responses. A new vocabulary had to be learnt, unfamiliar geography explored, new difficult terrain mastered, pioneering and pragmatic social relationships established.

The indentured dealt with challenges in their own way, modifying thought and behaviour, incorporating resilient threads from the old and frayed fabric. It was a difficult journey. Many perished along the way, but most survived – and not only survived but conquered the odds and triumphed.

This triumph of the human spirit over the adversities that defined 'girmit' and its legacy might be summed up in the words of Matthew Arnold:

> *"For he pursued a lonely road, His eyes on Nature's plan; Neither made man too much a God, nor God too much a man."*

In the struggle to unshackle their bondage, men and women scratched out niches with bloodied hands to write a chapter of their existence, a shared destiny and a common destination. From the fragments of a common past and a mutual predicament, another bond emerged – the 'brotherhood' of the crossing. Emotional, enduring and powerful, devoid of the vestiges of caste or religion, this bond – which became as intimate as real blood kinship – was cherished by men well into their twilight years as a memory of a shared ordeal and of solidarity against the antagonism and adversities of a hostile new world.

To fully understand the reasons for the emigration of thousands of Indians to remote colonies, we need to journey back in time and search for answers into European colonial history.

The growing humanitarian and liberal sentiments of the Europeans brought about the emancipation of slavery. However, their perceived success rested upon a critical ratio between abundant land and cheap labour, a ratio that slavery had served and which, after abolition, was replaced by a new kind of 'slavery'.

The economies of the colonies centred largely on labour-intensive plantation agriculture, predominantly, the production of sugar, facilitating the global development of British capitalism. Indenture was crucial in enabling the expansion of local colonial economies by cutting costs in the process of capital accumulation.

At about the same time, rural India was undone by increasing British revenue demands. Colonial rule had set a stage to be played out, and the agrarian poor acted their part. The industrial revolution transformed British wants and needs. From an established manufacturing power, India was suddenly downgraded to a mere supplier of raw materials. The intention and effect of this policy were to make India a supplier of crude materials, subservient to the manufacturers of Great Britain. Its task was to feed the British mass-producing industries which were on the rise. Affordable imported products and crafts from India were no longer required.

The introduction of railways and cheap British machine-made goods penetrated the Indian market. Even remote villages felt the effects of Europe's upsurge. Industries that once provided employment to a wide array of people, irrespective of religion or caste considerations, collapsed. Millions of commoners lost their jobs and income. Weavers, spinners, tanners, smelters, smiths, ceramicists and other village artisans were pauperised or forced into the already overcrowded areas of agricultural work where employment was seasonal and wages were at, or even below, subsistence level.

There was no way that the plagued lands could provide all those needy with their daily dose of dahl (chickpeas) and rice. Insufficiency became endemic; emaciated and penniless, many thousands streamed into Madras and Calcutta. Walking and on bullock carts, they chose this option to cheat death. Major famines crushed the colony. Localised famines occurred at least twenty times between 1860 and 1908. Entire villages were deserted as the frequent shortages drove many to leave their homes in search of a promise.

The large number who crossed India, away from starvation's tentacles towards the lands of prosperity, was driven by one goal: a better life. It was an escape from the unending insecurity of life in a country plagued by chronic famine and economic downfall. The British needed cheap labour and the Indians provided it, yet they were disposable cogs in the heartless wheel of a profit-driven plantation system.

Historians argued that "... indentured emigration from India to overseas colonies was a result of rational and deliberate choice on the part of the emigrants, prompted by hopes of bettering their future." Some emphasised that the push factors in India, such as famine, poverty and corruption, drove emigration, yet others regarded opportunities in foreign colonies as pull factors. Most regarded both factors being true, but both British and Indian authorities failed to apply countless policies that they promulgated to the detriment of the emigrants. Inadvertently, the Empire had stumbled on a machine that would satisfy the needs of their economy.

The Establishment of Port Natal on the Trade Route to India

On 25 December 1497, Vasco Da Gama, the Portuguese explorer, found his flotilla of four small ships off the coast of South Africa. He named this stretch of coastline *Terra Natalis* after the birth of Christ. Between 1497 and 1824, Portuguese, British and Dutch trading ships anchored in the safe harbour of Port Natal (originally named *Ponta Pescaria* by the Portuguese surveyor A. Manuel Perestrelo in 1575) to replenish their supplies. No European nation claimed sovereignty over *Terra Natalis* until 1824. The hundreds of ships that used Port Natal were bound for one destination – India.

British Settlement in Port Natal

On 7 August 1824, the British, under Lt James King and Lt Francis George Farewell, concluded negotiations with Shaka, King of the Zulus, for a cession of land which included the bay (Port Natal), and land 10 miles south of the bay, 25 miles north and 100 miles inland. Successive acquisitions extended the colony, notably that of Zululand (the area north of the Tugela River), which was added after the Zulu War of 1879, fought between the Zulus and the British. The land north of the Buffalo River was added in 1902. During the South African war (1899–1902) when the

British fought the Boers (the Afrikaner descendants of the Dutch settlers), the Boer forces invaded Natal, but British defences at Ladysmith halted the advance.

The Start of the Sugar Industry

Edmund Morewood, regarded as the founding father of the sugar industry, brought the first cane plant from Mauritius in 1847. The Milner brothers brought it to Natal on their ship, the Sarah Bell. Morewood later resigned from his position as manager of the Natal Cotton Company on the Umhloti River and concentrated on growing sugar on his own property, Compensation Flats.

The first indentured labourers were sent to Mauritius in 1834. Their horrendous treatment – the oppressive conditions and abuse they suffered – resulted in India's ban of further 'coolie' shipments in 1838, until such time that emigration could be transformed into a regulated system and one secured by legislation. In 1842, India was satisfied with the new policies in place and reopened emigration under proper safeguards.

In 1853, Morewood went to England to acquire improved machinery and started the commercial undertaking of the sugar industry with developments at Umhlali, Tongaat, Umgeni, Umbilo, Isipingo and Umkoomas, creating work for six mills. The first Indian cane was brought in from Coimbatore and planted at Compensation Flats. In 1854 the first sugar was exported, valued at £2.

Indian Immigration

The lush green hills of the coastal belt of Port Natal needed clearing to make way for the sugar plantations. In 1848 it was proposed to use British convicts for this, but the scheme did not get underway. In the same year, the Governor of the Cape made a proposal to bring Indians to Port Natal. The Government of India delayed many proposals for years, but on 7 August 1860, an Act was passed allowing emigration to Port Natal which met the legal conditions stipulated in India.

France allowed Indian immigration into her colonies, when kidnapping had been encouraged until Napoleon III passed a resolution to institute policies for India to provide labour. In 1863 emigration was sanctioned to the Danish colony of St. Croix, followed by the Dutch Colony of Surinam in 1872 and the British Colony of Fiji in 1885. Colonial documents frequently used the term 'coolie', which has disrespectful connotations. The word 'coolie' is a term of disputed origins, which some believe was derived from 'Koli', a tribe in the Gujarat region of India and others maintain it came from the Tamil word 'kuli' meaning, according to the Oxford English Dictionary, payment for occasional work.

Initially, the indentured labourers were collected through the agency of 'Duffadars', 'Sirdars' or 'Jobbers' – terms commonly applied to locally-based agents. This system was later changed due to exposures of corruption, and proper licensed recruitment agencies were established. Records also show that many people were lured into making the trip by strange and deceitful methods; for instance, tales were related of gold dripping from fruit trees. In addition, many Indians were kidnapped and torn away from their families, even their children. Thus, in many cases, compassion fell foul to greed.

Each shipment was supposed to include forty women for every hundred men, but in many cases, they numbered less than twenty-five. On embarkation, the emigrants handed their passes to the master of the vessel and were given fifteen rupees as a gratuity. This rate differed for different colonies. Every fifty persons had to be accompanied by a sirdar (supervisor) who was competent to interpret. Provisions within the Passenger Act required that the ship be seaworthy and properly manned, equipped, fitted and ventilated. The emigration officer would then survey the ship and approve the voyage.

The Protector of Emigrants granted a certificate to the master of the ship. A qualified European or native surgeon-superintendent was appointed to each ship. How much relief these surgeons were able to provide was questionable, considering the number of deaths that occurred on the voyages.

Main Recruitment Areas in India

South India

TAMIL DISTRICTS

A. TRICHINOPOLY
B. MADURA
C. RAMNAD
D. SALEM
E. TANGORE
F. CHINGLEPUT
G. NORTH ARCOT
H. SOUTH ARCOT
I. MALABAR
J. TINNEVELLY

TELGU DISTRICTS

K. VIZGAPATNAM
L. GANJAM
M. EAST GODAVARI
N. WEST GODAVARI
O. GUNTUR
P. NELLORE

North India

HILL 'COOLIE' DISTRICTS

1. SANTAL PARGANAS
2. HAZARIBAGH
3. RANCHI
4. MANBHUM
5. BIRBHUM
6. SINGHBUM
7. PALAMAU

BIHARI DISTRICTS

8. SHAHABAD
9. PATNA
10. GAYA
11. MUZAFFARPUR
12. CHAMPARAN
13. SARAN
14. DARBHANGA
15. MONGHYR

UNITED PROVINCES

16. BALLIA
17. GHAZIPUR
18. AZAMGARH
19. FYZABAD
20. BASTI
21. GONDA
22. GORAKHPUR
23. BANARAS
24. MIRZAPUR
25. JUANPUR

WEST BOMBAY

26. AHMADNAGAR

CALCUTTA

27. TWENTY-FOUR PARGANAS

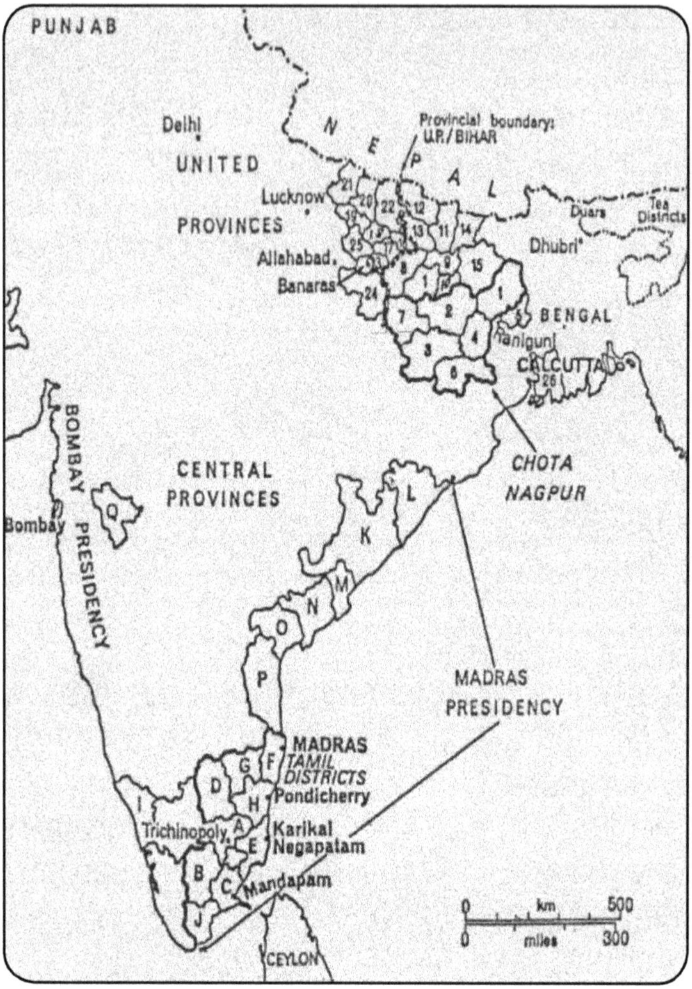

MAP OF INDIA: KEY TO RECRUITMENT DISTRICTS

The first ship leaving India (Madras) was the Truro arriving in Port Natal on 16 November 1860 and the last was the Umlazi on 21 July 1911. In total, 384 vessels were employed, of which 262 sailed from Madras and 122 from Calcutta.

Every indentured labourer was given a number, which was reflected on a shipping list. Number 1 was on the Truro and number 152184 on the Umlazi.

ARTISTS IMPRESSION OF SS TRURO – PADDLE STEAMER 16 NOVEMBER 1860

No immigrants were sent to Port Natal from India between 1867 and 1874, partly because of the economic depression in the latter years of the 1860s and when this lifted, the Government of India put stipulations on some of the conditions under which they lived and worked. This was mainly because in January 1871, returning immigrants on board the Red Riding Hood complained that the £10 bonus promised when they were indentured, was not paid on termination of the contract.

A commission of enquiry was set up under the chairmanship of Attorney General Gallwey. The report of this commission, which became known as the 'Coolie Commission' was published in 1872. Once new regulations were promulgated, the Government of India allowed recruitment to take place again in 1874, continuing without interruption until 1911, when the Umlazi carried the last immigrants.

In 1887, the Natal Government established the Indian Immigration Board. Mr Joseph Baynes was appointed chairman. He made several trips to India to fully understand all aspects of the indenture policies. In 1901 he opposed the two new Acts that were proposed by the government. One was to increase taxation for immigrants and the second was that Indians were not permitted to carry guns. Mr Baynes's objections were defeated and the acts were passed.

The taxation law was introduced in the wake of complaints from white settlers who objected to the continued influx of Indians. This Act would reduce the level of importation and promote re-indenture. The Tax Act penalised Indians after completion of their five-year period of indenture.

Following the Act, more than thirty percent of the Indians who arrived after 1895 returned to India. In addition to the indentured immigrants, a smaller group of Indians, referred to as 'Passenger Indians', came to Port Natal at their own expense. They came from a relatively distinct and comparatively privileged trading community engaged in importing and retailing only for the Indian immigrants, but over time they also competed with the white merchants. This earned them a great deal of hostility.

British colonies that used Indian immigrant labourers were Mauritius, British Guiana, Trinidad, Jamaica, Ceylon and the Federated Malay States, Fiji, St. Kitts, St. Lucia, Granada, Kenya and Uganda. Other European colonies that used Indian labour were St. Croix, Surinam, Reunion and Guadeloupe. Confidential reports reflect 'coolie' trade with Portuguese Macao and with Cuba. In 1820 the first group of Indian immigrants arrived in the US, but not as indentured persons.

In August 1878 Florence Nightingale wrote in the New York Times:

"It is commonly supposed that famines in India are due to the failure of crops and that the crops are cut off by sudden droughts which sweep over the entire country, but when in Southern India alone six million have perished by starvation in one year's failure, the causes must lie deeper beneath the surface … The land of India is not subject to famine the cultivators of the soil are industrious; the native races compare favourably with other races in their capacity to take care of themselves."

Nightingale summed up her accusation of the English nation with just one sentence: *"We do not care for the people of India."* By this, she meant that the British government had put such a burden on the Indian people that they had crushed them.

"For instance, salt, which costs 12s 6d per ton, has a tax of £7 per ton. This restricts the preservation of food and absolutely forbids native manufacturers. Where there is water there is no famine … then again, the native man has no voice, no education, and no method by which his grievances or sufferings reach the public ear. There is little to show in the British rule of India that the Government has had any higher idea than that of great returns for small outlays from that distant section of the Empire … human slavery … and also, whose only result is to make English rule in India a disgrace to civilisation."

1877/8 FAMINE IN INDIA – A PROLONGED LEGACY

Ayepakkum was a small rural village in the district of Tiruvannamalai, South Arcot, within the British-controlled Madras Presidency, which was situated along the eastern seaboard starting at the Telugu district of Ganjam in the north and reaching to the southern district of Tinnevely. Tiruvannamalai was a fertile district, fed by rivers and streams flowing from the mountain ranges of well-watered western regions. Hundreds of villages lay in the foothills of diminishing mountain ranges that snaked eastwards and then flattened into agricultural land. This land provided most of the food requirements of Southern India.

It was predominantly home to descendants of Dravidian clans, once ruled by the Chola (Thangavur), Pallavan (Kancheepuram) and Pandyan (Madura) dynasties. The Chola dynasty was a respected sea power controlling the Indian Ocean. It maintained a navy and its subjects not only conducted trade with lands both sides of India, but they also settled in considerable numbers on foreign soil, including Sumatra, Java, Sri Vijaya (Indonesia), Kamboj (Cambodia), Ceylon and the Maldives, three millennia, before the birth of Christ.

Dotted amongst the flowing fields of green were villages, each one consisting of about twenty to thirty households within earshot of each other. Almost all the villagers were agrarian, cultivating large patches of rice, cotton, interspersed with chickpeas, tomatoes and other vegetables used for their daily diet. Ayepakkum was one such village, nestled between small hills somewhere west of the town of Kanchipuram.

One homestead belonged to the Konar family; father Muthangu, mother Parvati and their two sons, Venkat, aged 16, and his 14-year-old brother, Suryan. Muthangu and Parvati also had two daughters, 12-year-old Saraswathie and Kantha, aged 10. Other households in the village were relatives and friends of both of Venkat's parents. It was a close-knit community, its folk religious and caring. Their main activities were agriculture, farming and rearing of goats to trade. The land was part of their destiny and the link to the land, as it was with almost everyone in pastoral India, bordered on the religious with festivals being held regularly to bless Mother Nature for her bounty.

The houses were made mainly of mud with palm-thatched roofs, neatly tucked amongst the tall coconut palms for shelter from the scorching heat. It was a charming expression of simplicity, a life deeply attuned to nature. Every village had its own temple that housed the village deity, which was kept alive with worship at auspicious hours of the day. Neat courtyards, decorated with powerful cosmological diagrams, invited good fortune and warded off negative influences. This life of reverence to god and the land was about to change drastically.

Between 1876 and 1878, famine struck South India. Millions lost their lives in British-controlled Southern India alone. The monsoons failed and with them, food production. It was a desperate time for all and no less for Venkat and his family. Three young children in the village succumbed to the famine. The consequences drove Venkat to go in search of a sirdar, his first steps on the long journey to Africa.

THE FLIGHT
OF
A STONE BIRD

CHAPTER 1

South Arcot, Tiruvannamalai District, Southern India - 1878

The second Carnatic war between the British East India Company and Nawab, Chanda Sahib, supported by French East India Company was fought in Arcot between September to November 1751.

Village of Ayepakkum (Located west of Kancheepuram)

It was almost two years since the rains wet the lands. Most of South India sweltered under the onslaught of the oppressive heat as it bleached the parched earth. The natural vegetation and the crops planted by the villagers lay withered. Green paddy fields which once rippled in the breeze lay barren as dust storms swept the countryside.

Sitting under the scant shade of their mud huts and drying palm trees, their dehydrated faces creased by the effects of the endless fight for subsistence and survival, villagers watched from the sidelines while nature frothed and fumed as she ravaged the land. Water was their lifeblood, and when there was no water, the flimsy thread that the villagers clung to broke and life itself was threatened.

Sweeping winds fanned wildfires, which, fed by the tinder-dry remnants of rice patches, raced through vast areas of the countryside. Many families stood by helplessly as their homes disappeared beneath raging walls of flame. Efforts of some villages to thwart the fires were feeble in the face of such ruin. It was an attempt, a futile gesture, but one worth trying, to resurrect their belief and find a way out of their ravaged existence. In the aftermath of the devastation, dejected victims consoled one another. Desperate and disillusioned, Venkat left home.

Leaving behind his family, friends, the ravages of drought and the inevitable signs of a prolonged famine, Venkat made his way to Madras from where he would board a ship bound for Port Natal.

A day into the journey, he sat beneath a tree and watched vultures, black spots against a crimson sky circling a dying beast. As the last rays of the sun disappeared, he drank from a tin cup and ate a portion of his rice. Resting his back against the trunk, he recollected the events that had brought him thus far; tired and mentally exhausted, he fell asleep...

The lifeless ground baked as the heat persisted. Vegetation had wasted away and where rivers once flowed, dried mud lay cracked in a mosaic of misshapen squares. Reeds lay tangled in the riverbeds. Monkeys searched for food and fights erupted periodically as they squabbled over meagre pickings.

Village life in India is one of unity: gentle people living in harmony, both with nature and themselves. It is a way of life that has existed for thousands of years and they shared the bounty that nature provided but at that moment, for some reason, the gods had overlooked their plight.

Without the sustenance of the summer rains, the once flourishing fields of golden rice lay parched and bone dry, dust-laden dreams of despair. The mountain peaks of the Western Ghats sourced rivers that flowed eastwards, but they failed to feed the rivers sufficiently to sustain their long journey. The unrelenting heat evaporated both the last remnants of moisture and the hopes of the people who depended on it for their survival.

Wildfires scorched the already barren land and leaping flames, swept by howling winds, reached out to touch the thatched dwellings that exploded into huge cauldrons of fire, everything within consumed. When the dark clouds of smoke lifted, the true picture of the disaster became clear.

"It will be night soon. Let us look for anything we can find to eat," an elder of the village suggested. Girls searched amongst the fire-ravaged homes for pots, utensils or any other items that might have survived the intense heat. Milk from burnt coconuts replaced water to quench their thirst.

Venkat, accompanied by his friend Ramu, went down to the riverbank to see what they could find. All they dug up was a handful of yams. Roasted yams and rice provided some relief from the hunger that was intensified both by the anxiety brought about by the fire and by the futility of their efforts to free themselves from their present predicament. Beneath a cloudless night sky, the stars shone brightly as the villagers huddled together, seeking answers from the divine.

The next morning, Venkat stood beside the ruins of his home. Frustrated by the sheer desperation of the situation, he kicked a bucket that only a day earlier had served their attempts to douse the flames that ravaged homes. Flying embers burnt holes in the only sari his mother owned. Smoke had darkened his mother's face and her tears left tracks in the soot which her younger son tried to wipe away.

Venkat bowed, touched his mother's feet with both hands and promised her that he would find a way to end the pains she endured. It was then that he made up his mind to go to Port Natal, using any means possible to get there.

Turning away from his mother, Venkat left and headed for the village of Ramapakkam and the home of a sirdar. He followed a path that skirted many villages. There were signs that they, too, had suffered a similar fate. Many families had lost valuable livestock; their cows, goats and chickens had either been burnt to death or were too badly injured to save. The villagers told similar stories about the devastating effects of the drought and ferocious winds on their crops. Venkat was puzzled; although the festivals and prayers to appease the gods were performed, the drought persisted.

Venkat expected to reach Ramapakkam just before sunset and he needed to locate the sirdar's residence, meet with him and start the journey back home the same evening. His plan was to obtain the relevant permit from the sirdar, walk to Madras, a port city and a British base on the east coast of India, and then board a ship to any destination, with one goal: a better life for his family. It was a simple plan, yet he realised the dire consequences it would have on his family if not managed well. Pushing aside all thoughts about the impact that his departure would have on his mother, he focussed on visions of flowing rice fields, green pastures, his family dining together, glowing brass lamps in the village temple and of his mother dressed in a beautiful sari welcoming him back home. Satisfied that this could be achieved, he shrugged his shoulders and journeyed on.

Venkat paused at places, taking in the beauty and serenity. It was a world away from his own village. Wells yielded buckets of water and children played games as the sun was about to dip behind the hills. There was joyous laughter all round, a sharp contrast to what he had left behind. Tired, hungry and anxious, Venkat surveyed the scene before him. A narrow, dusty road followed the contour of low hills and wound its way in a northerly direction. A short distance away more homesteads snuggled amongst plantations of bananas. Hoping it was the village of Ramapakkam, he wobbled unsteadily down the winding path and eventually took off his sandals to continue barefoot until he reached the courtyard of a homestead.

A young girl threshed rice on the doorstep of a neat, humble home.

"Is this Ramapakkam?"

"Yes," she nodded.

"Where can I find the sirdar's house?"

She pointed towards a mango grove.

He rested for a while, wiping away the perspiration and the white streaks that marked his face. Thanking the girl, he dragged his weary legs down the footpath to a house that stood in the shade of a mango grove. Weakened by hunger and exhaustion, he called out his presence. There was no answer. He sat on a log and mulled over questions he had to ask and, more importantly, the answers he needed to give to influence the sirdar's decision. As he dozed off, a gentle nudge to his shoulders woke him.

"How can I help you, son?" a middle-aged gentleman asked.

"I'm sorry I fell asleep. It is a long walk from my village," Venkat replied.

They both sat silently for a while. A young girl brought a bowl of fruit and a cup of milk.

In India, respect for parents, elders, customs and other religious belief systems was important; cultural and moral conduct were adhered to and very rarely broken, not because of fear but because of character. Addressing an older person would, therefore, follow such customs and Venkat addressed the sirdar in the way his parents and culture dictated.

"Uncle, my name is Venkatchella Konar, of the Idaiyar caste. Our homestead in Ayepakkum has been destroyed by fire, and I would like to go to Port Natal to find work. I need your help to get a pass to go there."

"You're a long way from home. Why Port Natal?"

"I don't really mind where I go, but friends from nearby villages are working there."

"How old are you?" Sirdar Vella asked.

"Sixteen."

"Aren't you a bit young to make the trip alone?"

"If I go, my father can take care of the family. Everything we owned was burnt by wildfires. My mother is devastated … so I'm here to plead with you for your help."

The sirdar sat for a few minutes, slapping his knee with an open palm, mumbling softly.

A nervous, perspiring Venkat prayed.

"We have no choice but to help you. I will provide you with the papers," the sirdar promised. Reaching out, he took Venkat's right hand and read his palm. Looking intently, the sirdar spoke: "Your path will not be easy. However, the four pillars of our existence will guide you through life. Your commitment and dedication far exceed that of any young man I know. Go with god."

Slowly pulling his hand away, and as politely as possible, he nervously asked, "When can I come for the permit?"

"You can send someone else if you have much to do at home. I need about seven days."

"Thank you," Venkat replied excitedly.

"We have also experienced droughts and shortages of food, but we have been a bit more fortunate than your family because we still have water in our wells," Sirdar Vella said. "You must stay over. It's already too late for you to go back home. We welcome you to our home and offer you a place to stay for the night."

The sirdar got up, threw a white cloth over his shoulder and went to ask his wife to give the visitor food and a cotton sheet.

The moon rose above the trees as Venkat cleaned out his plate. The heat of the day had not yet dissipated; he wiped away perspiration from his forehead, nervous and eager to go back home to make plans for his future. For the remainder of the night he was restless, trying to keep the whining mosquitoes at bay.

The next day, on reaching home when the sun was at its zenith, he called out to his mother. He found her sitting in a corner of the burnt-out remains of a section of their house. It teetered ominously and held in place by a few roof poles that survived the fire. Scorched, sun-beaten palm leaves were thrown over the cross-poles and his mother sat in the scanty shade.

"Do not come near!" she called out.

"Are you … are you alright?" he shouted.

"Yes, I've washed my clothes and I'm waiting for them to dry!"

Venkat sat on a mound of a collapsed wall and pondered his future. Beneath the mound were remnants of his family's possessions.

In the week following his meeting with the sirdar, Venkat kept himself busy, determined to rebuild the house before he leaves. He dug a pond in the moist bed of the dying riverbed. The next morning water filled the deep pond. It took family and friends two days to finish the mud walls, strengthened with thin dried bamboo and compacted by using a small makeshift ram. The day Venkat added the final touches to the roof, Ramu brought him news from the sirdar.

"Thank you for the message, my friend," Venkat said, accepting the note that carried the details of what he was required to do to make the trip.

"No trouble. It's only a short distance from the place I went to."

Mr Vella Chengai had successfully arranged for Venkat to go to Port Natal. He could collect his permit as soon as he had paid the sirdar a £3 fee. Venkat kept secret his intentions from family and friends, apart from Ramu. Weighing the options, mulling over the consequences, he concluded that backing down was not an option, as the indenture would provide the income needed to re-establish family stability. He intended to serve the required contract term in Port Natal and send home the money.

"Difficult as it would be, it seems your trip been decided already?"

"Yes Ramu, my friend, my brother, I'm happy with the choice I made, but where will I get the money Uncle Vella said I would need?"

"You have a bigger problem than getting hold of £3. How will Mother feel when you disappear? And don't worry, we will collect money to make up £3 and a little more," Ramu promised.

"Thank you, friend. It is a trip for my family and all those I regard as being family and when I return, we will lead the lives we always spoke of. It wasn't an easy decision; if I leave, I will not know how the problems will affect everyone and if I do not go, then we have no means of earning an income to rebuild our lives," Venkat summed up.

"We have survived the famine by the grace of god, and we shall survive the next few years without you," said Ramu, getting up and dusting the seat of his pants.

"My greatest fear is for my mother."

"None of us will really be able to know or understand how Mother will feel when you leave. We will do our best and be supportive," Ramu promised.

"I shall write a letter explaining what I intend to do, and you must give it to my mother ten days after I leave home."

"Ten days. Why?" Ramu questioned.

"I'll need at least two days to get to Madras. I'll spend another few days at the depot and then board the ship. I think I'll tell my parents I'll be at the mountain pastures with the herd."

"A good excuse, I think," Ramu considered.

CHAPTER 2

Ayepakkum

A day before his departure, the well-laid plan was set in motion. Five village boys huddled together for a short prayer, then Ramu and three of them left with the combined herds of the village – the first part of the plan. The second part of the plan was for Venkat to leave before sunrise the next morning to separate the herd and take some to the pastures close to the remote village of Surinder.

The rest of the afternoon, Venkat spent his time ensuring that urgent repairs to the house would be looked at and if possible, completed before he left. Although the walls and roof were rebuilt, the house still lacked windows and doors. So, he made frames of thin bamboo poles of the required sizes, covered them with sacking and, threading an awl with fibrous string, stitched the coarse material to the frames. He designed hinges from leather straps, and then hung the windows and doors with the help of his father.

"Anything wrong, son?"

"Why?" Venkat asked, surprised.

"You seem to be rather preoccupied with repairs to the house. You have not taken the herds out yet."

"Ramu has left with the goats. I'm joining him in the morning, so I have time to finish the house because I may be away for a few days. I also think that we have some goats which we can sell off," he answered his father while testing the hinges of the door. Satisfied with his workmanship, Venkat joined his mother, chatting for a while before he disappeared into a palm bush.

Hidden between the sloping branches of the young palm trees were his clothes and other items gathered from friends. Taking a small cloth bag, Venkat lined it with husk, placed an oil lamp and a chunk of marble inside, shoved more husks into the bag, knotted it and pushed it into a bigger cotton sack filled with shirts, pants and small sheets of cotton. In a second bag, he gently set small utensils, fruit, a small parcel of boiled rice and water to last him for part of his journey. It was anyone's guess how he would overcome hunger thereafter. He was ready just as dusk set in. He walked back home and joined his father, who was resting in the front yard. They talked about their future and aspects of their lives that needed changing.

Venkat's sister, Saraswathie, brought a pot of tea and a reed mat which Venkat unrolled and stretched out onto. The evening had cooled down considerably and a breeze had picked up. His father joined him on the mat. Venkat would later cherish the time they spent together, because their conversations held subtle details of life's lessons, and it seemed as if his father was mysteriously aware of the impending parting. Sleep was inevitable and when he woke up, he was alone.

The moon shone brightly. Looking up, he estimated that sunrise would be in another four hours. Venkat entered the temple and lit three of the seven lamps, knelt on the cold floor and prayed as the benevolent face of the deity Luxmi shone in the dull light. Walking out backwards, he gently touched the bell that hung from a rafter. Looking up at the moon once more, he assured himself that it was time. Leaving the temple, Venkat sat on the steps of the front door and reminisced. Memories of the village, family and friends, joyous moments and difficult times exhausted his already overwhelmed mind. Satisfied that he had made the right decision, he walked around the homestead one final time and, on entering the house, walked to where his mother slept. The smell of fresh mud still hung heavily in the air.

Sitting in the dark room, awash with lingering doubt and emotionally in limbo. Although it was dark, he knew perfectly well how his mother always slept, lying on a reed mat placed on the hard mud floor, her face resting on her palm and her other hand tucked under her chin. On balmy nights, perspiration dotted her forehead. Accustomed to the darkness, sitting next to his mother, he prayed. Leaning forward, he pulled the thin cotton sheet over his mother, silently promising to return, bringing with him the means to improve their lives. Stepping into the next room, he uttered a short prayer and knelt next to Saraswathie. The glow of the moon filtered through the holes in the sack window. Nudging her awake, he whispered the plan that he and Ramu had devised and kissed her on her forehead. Leaving the house, picking up his bags, he began his quest.

Venkat looked over his shoulder once more, as the moon began to dip below the roof of his house; sighed heavily as the enormity of this undertaking struck him. He had an overpowering urge to go back, and after taking a few steps, realising his weakness, he turned around and ran for a few hundred yards away from the house; now a silhouette against the light cast by the moon. Breathless, but now relieved that the bond that tethered him to his family and friends was finally broken, all thoughts of turning back became as remote as his intended destination.

Venkat reached Ramapakkam just as the sun reached its nine o'clock position.

"You're early," the sirdar said.

"I'm in a hurry to get started."

The sirdar welcomed Venkat into his house, offering him a cup of milk and gesturing to a plate of pancakes on the table.

"I was expecting you, do you see? Let us first eat and then talk about your trip."

Once they had eaten, they discussed matters about indenture and its processes.

"I have written this letter for the official in Madras. Give it to him with the permit and do not open the pouch. You're a boy with the fire of a man. I wish you well," he told Venkat as he handed over the cotton pouch containing the permit and the letter.

Thanking him, Venkat gave him the £3. Threading his hand through the loops of the bags, he slung them onto his shoulder and adjusted the straps as it settled on his back.

"Here, take these sandals. You will need them for your walk," Sirdar Vella said as he handed Venkat two new pairs of handmade leather-strap sandals, strung together. He gratefully accepted his gift, threw them over his shoulder too, and set off on his journey.

The road to Madras was dusty and energy-sapping, causing Venkat to feel as if he was paying penance for not informing his family about the trip. Soaking up the punishment dealt by the oppressive heat, he covered his head with a cotton cloth and counted his steps.

He passed drivers of ox-drawn carts sitting in patches of shade, the beasts chewing cud as they waited for the heat of the afternoon sun to abate. Venkat had short conversations with equally exhausted boys, offering fruit from his bag. In return, one driver shared a meal with him and gave him a ride to the next village.

"Where are you sleeping tonight?"

"I will find a place somewhere."

"Take this mat; you will need it." The driver tossed the mat to him.

Thanking the driver, Venkat slid off the cart and pressed on doggedly. Sirdar Vella's instructions had been clear; he must be in Madras by the third morning and, if he's accepted, the next part of his journey would commence in a week's time.

The sun began to fade as he nibbled on the crusty food he had brought. Reaching into the sack, Venkat eased out the tiffin and swallowed several mouthfuls of rice. He sipped water to wet the dryness in his mouth and throat. Thirst quenched, he placed the bag at the foot of the tree, unfolded the reed mat, rested his back against the tree trunk, brought up his knees close to his chin, shut his eyes and tried not to fall asleep. His tired body couldn't resist the inevitable, and from deep within, serene music lulled him to sleep.

A bullock cart rattled past, startling him, bringing him back to the present and the foreboding challenge ahead of him. Realising his stupidity for losing many hours, he hurriedly got up, swept his possessions together and continued. The dusty road was lit white by a full moon and millions of stars. "It is a good sign," he mumbled.

A few hours before sunrise on the third morning, Venkat, numbed by exhaustion, reached his destination. Sitting against a damp, moss-covered wall, he waited for the gates to open. He was one of many hundreds waiting for the promise of a better life. It was this indelible picture that would fortify his resolve in later years. Thousands waited, voiceless and anxious, a future once again in the hands of colonialists and a fate lacking compassion.

Jostling groups of people, eager to forsake the land of their birth, crowded the entrance, pushing, shouting and pressing measly possessions through unhinged, crumbling gates. Guards armed with long bamboo sticks freely whacked men, women and children who they felt needed to follow orders.

Against this backdrop, Venkat waited patiently. Sapped of energy, hungry and weary from the walk, he endured the melee. It was a few hours wait before he entered the recruitment centre; his frayed pants and shirt tore in the scrimmage. A giant of a man, his blue eyes piercing and his brown beard covering most of his face, jerked the letter from the pouch.

"How old are you?" a sirdar translated.

"Sixteen," he replied, petrified and weak.

Shoving the pouch into his pocket, the man directed Venkat to the surgeon's tent.

"After the medical go to the row of tables there," a sirdar instructed.

One great hurdle awaited Venkat. Sirdar Vella had stressed the importance of the surgeon's medical examination.

"If you fail the medical examination, you will not get a girmit," had said Sirdar Vella, adding a damper on Venkat's enthusiasm as he nervously waited for an agonizingly long time. However, he was examined, passed fit and was declared that he was 5ft.3 inches in height and had a mole on his left shoulder.

It seemed an eternity before he was accepted to serve an indenture in Port Natal. Flooded with relief, he sighed. He was able to answer the questions – inaudible at times – under the din of misunderstood dialects and languages, compounded by caste complexities.

It was almost late afternoon when Venkat stepped out of the building. Overcome with relief, he searched for a quiet spot, knelt, raised his hands in prayer and thanked god for the intervention.

When he opened his eyes, it was to the sight of his equally exhausted family facing him. Petrified, he picked up his possessions and faltered as he searched for a valid explanation.

"How did you find out?"

"Sirdar Vella brought gifts for your mother and sisters. He also gave us three pounds and told us about your trip."

"I shall thank him someday," said Venkat, who, although looked devastated, was relieved.

Small groups gathered as the night closed in and for Venkat, it was a moment of joy and relief on the one hand and one of great sadness on the other. Confronted by his parents, his mind racing, he tried to explain his actions.

Venkat outlined the details of his indenture, and it was agreed that they would spend the night together.

Finding a sheltered spot behind a cargo shed, shielded from the wind that blew in from the bay, they planned to settle for the night. However, it was not to be. As the night wore on, other wouldbe emigrants were drawn to the inviting fire. Wide-eyed and nervous, each face was a story waiting to be told. Every story was one of sadness and human tragedy, of starvation and a search for dignity and a life worth living.

Venkat took his turn. In the glow of the flickering embers, he spoke of the drought and the fires that ravaged his district and he introduced his family to the crowd.

Muthangu, Venkat's father, got up, adjusted his white turban, cleared his throat and thanked the crowd for allowing him to say a few words. Holding his son's hand, he spoke.

"I am here today saddened by the fact that a son is embarking on a journey and taking on the responsibility of a father. It also saddens me that the land he will go to crosses not only an ocean but our own imagination and the dreams that we carried for our children. We may have amongst us those who have been to the place where some of you will go to. We must all respect their knowledge and let's pray that their guidance will benefit those who listen to them."

Venkat was urged by his father to say a few words. A nervous Venkat, after a while said, "My father has for years been burdened with the responsibility for the family and he has endured much more than he can. I was once told that god does not give you a yoke that is heavier than what you can carry. However, my father has and for that reason, I, from now on, will happily carry the yoke for my family. I shall become the man my father was, and I will succeed. Thank you."

Guru Sundrum, who just joined the crowd with a group of people, stood amongst them. The rising flames reflected off his long white cotton shirt.

Introducing himself, he spoke with tranquil fluidity and carried an aura of calm authority. Even the most exhausted person could not wait for him to speak.

"Many of us believe that we are bound by destiny. Whether that is true, we must find answers by ourselves. Unfortunately, we leave our land behind in search of all that our Mother has provided for us for thousands of years. Yet, here we are today, unhappily gathered, waiting to go on a journey which will give the very people who tear the world apart for power a way to increase their wealth. We shall do what is necessary. Fathers, brothers and sisters, sons and daughters, mothers and children, everyone we leave behind and those who are here are making sacrifices for the simplest of our needs – to be free, to care, to have food and dreams for our children. The life that we will lead in a new country will be difficult and painful."

"Our brother Rathna would like to say a few words, as well," Guru Sundrum told the sombre crowd.

"Soon we will reach a place we will call home for as long as we live there and must bless the land with our prayers as she shares with us all that we need. There are three important actions that define who we are; those are, having faith, giving a person light to remove darkness and sharing bread with those who are hungry. If we do not fight for each other, we lose our humanity…"

"Stitch by stitch we will thread together our future. When you are planning your future or when you are faced with problems, don't scatter your thoughts onto many ideas in trying to find solutions. Get help from older people because they have the wisdom to know differences and how to manage the problems or successes. We need to protect ourselves because the system does not. I thank Guru Sundrum for his words of wisdom and thank you for listening to me."

The darkness accentuated the silence. The fire crackled and sparks pierced the darkness. Guru Sundrum continued, "I would now introduce to you all, Sushila and her daughter Victoria. I shall ask her to tell her own life story, a story that we must take as if our own, as we are all one."

A young mother walked over to where Guru Sundrum was standing, accompanied by her daughter. In the dim light, their European parentage was quite evident. Hushed whispers rose from the crowd. The daughter spoke in Tamil.

"My name is Victoria Payton. My mother, Sushila, and I also seek a new life in a new land. It will be a journey to find solutions to our own problems. For many years we laughed and played together as one, all children of Mother India. It was joyous. We are no different; we pray to our gods just as you do. However, as we grew older, our life began to change. My mother, being Franco-Indian and my father British, we were also exposed to part of the English way of life. All parents provide for their children and we live as they want us to. Unfortunately, it brought us pain and we missed the fun of being children.

"I share two worlds, both British and Indian, and it brings us into conflict with the problems from which our people now suffer. I was not responsible for being who I am, nor is my mother as the universe has its own set of plans. We sympathise with all who are here for the wrongs of those who prey upon our poor and voiceless people.

"My father, a British Army Officer, does his best to change the way our people are treated, but one voice against an ocean of rules is a challenge too big. I think he also suffers from being my father. I shall live with the pain, but it will be my life's work to bring relief to as many as I can. However, my mother and I join you on this journey and hope you can forgive us as we are also now trying to build ourselves a new life. Within this rationality, within this complexity, my mother and I believe that there can be found reason for hope. Hope, that we can reclaim the life we once lived; hope that we can join in a common cause for improving our lives; hope that we can extend our hand, and our good faith, mostly for the benefit of our people. We thank you and god bless you all."

"Victoria, you will make Port Natal a better place for all," Guru thanked her and continued, "Finally, all of us know what the people of India face. Historically, many outsiders ruled our land and even now our leaders place their trust in god. Sadly, it is easier to perish in a world we understand than in one which makes a mockery of who we are. Those who passed on have left behind a legacy of the people we were and hopefully, we must keep them as lessons for the future. The story of our land will be told and retold many times over but remember, let that not hinder progress and let us not dislike the British people themselves as they are characters caught in between their kingdom and us. Till the ropes that tie us down breaks, we must live, pray and be joyous as we have each other. Thank you and god bless."

Silence and darkness closed in as the flame flickered its last breath just as the Guru finished reciting a prayer and thanked the crowd. Very few slept for the rest of the night.

The peace of a balmy Madras morning arrived with the sunbeams breaking through the trees. Small groups loitering around the emigration depot lazily began to assemble at the iron gates. Families and friends burdened by the weight of separation, emotional, spent and tearful were now forced to say their last farewell.

Young Venkat, nervous and hesitant, would then join hundreds of emigrants to spend time at the holding depot before departing on voyages that would break the emotional family bond that had stood firm against the adversities thrown by man and nature. Every step he took was filled with fear, not so much for the unknown in a new land but for his parents and their ability to survive in the old one.

Muthangu held his son's hands in his own and recited a prayer. In those few moments, Venkat was aware of the torment that his father endured. It was the first time he saw tears rolling down his father's face as he embraced him goodbye. It was strange to see his father like that as he had always fought the elements that threatened his family and never yielded to emotional weakness. Yet there he stood, silent and at a complete loss for words.

At first, the idea of seeking employment in a foreign land and providing income for his family had seemed both an adventure and a necessity, but at that moment he stood on the edge of a precipice.

Looking back at his mother, her face etched with sadness, shoulders drooping and body limp, barely able to stand. Venkat hoped that she would see this journey was a way out from the drudgery of poverty, turning to his mother, holding her close, knelt, touched her feet, getting up, brought his hands together in prayer. Wiping away her tears, he walked through the gates, leaving behind his entire past. Her tear-filled eyes were a sight that would remain as a memory, never to be forgotten.

The familiar vanished beyond the lofty walls that surrounded the depot. Inside the packed barracks was an air of incarceration – a picture of plantation life. The migrant-to-be was left surrounded by a shipload of strangers, soaking in new and strange experiences while feeling a sense of fear and alienation far more frightening than anything he had imagined.

Yet, Venkat found solace amidst the mayhem; armed with the contract, he was a transient waiting to board, driven by youthful optimism and with a past soon to vanish beyond recall.

In the middle of the monotony of depot life, which was typified by unhygienic conditions and scant food rations, lived men caged between rhetoric and the reality of contractual obligations; along with them, mothers with children, widows and single mothers banished by their in-laws – the products of dowry customs – soon to be cast adrift on an uncompromising ocean to await salvation.

For the thousands who would embark in either Madras or Calcutta, every crossing would be a voyage of emancipation. Sincere friendships and new bonds developed between the emigrants, such as the one between Guru Sundrum and Venkat. Young, alone and vulnerable amid a rolling crowd of strange and anxious faces, he needed counsel, and the guru provided it. He was a man of great knowledge, religious, charismatic and compelling, providing the young man with a sense of belonging. Guru Sundrum would become the surrogate father upon whose shoulders the boy would rest his entire future.

Excitement grew with the news that the Dunphaile Castle would be sailing from Madras around the fifteenth of March 1878 and that all those in the depot were bound for Port Natal. When the day finally arrived, all the emigrants were cleaned, inspected and numbered with a tin disc hung around the neck.

They boarded the ship in parties of six at a time: single women first, followed by married people with children, and finally the bachelors. Most were pleased and amused by the novel experience. Venkat looked back at the pier, but his family was nowhere to be seen. Guru touched him on his shoulder and reassured him, "They will always be with you and you with them."

CHAPTER 3

Some women, decked out in their brightest beads and ornaments, wept and wailed as the reality of the parting dawned on them, but calm soon returned as the ship chugged out to the open sea and duties were assigned. Some of the chores were sweeping the deck, cleaning toilets, washing clothes and utensils and preparing food.

The voyage itself was traumatic for many, as the majority has not seen the sea before. In the crowded confines of the ship's cabins, old rituals and ways of doing things could no longer be sustained. People ate, cleaned, washed and played games together, bound by a common goal. It was also a concentration of massive social transformation. Men and women of different ages, often speaking a variety of equally incomprehensible dialects and with contrasting expectations of life, met and mingled. Out of that enforced interaction in the confined and constricting space emerged a new culture. In this new environment, people's old habits were buried by the new set of rules forced upon them.

Fairly calm seas along the Coromandel Coast made the first few days unexpectedly pleasant. Most of the time, Venkat could be found outside the claustrophobic cabin where he spent many daylight hours looking out towards his beloved homeland as it gradually disappeared. Even at night, he slept outside the cabin or on deck. Some evenings Victoria joined him. Encouraged by her mother, they became close friends, sharing their experiences, hopes and dreams.

In the beginning, their friendship examined their past and dwelt on the present. Later it grew to an extent where both shared a bond so strong, honest and innocent that it overcame the challenges of suspicion, guilt and taboos. Victoria gave Venkat a platform that stood him in good stead for the remainder of their friendship and shaped his life in a turbulent new world. For Victoria, it was a friendship that chased away the ghosts that haunted her for being of mixed parentage. If that friendship failed to withstand the inflexibility of social paradigm, a new bridge would have to be built. Venkat knew theirs was a friendship with lessons for them both, swayed by the nuances and the mysteries of human co-existence.

Passengers who had made this trip in the past were in better shape and paid no heed to the creaks and groans or the gentle swaying as the ship rode the neverending swells and troughs. From the second week onwards, the once-calm seas changed; the waves were taller, and winds grew in strength. Many women, children and even Venkat endured bouts of nausea, seasickness and diarrhoea.

Venkat spent his mornings washing the forward deck. It kept him away from the cabin and the rank odours inside. Despite the taunts from the officers, which he tolerated grudgingly, he completed his job to the satisfaction of the surgeon-superintendent.

Guru Sundrum's morning and evening meditation sessions, once conducted indoors, were now held on deck to the amusement of some of the officers. To them, it was a pagan act that prompted derogatory taunts and jibes against the group. Guru complained to the Protector of Emigrants, but as he wasn't an Indian national, he sided with his employers.

Onboard life was barren, brightened only by the three meagre meals a day. Individuality almost ceased to exist; uniformity bloomed as caste and custom were left behind in the motherland. Every Indian ate the same, experienced the same and wore the standard outfit. Without exception, they were serfs subjected to a shared regimen of waves and weather and the authority of the surgeon-superintendent. Together they faced the fatality of cholera, fever and the ferocity of seas and storms.

Among the passengers were widows with children, young ladies with remarkable courage and self-respect, and on these voyages, new relationships blossomed. Some of the females accepted the proposals of men, afraid to face the new world alone, while older passengers scorned illicit liaisons. Squabbles broke out between would-be suitors, as men far outnumbered the few women on board.

In tiny cabins tempers frayed and arguments flared up. Guru Sundrum, aided by reprimands from the officers, quelled scuffles. Dingy, rancid, smelly and unhygienic conditions gave rise to a multitude of illnesses. Inadequate diet and congested living quarters aggravated the spread of diseases. The surgeon-superintendent had his hands full as a shortage of medicines compounded the risk of heart-rending infant suffering.

A month into the voyage, a mother and her six-year-old child died of cholera. The next morning at sunrise, their bodies, wrapped in white sheets, slipped beneath the waves as the board tilted and touched the surface of the water. The woman's surviving eight-year-old son clutched Guru Sundrum's hand as they walked back to the lower deck.

"We will have many more deaths before we reach land," Guru told the people sitting in their stuffy cabin.

"Guru, how can we prevent it?"

"We need to be clean, we need to keep the cabin clean and pray that the others do the same."

Venkat stepped out of the cabin, saddened by the tragedy. He sat depressed, took the lump of marble from his cloth bag and filed away at it. A winged creature started to take shape. Venkat missed the warm embrace of his mother. Carrying in his heart the love for his family, he was now creating a make-believe world, fortified by a sister in Victoria, a mother in Sushila and a father figure in Guru Sundrum. This family helped him to shed the sadness of being separated from his real family and to face the fact that his life was destined to change irrevocably.

"When will the carving be finished?" Guru asked, startling Venkat and Victoria.

"I'm not sure."

"Why the sadness?"

"Guru, I'm in your hands, in god's hand. I know very few people on the ship, nor their god or their language, yet we're all sailing to a new destination without knowing how to build a new life for our families."

"All the rivers lead to one big ocean of faith. Do not be afraid," Guru promised.

It was a difficult trip for Venkat, for his young mind was overrun by trepidation, yet he felt proud that he would contribute to a better future for his family. His thoughts kept returning to the comforts of home and the closeness of his family. When he questioned himself – whether he made the right decision – he found solace in his father's parting words. However, after listening to Guru Sundrum, he found himself dreadfully confused as his father's words were now challenged by the wisdom he found in Guru's teachings.

"Guru, I need an opinion, but I'm afraid to ask the question."

"You may be foolish not to ask it."

"In the dead of night when the moon is up, I'm drawn to the light of the moon, the stars and the heavens beyond. When nature herself falls silent, looking up, I find the moon most compelling, and in her light, I think I see signs of things to come," Venkat grinned sheepishly.

"You have a gift," Guru replied.

"I hope it helps me find solutions to the problems back home."

Guru Sundrum turned around to ask Victoria, "Can you teach him your language?"

"My language is Tamil," Victoria said, cheerfully.

"No, please help him with English."

"I'd love to. My dear friend will be my first student. Lessons start tomorrow."

"I shall leave you two children now," Guru Sundrum said.

"We have no books or pens," Victoria realised.

The lack of pencil and paper was creatively solved by Venkat who, during his chore of washing the decks, selected ideal spots to spread a thin film of soapy liquid, and then allowed it to dry. As pencils, he found pieces of wood which he shaped into pointed sticks. So, equipped with writing tools and the deck as a board, lessons commenced in earnest. It became the primary activity that consumed Victoria and Venkat's time on the hitherto dull voyage.

Six weeks into the voyage, tragedy struck the Dunphaile Castle. Two men and a child died, and a young woman jumped ship unable to face the world; so humiliated was she after having been sexually assaulted. The perpetrator, a member of the ship's crew, was identified and the captain recorded the incident to be reported to the authorities when they made landfall.

In the ensuing days, Victoria spent more time with Venkat as their friendship gradually overcame the barriers that existed between her and the society she grew up in. As 'Passenger Indians' Victoria and her mother were allowed more room, a better cabin and even dinners with the captain, but Victoria preferred spending time in the lower decks as she was with the very people she loved very much. She was beginning to enjoy their innocence and their aspirations. The deaths and the callous rape of the young girl shocked Victoria. Her sheltered life had shielded her from the news of the ongoing deaths of many thousands in villages close to their home. The sight of lifeless bodies struck home the reality of what India had become.

"Your life and that of the poor means very little," Victoria complained to Venkat during a visit to the lower deck. Finding him at his usual spot, she tucked in next to him under a makeshift shelter.

Soft rain and salt spray wet the sacking and droplets seeped through the tiny pores. It provided relief from the clammy, pungent and overcrowded cabins.

"I am happy to be with you," Victoria said.

"I am happy as well."

"Still, I can feel the tragic life you and your family went through."

"Princess, the lives we lead are very different. Yet, over time we are conditioned to what is given. I saw the death of the people shocked you to tears. I'm saddened by another life lost too, but I'm also aware that there remain other battles to fight and lives to save."

Sitting beneath the porous sacking, they were wet. Water dripped through, soaking them. They sat shoulder to shoulder, and it was a special moment for Venkat, as a lack of water was the deciding factor for him to undertake the journey. At that moment he enjoyed every minute of the torrent.

"Do you want to go in, Princess?"

"No, I love being out in the rain. Let us talk about happier stories," Victoria suggested.

"Princess, though you explained the reasons for being here already, is there more to tell?"

"I wish I were a princess. I would change the world. Tell me first, what do think about us searching for a fresh start?"

"To leave a life of comfort, food, clean water, good clothes and rickshaw transport is foolish. Yet, you are here, forced by events that you had very little to do with. However, it pains me to see you and your mother with us, the destitute and the poor and those who society willingly tends to forget," Venkat replied.

"Let's not judge who we are. The pendulum of life swings."

"Princess, there is so much to tell, and the most difficult to explain are the emotions and sense of failure that my parents must have felt when they found me at the emigration depot. The disappointment of them finding me was torture."

"It must have been unpleasant."

"Yes, it was. Tears, imminent separation and the sheer weight of not knowing whether I will succeed saddled my thoughts and being the eldest son, I now have the greatest pleasure to carry the hope of a better future for my family and friends."

"Yes, when you knelt before your family so much was said without anyone talking. My mother shed a tear for you."

Surprised, Venkat replied, "I'm embarrassed that you saw my weakness. Well, we lost everything and yet it was insignificant compared to the pain I felt when I left without getting the blessing of my parents. I made this decision to shield them from the very sadness they felt when they found me that afternoon. I walked for two days and most of one night to get here on time and all through the journey, my dreams of the future and its rewards carried me down valleys and over hills, crossing dry riverbeds and burnt villages. The sight of broken fathers and mothers and starving children drove me. Hunger and thirst were my constant companion."

"I would like to share my experiences as well," Victoria suggested.

"Only if you want to."

"I am fine. You already know what my father's responsibilities were. So, how do you think the people reacted? It was their harvest and they had every right to rebel. Later we felt the wrath of the people. We were estranged from our own friends and the villagers whom we loved so much. My father went to Britain, taking my brother with him to enrol him in school and to get answers to the ration fiasco. So, we were alone and at the mercy of angry villagers. When we received news from the fort that many families of officers in the northern frontiers were killed, we moved from village to village, home to home, hiding our identity and appearance. Due to our family ties we were painted as collaborators."

"Your Tamil is better than mine."

"I am more Tamil than you think. I read, write and speak it. It is Mother India's gift to me. You may not believe it, but it's true."

"I believe you."

"For more than two years, my mother moved around alone, and I felt it was time to leave school and protect her. More people were dying, and so was our future. We packed some of our clothes, money, food and did what you did; we came to Madras. So now you know why. The state of India affects all of us and I'm proud of you and your commitment to your family. I'm with you now and I'll be with you forever."

"Life has twists and turns and we will let the universe decide our futures. I will take care of you as I would have my sisters," Venkat promised.

"Lastly, your education is important, and it must continue even late into the night," Victoria re-iterated.

"Education is going to kill me before we reach land."

"Even when we reach land, it will not stop. I'm surprised you are a very good student. So far, what might have taken me years you have accomplished in a few weeks. I'm impressed."

"Princess, have mercy on me!"

"I shall see if you are worthy of my compassion!"

The voyage was into its seventh week when, to everyone's surprise, an officer made the announcement that it would take two more days for the ship to reach port.

The excitement was intense for those who were making this journey for the first time. A thousand thoughts raced through Venkat's mind and it showed.

"We are still far away," Guru Sundrum said.

"I'm excited yet frightened at the same time. Guru, I had a dream of my sisters dancing."

"You are blessed, young man."

Guru Sundrum took Venkat to a quiet spot on the ship and sat him on a barrel.

"I have been indentured before and what I have to say to you I have been keeping from you until now because I did not want to frighten you. Your undertaking is very important; do not let problems make you forget the reason you are here. We will have to endure insults, beatings, hunger and other hardships inflicted by the people who employ us. Our minds will need to be strong and we shouldn't let them break our spirit," Guru counselled him.

Venkat looked out to the azure sea and Guru held him by his hand, knelt on the wooden deck, took a deep breath and spoke softly. "Life is like a storm. You will bask in the sun one day and be shattered against the rocks the next. The way in which you overcome challenges determines how you grow as a person. The success of a person goes beyond his limitations, and in the imperfections of man are valuable lessons for us."

"I shall be a man and my purposes are that of a man."

"Son, we will need to look at old customs, find new ways to adapt to the changes that will be brought on by a new set of rules and look at our ability to change things that we must."

They walked back to their cabin as dusk darkened the ship. The mood in the cabin was sombre as each one looked to Guru Sundrum. Searching for answers, he said, "Let us pray for that which lies ahead and for wisdom from god, as our future is in his hands."

Sitting cross-legged with their hands held in prayer, they closed their eyes for a one-hour union with the divine being. Later, sallow, holloweyed, confused men and women faced Guru Sundrum who, totally at a loss for words, searched his mind for any flicker of hope that he could provide for a group so eager to start a new life. However, it was beyond his reach to give them the thread that they could cling to.

Finally, after much deliberation, he spoke, "At times it will be difficult to understand whether religion leads us to god or whether god gives us the benefit of religion. Spirituality is the ultimate necessity for a life of contentment. I may not see most of you, as soon, we will part ways. Know also that life is of tempests and tranquillity and both teaches the way to live. We have lived through the experience of the worst kind and living in self-pity is futile. Carry the memories of those we left behind in our hearts and minds. We are living a new chapter and although our lives have been desecrated, both by the folly of our own leaders and by the greed of outsiders, we must build a future filled with the joy and expectations of a new beginning. Misfortunes bring out the best in us. God bless us all."

Venkat led Victoria out into a fresh gust of moistureladen wind. Leaving her on the upper deck, he headed back to his cabin to wait for daybreak.

Nervous anxiety gripped the passengers as they waited for daybreak. The bonds and the companionship that were forged during the voyage would be broken by sunset. Each would embark on his or her own journey, yet they would all be united in their efforts to build a foundation of hope and prosperity.

The last day was taken up by ensuring that all their possessions were well packed and their papers easily accessible, and now the wait dragged on. The ship's crew scurried from cabin to cabin, making sure that all the final preparations were in order. Venkat sat against the cabin wall with the straps of his sacks hooked over his arm.

"Are you ready, son?"

"Yes, I am, Guru."

"Unfortunately, we shall be holed-up in here for another day."

"Guru, it is tiring to wait when we know that we are near the end of a long voyage."

Darkness was setting in and there seemed to be more lights on deck. The moon made a golden path as it lit up the surface of the ocean. The water shimmered black and gold and the path seemed to lead all the way back home. Guru and Venkat leaned on the rails and admired the beautiful sight of gold-rimmed cloud bundles as they floated by just above the rising moon. Suddenly they were brought back by the sound of the ship's horn. They looked back and people pointed towards rows of dull lights. The Dunphaile Castle made for the port as more lights popped up against the dark background of the landmass. Messages were sent around that disembarking would be at first light. Some of the passengers trundled back to their cabins to spend another tardy night.

Night became morning and Venkat awakened, disturbed by the noise of feverish activity flooding the ship. The ship slowly entered the harbour and dropped anchor. The crew signalled to the workers waiting on the wharf to tie the mooring ropes onto stout wooden bollards.

CHAPTER 4

Officers and crew lined the wharf and barked an unending stream of instructions to ship's agents who spilt out from warehouses bordering the pier. The immigrants were herded into groups as teams prepared to hose them down to remove any infection or diseases that they could have carried with them from India.

"A sorry looking bunch, this lot!" a uniformed officer chuckled.

"They're only going to work on the cane plantations, sir," his colleague replied, enjoying the moment.

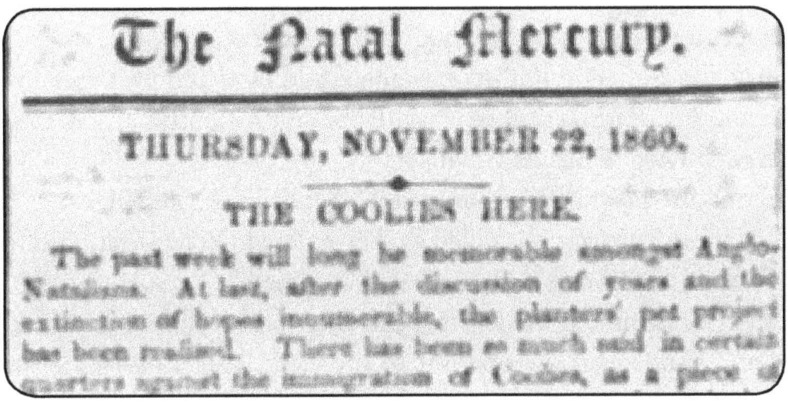

The Natal Mercury.

THURSDAY, NOVEMBER 22, 1860.

THE COOLIES HERE.

HEADLINES – A PORT NATAL NEWSPAPER

Newspaper article: "The Coolies Here from the Natal Mercury", Thursday, November 22, 1860 – Actual arrival date – 16/11/1860

"The past week will be long remembered amongst Anglo-Natalians. At last after the discussion of years and the extinction of hopes innumerable, the planters' pet project has been realised. There has been so much said in certain quarters against immigration of Coolies, as a piece of national policy."

Cleaned up, the men, women and children waited to be listed (shipping list), cleared for recruitment and once registered, dispatched to their various plantations or commercial enterprises.

In the melee at recruitment stations, huddled groups were addressed by men in suits. Sirdars interpreted feverishly as regional dialects baffled them. Ladies, adorned in all their finery, gathered in the shade of the sheds to await the outcome of the many discussions in progress with the recruiting agents. Photographers had a very busy morning as well. Bulbs exploded into sheets of grey clouds as group after group posed for pictures. The boy whose mother and sister died at sea was taken in by another family. The newly-formed family's inner happiness reflected in joyous smiles, captured as a memoir of the compassion of the human spirit.

Rathna Pillayiar, a close friend of Guru Sundrum, grew fond of Venkat during the voyage. Lauding Venkat for carrying the responsibility of seeking a solution to his family's predicament, he declared, "You are a young man filled with courage and determination. You will succeed."

Guru Sundrum and Rathna exchanged addresses and promised to write to one another. Rathna walked towards the administrative offices to secure a passage to King Williams Town.

"Let us also go and sort your girmit," Sundrum suggested.

"I'm afraid," Venkat mumbled as they entered the registration office.

"There is no courage without fear young man."

Guru Sundrum led Venkat through the steamy, cloistered registration office and handed his own permit to the clerk. Guru, being a returning labourer indentured to the same plantation and well known to the officials, spent a few minutes with them. He then handed Venkat's papers. Venkat waited, nervous.

The official addressed Guru Sundrum, "We have a problem with the young man. We can offer him an indenture, but the only option open to him is the Natal Railways and that has its own complications as he's unsuitable to the rigours of hard work because he is young. We shall offer him an indenture assigned under your temporary guardianship because he is already here, and we cannot send him back. I suggest he continues to look for employment as a servant or a dishwasher. When he finds an employment contract elsewhere bring him back here and we will change his details. That is all I can do for now, Mr Sundrum. I wish you well."

Thanking the clerk, Guru Sundrum turned around, and placing his arm over Venkat's shoulder, he led him out to explain the crux of his indenture.

In the already oppressive surroundings worsened by the clamouring crowds, Venkat, tense and close to tears, approached Victoria.

"Why the sad look?"

"I have no contract yet. I've been indentured under the care of our Guru."

"That's a good sign," Sushila consoled him.

"I'm afraid I may not be able to fulfil my promise to my parents."

"You're here, and it's not the end of the world. We're with you," Victoria tried to reassure Venkat.

Perspiration poured down his face partly due to the intense heat and largely because of the uncertainty that surrounded his future and the promises he held in his heart.

"Now, ladies, it is your turn." Guru once more led the way into the cauldron.

Sea birds skimmed the calm surface of the water, dipping down to pick up scraps of food tossed overboard by the crews of an anchored ship. Across the bay, the long landmass of the bluff stretched out to the sea.

A dejected Venkat found a spot beneath the tall palms and soon fell asleep.

The British who had recruited them to work in the African colony were facing challenges themselves. Although thousands of miles separated them from their homeland, they were driven by their unwavering loyalty to Crown and country. The British military had recorded numerous victories and were in the process of signing many treaties to ensure the expansion of the colony.

The frontiers of the colony stretched westwards and to maintain stability, forts were constructed to subdue any uprisings. This allowed remote areas to be occupied by settler farmers. A strong and viable economic platform was needed to support expansion programmes and to provide resources for the large numbers of British immigrants who were arriving to establish commercial, agricultural and industrial enterprises. The British government saw India as a good source to satisfy the need for cheap and productive labour.

Port Natal was the hub of all economic and military activity and was home to the governor. It was a bustling town where the British established a good commercial and transport infrastructure, and it also served as the main harbour and the gateway to the expanding interior.

The entire coastal region from the Cape of Good Hope all the way to Port Natal was in the hands of the British. The famous Frontier Wars between the British and the Xhosas (an independent African nation living far south of the Zulu kingdom) and the subsequent defeat of the Xhosas resulted in the gradual occupation of the interior.

King William's Town, founded in 1835, was named after King William IV. It was the capital of the British Protectorate from 1847 until 1865, when it was merged into the Cape Colony.

The Zulu nation comprised of numerous small clans unified into a powerful nation by the great warrior king, Shaka kaSenzangakhona, also known as Shaka Zulu, some fifty years earlier. The kings who succeeded him were responsible for approving and signing treaties with the British and with the Boers (descendants of the Dutch who had settled in the Cape of Good Hope centuries earlier). The Cape sea-route was of strategic importance to all the European nations intending to conduct trade with India and the Far East.

The Dutch had annexed the Cape Colony and were the first to set up a way-station at the Cape of Good Hope in 1652, importing slaves from Asia and African countries. It was there that the sailors rested and took on fresh vegetables and meat for the arduous voyage to the East. Later, the British ousted the Dutch and took control of the Cape Colony themselves.

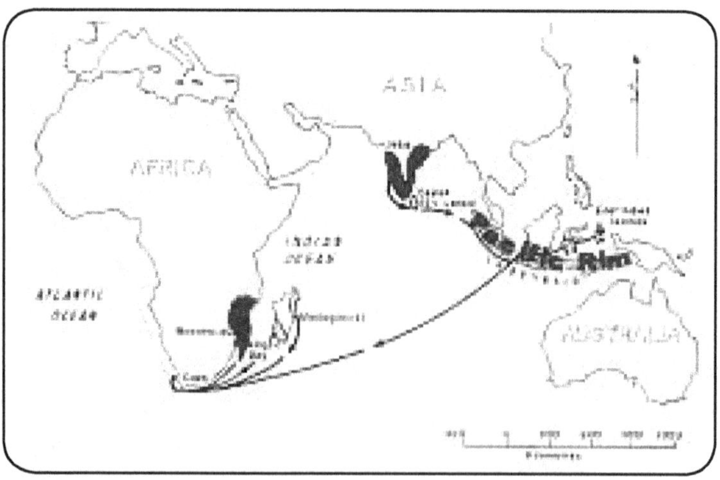

The historian Robert Shell has estimated that between 1652 and 1808, when the slave trade was abolished, an estimated total of 63,000 slaves were imported to the Cape from the African continent (26.4%), Indian sub-continent (25.9%), Madagascar (25.1%) and Indonesia (22.7%). Thus, the Cape Malay ancestry is a combination of African and Asian descent.

During the reign of King Shaka and in the battles that ensued, many tribes were decimated during the unification of the Zulu nation. Thousands fled into other areas to avoid facing the onslaught, thus reducing the local labour required by the British for their many new developments. It was also difficult for the British to influence the Zulus to work on the plantations that were being set up, or even in commercial enterprises.

Young Zulu men were recruited mainly for police units and some for construction-related industries.

"Again? Who is it this time?" the clerk questioned. Introducing Sushila and Victoria, Guru indulged in quite a long monologue detailing the plight of mother and daughter. Looking at the ladies, eyes fixed, the clerk commented.

"Charming indeed, delightfully charming, I must say."

"I expect it to work to their benefit," Guru chuckled.

Checking, the forms the clerk advised, "I wish it were possible. I do regret to say that we are in no position to assist them as they are Passenger Indians, and it's therefore out of our mandate to provide them with an indenture."

In that cloistered, humid, confined space, the ladies looked at each other, searching their minds for an outcome that could give them a second chance at a life once enjoyed.

"Young man, they are British nationals as well, do your best or suggest any options available to give them a fighting chance," Guru pleaded.

The clerk conferred with his colleague.

"Mr Guru, there could be an opportunity open at Rosehill Estates. Mr Harrisford, just a month ago, sent his manifest of the workers he needs. I can't recall the details, and my colleague doesn't remember either. It would be best if you approached their agent directly."

"Where are they?"

"Down the road in the recruitment depot. I wish I could help you more. Delightful – meeting such fine women in this dreadful place!"

Thanking the clerk, Guru left the testing conditions in the office for the cool breeze that wafted in from the ocean.

"Mother, we are in trouble," Victoria lamented.

"Not just yet. I have a plan," Guru promised encouragingly.

Just then, a tall, slightly chubby gentleman, grinning, hugged Guru Sundrum and spoke in Tamil. "I've spent more than ten days coming here, waiting for you. I just about gave up, Guru," Patrick joked.

"Don't be surprised. He sings our songs and prays to our gods as well." Guru Sundrum introduced Patrick Cele (a Zulu) to the ladies.

"Glad to meet you, sir." Sushila bowed.

Victoria walked over to Venkat and shook him awake. Picking up his bags, he dragged himself to join them.

"This is my young friend, Venkat. He came with us. Patrick, I need your help. A few months ago, your memsahib mentioned that she will be needing a person to work in the bungalow. Has she employed anyone yet?"

"Not yet, but this one is only a boy."

"A boy he is, with the determination of a man."

"Okay, I will try to sell the idea to the captain and Mrs Nessfield. Did you bring my gift?"

Patrick accepted the small package from Guru Sundrum, thanking him profusely and picked up Venkat's sacks.

"Go with him. He is our friend and a good teacher as well. Don't be afraid," Guru assured the hesitant and nervous boy.

"Son, we will meet soon."

Venkat promised Victoria and her mother that he would find them and visit. He bowed to Guru Sundrum, waving goodbye as he rushed off to catch up with Patrick.

Looking up at the sun, Guru suggested to the ladies to find accommodation for the night so they could begin the task of finding them work in the morning. They agreed willingly and walked towards a nearby inn.

"I will meet you here in the morning."

"Where will you sleep?"

"Sister, I will find a place under the stars. It's pleasant."

At the crack of dawn, Guru Sundrum visited the overcrowded recruitment depot filled with agents who acted on behalf of businesses and sugar barons to negotiate terms with prospective labourers. He searched for the Rosehill Estates team, and on finding the estates' agent, the guru approached him confidently.

"My name is Sundrum," he said, introducing himself to Agent George Ogilvy, who, on listening to Sushila and Victoria's predicament, referred him to Sirdar Murugappa Naik, who oversaw and held the recruitment manifest on behalf of Mr Harrisford, the Baron of Rosehill Estates. A lengthy, confrontational discussion between Mr Ogilvy and Murugappa ensued, with intermittent questions posed to Guru Sundrum, the men agreed to meet the women. Guru Sundrum, who believed that meeting the ladies would influence the men's decision to recruit them, went to the inn, satisfied that the door had been opened.

Sushila and Victoria waited anxiously, as finding employment was uppermost in their minds and their future depended on it. The dust swirling around worsened the balmy morning. Guru Sundrum, relieved to see them waiting outside, picked up their bags, but later regretted the offer to carry them as he laboured under their weight.

"Is there gold in these bags?"

"Can I carry one of them?" Victoria offered.

"No, it's not far now."

Dropping the bags, Guru took a deep breath and introduced the ladies to both Murugappa Naik and Mr Ogilvy.

"It is indeed a pleasure meeting you both," Mr Ogilvy smiled at Victoria and her mother. Turning to Guru Sundrum, he said, "Mr Sundrum, I have considered the situation the ladies are in and I'm afraid there are no positions in the manifest that require skills other than plantation type. However, now, after careful consideration, though detrimental to my wellbeing, I think I have a plan that could influence the Harrisfords to look at a new option that may suit the estate."

"We are pleased by your efforts, sir, and thank you."

"No need to thank me just yet, Miss," Mr Ogilvy replied. "Victoria, is it?"

"Yes."

"Miss Victoria, we hope the Harrisfords accept the yarn I'm going to knit. It would be my greatest pleasure to have you both on the estate. You will serve them well. I'm certain of that."

"You are very kind, sir," Victoria thanked him.

"I will go ahead to introduce my plans and you can join the group of labourers who will leave here mid-afternoon by wagon. Don't miss the transport."

"Thank you, brother, Mr Ogilvy," Guru Sundrum thanked the two men who solved the greatest challenge he had carried during the entire voyage, now more confident that the ladies would enjoy British hospitality in an environment more suitable to the lifestyle they were used to.

Rosehill Estate

As the last rays of the sun dipped below the low hills, the wagon pulled up in front of a splendid white building. Beautiful flowers adorned the lush manicured gardens. The setting reminded Victoria of the luxuries enjoyed by the British back home in India. She helped her mother off the wagon and Mr Ogilvy collected the bags and placed them on the patio.

Sitting in the coolness of the afternoon, Mr and Mrs Harrisford welcomed them, requesting the servant to offer chairs to the ladies and to bring a pitcher of fresh juice.

"It must have been a tiring day for you both," Mr Harrisford said as he filled two glasses with refreshing drinks.

On the road

Clouds of dust rose as wagons hurtled along dusty streets. Muscular, sweaty men pounded into the virgin, sunbaked earth, gouging deep trenches. Piled in spaces between motley buildings were crates, bags and boxes of varying sizes. Uniformed Zulu men, watchful, stood guard.

"You are very young," Patrick remarked.

"I am young but determined to be a man tomorrow. You speak my language very well."

"I was taught well, and I am learning about your gods as well."

"Our gods are for everyone." Venkat managed to complete the sentence although he was out of breath.

Nessfield Manor

As the day was about to end, Venkat reached a beautiful white, colonial-style house. On three sides ran a white wooden fence. Rows of palm trees, trunks painted white, stood steadfast in circular beds of low, flowering shrubs and stubby succulents. Familiar smells of salt and sea drifted in from the ocean. The backyard of the house stretched deep into a thicket of trees and matted bushes. Patrick led Venkat around to the back and offered him water.

"This is my house," Patrick pointed to a section of the stable that was converted into a house. He pushed open the stable doors, directing Venkat to rest where it was comfortable. Venkat looked around, rearranged a thick sack between two barrels, and dropping onto it, he immediately bedded down on the stable floor.

CHAPTER 5

Rosehill Estates

Agent George Ogilvy sat opposite Mr and Mrs Harrisford. He was about to elaborate on Sushila and Victoria's predicament that led up to them being there.

"Thank you, Mr Ogilvy, I have read your report and I would like Mrs Payton to tell us more," Mr Harrisford requested.

"Thank you, sir. I am an Indian by birth and my husband, Colonel Alexander Payton, is a British Officer formerly based in Madras, where I served in an army base as a nurse. He left India about four years ago with our son Jasper, who he felt needed an English education. He also wanted to finalise military and family matters.

"We haven't seen him since and I'm not certain of his present whereabouts though his original destination was Putney. His absence has caused my daughter Victoria and I great hardship. My husband was a senior official guarding the food stockades. The food was meant to be distributed as famine relief, but it was held back by authorities. The people blamed him."

1877 – MADRAS – RICE AWAITING SHIPMENT. NEARBY, MILLIONS ARE DYING OF FAMINE

Mr Ogilvy poured a glass of water and handed it to Sushila. Thanking him, Sushila continued, "Naturally, the people were very angry, considering it was their harvest that was stored in the stockades. We, being who we are, faced the brunt of the peoples' animosity. Leaving our home and drifting for almost four years, we wandered from place to place, avoiding the wrath of people. The only choice left was for us to emigrate and begin a life in a new country."

"I sympathise with you and your lovely young daughter and I fully understand the predicament. Mr Ogilvy and I discussed your nursing skills at length, and you will be pleased to know that we will offer you employment and everything else you need to rebuild both your lives," Mr Harrisford informed Sushila.

Sushila thanked him and bowed.

Mr Harrisford continued: "You do realise that the indentured workers, without a doubt, have brought their beliefs, customs and traditions with them and regardless of your isolation, their anger could still exist."

"Yes, that may be so. However, on the voyage across, every person had one shared vision and a united goal and had discarded the remnants of the recent past."

"Good, as long as you fully understand your position in a difficult and remorseless environment, Mrs Harrisford and I will help you both."

"Victoria, is it?"

"Yes, sir," Victoria answered.

"Young lady, you look more British than Indian, even your mother would concur. Your good looks could pose your mother a problem or two, as young men outnumber girls here. Though I guess you have endured a lot in India, my advice to both of you is to stick to a disciplined life. You hold your future in your hands and after a rest and acclimatisation, we shall see how we will proceed further."

"Mr Harrisford, Mrs Harrisford, we thank you and will forever be indebted to you both." Victoria thanked them, bowed and followed Arvin, the servant, through the backdoor and onto a long balcony that led them into the guest house, an extension of the stately manor.

Inside, a beautiful home surprised them. They entered a beautiful kitchen fitted with Victorian-style cupboards. A dresser and a bamboo bin stood against the back wall and a round mahogany dining table and three solid hand-carved matching chairs stood in the centre. Persian carpets covered wooden floors. In the bedchamber (bedroom), luxurious linen covered a splendid hand-carved bed, complemented by equally impressive furniture. A room attached to the bedroom served as the parlour (living room) with beautifully crafted furniture and leather couches. An immaculate white door separated the parlour and the ornate privy (bath) room.

"Mother, this is a dream."

"Yes, this is a lovely home," her mother agreed.

"Mother, this is thanks to our Guru."

"God bless him," Sushila replied.

Mother and daughter, alone after an overwhelmingly emotional journey on the sea, surveyed the beautiful setting and wept.

"Tomorrow is the beginning of a new life. Let us sleep."

"Yes, Mother. We will prevail. God bless our Guru."

Nessfield Manor

The next morning Patrick and Captain James Nessfield, his new employer, stood over the sleeping Venkat.

"Rather young, isn't he?" Captain Nessfield remarked as he handed Patrick the reins of his horse.

"He says he's a man."

"We will see about that!" the captain remarked. He kicked the sleeping youngster on his legs. Startled by the impact of the boot, Venkat got up.

"Where are you from, coolie?" Nessfield demanded.

"Madras," Venkat replied, one hand on his knee and the other resting against the stable wall.

"Do you speak English?" Patrick translated for the captain.

"I am learning now," Venkat replied nervously.

"You better do that. If not, you'll be going back on the next ship to your godforsaken country," instructed Captain Nessfield, accepting the reins and walking out of the stable. Turning around, he shouted, "Employ him. He's your responsibility."

"Thank you, sir. I will teach him well," Patrick accepted the task, relieved that a promise he made to Guru Sundrum was fulfilled.

"Do not be afraid," Patrick comforted Venkat and suggested he get ready to meet the memsahib.

Patrick, with Venkat in tow, knocked on the front door of the beautiful manor, careful not to soil the mats that ran the length of the patio floor. He removed his work-worn hat. The door opened and standing at the entrance was an English woman dressed in more clothes than her frail body could carry.

"Are you Madras?" she asked.

"My name is Venkat," he corrected her.

"The captain has made a mistake then. Patrick, will you translate as I explain?" she turned and invited them in. "Will you teach him English, Patrick?"

"Yes, I will, memsahib."

Leading Venkat to a table, Patrick pointed to the spot on the bottom of the page of a contract that confirmed his legal status as an indentured labourer in the Colony of Natal.

"Make a mark here," he told an excited Venkat.

"I am happy now. Can I give Guru the details of my contract?"

"We will, soon."

They followed Nancy Nessfield around as she laid down the rules and outlined the chores Venkat had to perform. As Patrick translated, he nodded, confirming that he understood. Venkat was totally overjoyed with his contract and more so with the fact that his family's future was bound to get better.

"The captain has other tasks that he will want you to do," Nancy added as they walked out of the house.

"Do you think you can do all this?" Patrick enquired.

"I'll be able to do it. Victoria was teaching me, but as she's not here, I will need your help."

"You start tomorrow. Today you will rest."

"Where did you learn English?"

"At the Catholic Mission, where I was first schooled."

"Tamil?"

"Our Guru. We met at the market and he helped me when a horse knocked me over. I will learn more from you, I hope."

"We will learn from each other," Venkat replied.

Two weeks passed and Venkat, who was now called 'Madras' in the Nessfield household, worked tirelessly to the satisfaction of Patrick's wife, Gertrude the housekeeper and Nancy Nessfield. His chores were monotonous, but it was a way to earn an income for his family.

"Uncle, back home in India, sleeping outdoors was normal. Here, in a new place, I'm a little afraid. Could I have a small space which I can call home?"

"For that, we must ask the captain."

It was dusk when Captain Nessfield arrived home.

"Madras respectfully requests for a small place he can call his home," Patrick addressed the captain.

"He makes demands already?" the captain questioned, irritated as he ran his fingers through his golden-brown hair.

Patrick led the captain's horse into the stable and dropped hay into the feed box. He then went out to see whether Venkat had completed his daily tasks. He waited for a little while until Venkat came out of the house.

"How was your day?"

"I'm a man doing the work of a lady and my name has changed! This is all very different from home."

"Home is very far away, and you must accept changes even if you don't like them," Patrick consoled the dejected young man who struggled to come to grips with the type of work he was doing.

"Memsahib wants me to use a uniform as soon as she gets one," Venkat mumbled, as they walked around the building.

"Uniform," Patrick laughed.

"The captain's request."

"My wife will cook food for us," Patrick mentioned as he marched off into the bushes with a sickle tucked under his arm.

Collecting a bucket of water from the rain tank, Venkat undressed behind a bush, poured bowls of water over his head and lathered himself with an overused piece of soap. Emptying the bucket over his head, he dried himself, changed into a fresh set of clothes, sat on a crate and took in the grandeur that spread out before him.

Patrick had just returned with a huge bundle of fodder on his shoulder, and after tipping it onto the stable floor, he joined Venkat.

"I will help you in future."

"Thanks," Patrick accepted the gesture, just as Gertrude announced that food was ready.

"My wife is a good cook. She will cook our food. She even cooks for the British."

"Every day?" Venkat asked.

"Yes, every day!"

"Hunger was a regular guest back home," Venkat remarked as they accepted the food from Gertrude. Patrick turned around and passed a curious glance. "I shall pay you for the food."

"You do not pay for food. It's part of the wage and rations scale," Patrick confirmed.

"The captain was very angry today," Gertrude told them.

"This is very good," Venkat mumbled as he spooned up the steaming stew.

"I think they are planning a war," she continued.

"The ship with the soldiers hadn't arrived, which annoyed the captain."

Captain Nessfield led many campaigns against the Zulus and was highly decorated for bravery. Many Zulus who had once adopted the Christian faith were dissatisfied, as their age-old tradition of rule by chieftainship was being undermined. So, they established their own faith whereby they practised both the new and their tribal, deep-rooted beliefs.

The king and some of his chiefs were adopting the British rule of law, but lower-ranking chiefs were against it and were garnering support from clansmen for an uprising. It was also at a time when the Natal colony was engaged in expansionist ideas to annex the Kingdom of Zululand.

The Governor of the Colony was steadfast in his belief and had equally faithful men to implement his orders. Many settlers joined the army to fight and protect their own interests and their farms.

When night fell, Venkat pulled the flimsy covering up to his chin and tried to fall asleep. Along with the storm that raged outside, one raged within his mind. Drops of rain fell incessantly through holes in the tin roof.

"It's still much better than home," he told himself. He tried to fall asleep, but images of the fire-ravaged house, his mother sitting between the fallen debris and the depressed features of his father consumed his thoughts. Close by, divided only by a wall made of planks, Patrick and Gertrude slept, oblivious to the problems of the world outside. The fury of the winds and the creaking of the timber beams as sheets of rain pelted down made the horses restless. Venkat fell asleep late into the night. The next morning, however, as the sun rose above the orange sea, he awoke determined to face the day's obstacles and as premonition would unfold; there were to be lots of them, just as Patrick had foretold.

"Patrick, Madras, come here!" Captain Nessfield shouted. They stood facing him as he slapped his whip against his boot. Polished buttons gleamed in the morning sun, his red uniform pressed to perfection and his black boots a testament to Patrick's skill at polishing. The whip swished, striking Venkat across his right cheek.

"So, you want your own bloody room?" he scoffed.

Venkat shifted his footing to brace himself against another possible strike.

"He only asked," Patrick intervened.

The captain's wife was leaning against the concrete pillar of the patio and called out in protest to her enraged husband.

"Beggars sleep in bloody gutters. You will obey the madam at all times," the captain hissed.

"I always do," Venkat replied, his palm covering his right cheek.

"Ready my horse. Patrick! The stable is for the horses," Nessfield warned, pointing his whip at Venkat. He turned on his heels and marched into the house.

Patrick led the way to the backyard and Gertrude offered each of them a plate of food.

"He really is furious!" Venkat muttered while dabbing his cheek with a wet cloth.

"I've been through much worse," Patrick tried to console the frightened boy who still managed to swallow his breakfast.

Feeling better, Venkat entered the house. Captain Nessfield had already ridden off and Nancy was sitting in the dining room having breakfast when he walked in.

"I am sorry," she said to him.

"Thank you. The master was angry," Venkat accepted the sincere apology and rushed to do his chores.

It was during a voyage from India to England to take up a new commission that Captain Nessfield's ship anchored in Port Natal, mainly to conduct minor repairs and pick up fresh food and water. They spent more than a week, and during the stay, he visited the fort and nearby military sites. On one such visit he identified weaknesses in the defensive installations and senior military personnel; taking his expertise into account, he was offered a posting, which he gladly accepted. Captain Nessfield delayed the acceptance of the original War Office commission and instead, sent for Nancy, with the plan that the family would settle in Port Natal.

The captain actively involved himself on reconnaissance expeditions to examine the forts and implement plans to improve their defensive positions, and his vast knowledge gained in India was an added advantage to the military personnel. The military strategists planned incursions into the Zulu heartland to make sure that the Zulu king complied with the ultimatums presented to him by the High Commissioner of the British Empire.

The intelligence personnel expected imminent attacks, but it was a gamble predicting where they would occur as the Zulu armies used the rugged terrain of the land to their advantage. To eliminate surprise attacks, Captain Nessfield identified locations where temporary camps could serve as forward positions, coinciding with the overall strategic plan developed by Lord Chelmsford (Commander-in-Chief of the British Armed forces).

The task that consumed much of his time was overseeing the movement of military hardware and ensuring its safe passage to far-flung destinations. Captain Nessfield's priority, however, was to improve the tactical capabilities of the garrisons and to enable them to inflict the maximum damage to an army that outnumbered the Empire forces by almost twenty to one.

Nancy had contracted an illness in England and Captain Nessfield had hoped that the warm sub-tropical climate would help her to recuperate. Her recovery was taking longer than expected, but the doctors promised that she would be well eventually. However, her condition worsened, and Gertrude took complete care of her. The constant dangers that her husband faced and her yearning to see her five-year-old daughter, Agatha, who was living with her mother-in-law in England, was aggravating an already depressed mental state.

Even in her condition, Nancy maintained a good rapport with the staff, always kind, poised and dignified.

"It will be two weeks before Agatha arrives by ship from England," she addressed Gertrude and Venkat. "Clean the room at the end of the passage and we must decorate it beautifully. The captain demands the best, as we have not seen her for many years."

They nodded in agreement.

"I will speak to the captain about your room," Nancy told Madras later, as she left the dining table. She went to sit in the rocking chair on the patio and looked out to sea.

Venkat worked throughout the day without resting, and when he walked into the stable, he found Patrick busy.

"How was your day?" Patrick asked him.

"Worse than I expected."

"The British are a strange race. 'We bring civilisation to a dark place'," Patrick mimicked the captain.

"All I'm here for is the money and if my being here angers him, I will look for work in the sugar plantations or join the railways. I am stronger now," Venkat continued as he washed his hands in the wooden box which Patrick normally used as a dip for red-hot metal from the forge.

"You think it's easy out there. I was taught about heaven and hell, and this is heaven!" Patrick clarified the situation.

At that moment, the captain clip-clopped his sweat-covered horse into the stable.

"Wash him, wipe him and feed him. He saved my life today," the captain told Patrick as he handed him the reins.

"The Impi must have had a good day today," Patrick muttered.

The fearsome Impi was the fighting unit of the Zulu war machine. The influence of King Shaka was still evident in the Zulu military strategy, battle formation and in their pride at being victorious. The much better-equipped British forces underestimated the awesome power of the legions. It is said that the Zulu Impi could run fifty miles in a day and at the end of it, they still had the strength to catch fleet-footed gazelles to feed their soldiers.

Opening a window, Gertrude shouted, "The captain wants to see Madras!"

Venkat nervously rounded the corner of the stable and tiptoed onto the patio. Gertrude invited him in. He walked into the house to find the captain sitting on a chair, pants rolled up to his knees, a towel draped over his shoulder and a basin of hot, steaming water next to his feet. The once magnificent red military jacket lay on the floor, torn in many places and spotted with dark blotches.

"Massage my feet," the captain ordered Venkat as he poured salt into the silver basin. Venkat went down on his knees and kneaded the captain's feet, hoping he was doing it correctly. Captain Nessfield leaned back in his chair and relaxed, thoroughly enjoying the ministrations. Gertrude ensured the water was kept hot. Venkat removed the round stones from the basin as they cooled, and Gertrude dropped hot ones in their place. Wisps of steam rose as they fell into the water. An hour later, the captain ordered him to stop and dry his feet with a warm towel.

"Build your room where you want to," the captain grunted.

"Would you help me build my room?" an excited Venkat sought Patrick's help later that night. "The master gave me permission to build a room."

"That's good," Patrick agreed. "Where will you get materials from, young man?"

"We could buy old crates from the British at the docks or from the market. I have some money."

"Then we need to take the wagon to carry them."

Immigrants who had completed their indenture, together with Passenger Indians and British merchants and traders, established thriving fresh produce and commercial businesses along pavements. They served the needs of the fast-growing Indian and British population. A few concession holders also benefited from supplying the military, shipping companies and the growing hotel industry. The Indian traders became important members of the commercial community in Port Natal, which was by then re-named Durban, after Sir Benjamin D'Urban, the Governor of the Cape Colony. Emigration officials in India continued to refer to Durban as Port Natal for many decades since the departure of Truro in 1860.

It was Venkat's first venture away from the Nessfields. Patrick drove the wagon and they bounced along the track towards the bustling marketplace. Patrick urged the horse to go faster, clipping its rump with the whip.

"I'm no different to the horse," Venkat thought to himself.

The street market was abuzz with frenzied activity and Venkat eagerly walked around the heaps of vegetables and fruit lining the pavements. Meanwhile, Patrick tied the horse to a rail, then he hurried off to reduce the boy's youthful excitement before it got the better of him. Patrick spoke to some stallholders about empty crates. None of them had any, but he was referred to Mr Chandrakanth Patel, a seed and groceries merchant.

Low-rise buildings lined unpaved streets. Indian traders rented these units from the town authorities. Lack of sufficient money led to negotiations and most often, the customer won after being told, "At that price, you are killing me and my business."

Mr Patel's business was in one of those buildings and was easy to find. Venkat and Patrick passed a tailor's shop and asked for directions from another merchant.

"Just two shops away," the owner directed them.

They stood in front of the store. Bags of various sizes were stacked against the wall, rows of small bottles filled with seeds lined the counter and against the rear of the shop wooden shelves held various sizes of rolledup sacks. Mr Patel welcomed them in.

"I'm want to buy old crates which we can use to build a room for my young friend here," Patrick spoke in Tamil.

"I'm from Surat in Gujarat," Mr Patel responded. "I admire your proficiency in the language. Even though I'm Indian, I don't speak it myself." Then he turned to Venkat, "When did you come to this place?"

"Three months ago."

Mr Patel offered them tea and discussed the proper construction methods for building a room and drew a plan, after discussing the size of the room.

"Crate planks is not the only material you require." Mr Patel confirmed. "I will give you as many crates as you need. Do you have sufficient money to buy all the material you would need?" he asked Patrick.

"No. sir. I don't think so."

Mr Patel drew up a complete list and wrote other details in Urdu.

"Give this note to the owner of the shop. If the cost exceeds the amount you have, then I will pay the difference. Mr Aboobaker Amod's spoken English is not as good as yours, but he is a friend from Porbander, Gujarat."

"How do I thank Mr Amod?"

Mr Patel wrote down on a separate piece of paper, greeting and gratitude formalities, which Patrick would practice all the way to the shop.

"Thank you, sir," Patrick and Madras thanked Mr Patel.

"You must come and visit me on Sundays, when possible, because there are lessons to be learnt."

"I promise I will visit you whenever I can, sir!"

Madras and Patrick hastily loaded the crates and headed in the direction of Mr Amod's trading store.

"Salaam, sir," Patrick greeted Mr Amod as he handed him Mr Patel's note.

"As salamu alaykum," Mr Amod responded as he accepted Mr Patel's letter and the money. He gestured them to wait. They waited, nervous as to the outcome. An hour later, store assistants loaded the wagon with planks, long timber poles, cement, tar sheet, wood tar, paint, nails and a six-paned window.

Mr Amod returned the money to Patrick, who stood hesitant for a few seconds.

"It is a lot," Madras whispered to Patrick.

"Jazak Allahu Khairan," Patrick thanked Mr Amod.

"Wa iyyak," Mr Amod replied, as he waved them off.

Patrick nudged a bewildered Venkat, who immediately bowed and thanked Mr Amod.

"People of your country are strange," Patrick commented.

"Why."

"Boy, two strangers give us a wagon full of goods to build a home for another stranger."

"Yes, we are strangers and helping others in need is not strange. Our culture says, giving without expectations, is a blessing, if not here, then, in the spiritual life and one is not compelled to give and yet give, we do!"

"Is there fear of retribution in the spiritual world if you do not give?"

"Is God a punishing God?"

"Heaven and hell come to mind."

"Uncle, if there are heaven and hell, then this is hell. Where then can we find heaven? Life exists here and in the spiritual world and our destiny is pre-planned or attained and for those who commit sins and pass on, their souls, whether it attains absolution or not, are reborn.

"Difficult as it is, I will accept your explanation."

On the way back, Patrick made a quick stop at Mr Patel's store to return the money which Mr Amod gave back.

"Keep it. It is our gift to the young man."

They started back and hoped that the captain had left before they reached home as Patrick had taken the horse and wagon without his permission.

"We can always say we're sorry," Patrick planned.

The horse turned into the yard and as they passed the white fence, Captain Nessfield called out to Patrick. Jumping off, Patrick stood next to the horse, rolling the rim of his hat and looking very nervous.

"I thought you two bloody fools stole my horse and wagon… and where did you steal the building material from?" Captain Nessfield growled.

"They were given to us by Mr Patel and Mr Amod…" Patrick tested the mood of the captain.

"I quite doubt that."

"Where should we build it?" Patrick pushed his luck. All the while Venkat kept very quiet and out of sight.

"Somewhere in the blasted backyard. Remember, we are not in India." The captain climbed three steps and sat on a rocking chair next to his wife.

"God saved us today!" Venkat exclaimed to Patrick.

"No, it was the memsahib."

Patrick unhitched the horse and slapped him into the stable. Then they both made a late start to an already monotonous routine.

That same afternoon, the two men sketched their plans given by Mr Patel, on a board with a piece of charcoal. They then broke down the crates, separated the boards from the thick, greenish oil paper, removed the nails and placed the flat sides into a neat pile.

"We have all we need, so let's start on Saturday," Patrick suggested.

"I cannot wait!" exclaimed Venkat, excited at the prospect of having his own room for the first time in his life.

Most of Saturday was spent completing the wooden framework of the room and continuing till Sunday afternoon, when the room began to take shape. The solid stable wall was shared, thus providing the strong support that was needed for the rest of the structure. Venkat, due to his small stature, was tasked with completing roof work. He covered the roof framework with the thick oilpaper, nailed the boards over them, ensuring a thin edge of the boards to overlap each other. Once the roof was completed and after getting approval from Patrick, Venkat spread the wood tar over the boards, as a protection against rain runoff or the effects of moisture carried by coastal winds. Patrick helped Madras to run the tar sheets over the moist wood tar so that the heat of the sun could bond the two together, solidifying and waterproofing the roof.

"Mr Patel is a genius with a heart full of kindness."

"Yes, he is and has a precious gift," Madras agreed with Patrick.

"I will cover the floor with planks later, as Mr Patel suggested."

"Uncle Patrick, can I cut out the window slot with this hand saw."

"Don't cut yourself."

"I'll try not to."

"Boy, you need to cover the outer walls with tar as well and paint over once dried," Patrick suggested.

"I will do the cement border around the outer walls, the window and the shelving next weekend."

Patrick agreed.

"Thank you, Uncle. It will be dark soon."

Venkat unrolled the cloth and it fell to cover the 'window'. Emerging from the stable, all smiles, Venkat carried the bamboo bed that had taken him two nights to string together. Onto it, he dropped a sack mattress filled with shredded coconut husks, covered it with a calico sheet (given to him when he had cleaned out the room for Agatha) and finally placed the pillow that Nancy had given him. It was Sunday afternoon and they celebrated their achievement by having a pot of tea and the best of Gertrude's biscuits. Nancy was satisfied that the room would receive the captain's approval.

"I have a lot more than I had at home," he shared his feelings with Patrick. "I wish my mother could have this as well."

CHAPTER 6

A few months had passed and Sushila and Victoria settled into a comfortable routine. Sushila was employed as the field nurse, attending to injuries sustained by the workers. Minor cuts, bruises, blisters and insect bites were cleaned up, sanitised and, when necessary, bandaged. More serious cases like knife cuts and diseases were treated appropriately and sick days were recommended. The workers appreciated her skills and many female workers valued her advice on feminine matters as well.

Victoria was Mrs Harrisford's newfound daughter, whom she loved as her own.

Workers were subjected to insults, whipping, scorching heat and agonisingly long hours. The oppressive condition caused exhausted females to faint, and their male colleagues weren't allowed to help carry their workload. Smelly, bloodstained, perspiration-soaked rags served as bandages. These conditions enraged Sushila. Eventually, she drew on her courage, undaunted of the consequences and, with the help of Victoria, she prepared a report about the unfair treatment that the workers endured. In the coolness of the afternoon shade, facing Mr Harrisford, Sushila addressed him confidently. Victoria sat next to Mrs Harrisford.

"Mr Harrisford, sir, I fully understand that my employment does not extend beyond treating plantation workers. However, I feel it is only just to notify you of the appalling conditions that the people are forced to work under. The ill-treatment of workers only reduces their performance, thereby lowering the work rate rather than increase it. The sirdars may feel that the workers are beasts of burden and the only tool to increase their work rate is the whip. With the help of Victoria, I have therefore prepared this report to outline the conditions that prevail on our estate. Mr Harrisford, I do hope that by preparing this report my employment is not compromised. We are in debt to you for the opportunity to earn a living. We are loyal and therefore hope to be judged accordingly. Our workers, as men and women need better treatment, sir."

Taking a sip of water, Sushila asked Victoria to hand the report to Mr Harrisford.

Mr Harrisford accepted the report and thanked Sushila with the undertaking that he will read it after dinner. Satisfied that she did her best for the workers, Sushila and Victoria were about to get into bed when a knock on the door surprised them.

"The memsahib would like to speak to Miss Victoria."

"Thank you, Arvin."

Victoria hesitated and looked at her mother.

"Go," Sushila prompted her.

As Victoria entered, Mrs Harrisford guided her to the dining table.

"Are you comfortable here, young lady?"

"Very much, madam."

"Victoria, did you prepare the report?"

"My mother explained, and I put the words together."

"Brilliant penmanship. We are impressed."

Arvin placed two logs in the fire, waited and then asked for permission to leave, pulling the door behind him as he left.

"Are you planning to study further?"

"I aim to, madam. Education is an important part of my future."

"I'm glad. The young need a good education," Mrs Harrisford concurred.

"However, for now, my mother and I are trying to pull the pieces of our life together. Our lives are divided, and she is clinging to the threads that unite the French and Indian in her and the British in her children. She carries that burden and still protects and preserves our Indian heritage. I cherish her commitment."

"She is a remarkable woman. Where does the French heritage come in?"

"My maternal grandmother is French and my grandfather Tamil."

"Victoria, have you considered the direction of your future?"

"Not yet. We must first put to rest some of the ills of the past, madam."

"What may that be, dear?"

"Growing up was fascinating, and social differences did not matter. Then, there was a gradual change in attitude. Parents prevented us from playing with their children, so we grew apart, which affected my brother and me. We saw no difference between us and the children from the village. The joys of childhood suddenly vanished, we were isolated. The cracks that emerged had its roots in the injustices committed against the poor, simple rural folk who clung to the threads of their ancient culture. They were now at the mercy of the British – my paternal half."

Dipping a biscuit into the cup, Victoria took a few minutes to finish the tea.

"Their reaction was a natural response to the travesty that swamped a nation. We were exposed and open to insults. My mother was painted as a harlot and my brother and I as half-breeds, lower than the untouchables. She shielded us, standing steadfast against a tirade of insults. Our position wasn't helped by the fact that my father was away. We were ostracised and eventually, my mother, exceeding the limits of her endurance – crumbled. The only option was to emigrate. So, we joined the very people who despised us, on a long voyage. During that voyage, a new friendship evolved, a merger of opposing pasts now on a path to oneness."

"You have quite a grasp of the English language, my dear. How is that possible?"

"I started learning English and literature from the age of three, and I think philosophy, history, arithmetic, art and Latin a bit later. We attended the best private schools my father could afford, and I loved it. At fourteen, I was compelled to leave school to be with my mother. I am well-versed in Tamil as well, and my religious beliefs are defined by the lessons learnt from ancient texts and scriptures from the Gita. I am proud of my heritage, as complicated as it may be."

"As you should be," Mrs Harrisford paid her a compliment.

"My British grandparents filled us with Homer, Virgil, Shakespeare and Milton while my Indian grandparents sent ancient texts as well as my grandfather's recollections of the history of our culture spanning thousands of years."

"That's brilliant, dear."

"It was sublime, and it consumed me."

"Such an education could certainly help Mr Harrison in solving some of our worker problems on the estate."

"There are no problems for the barons. Pardon me, mam, common-sense solutions are required to support workers on the estates. Barons, managers and the workers have one commonality."

"What is it? Pray, tell me," Mrs Harrisford prompted Victoria.

"Plantation workers are as human as the sirdars, managers and even the barons. Yet they seem to carry the burden of responsibility for the success of the estate on their shoulders and with their bloodied hands. The estates seek profit and the workers seek better treatment. If the former is achieved, only the barons enjoy the benefits that contributes much to the capitalistic ideals of the Empire.

"My girl, do you pity them?"

"Yes, firstly for the physical punishment they are subjected to. Secondly, most carry scars of the punishment meted out, but they ignore its emotional consequences. Indentured labourers endure this misery to change the course of their lives. Punishment is only a phase in their quest for freedom and success," Victoria poured out her thoughts.

"Dear, what do you mean by that?"

"Madam, the teaching back home is that the present generations own the world they live in and shape it for future generations. Thus, the fathers, mothers, brothers and sisters, who now carry the responsibility, are moulding the future of their children and generations that follow. It is a sacrifice so profound, yet simple. The human mind can't be flogged. You can kill the physical being, but the inescapable idea is carried in spirit. Victory is inevitable. Bloodied hands and broken bodies are testaments to their courage and strength of will."

In the balmy evening, the breeze fanned the flickering flames.

"I doubt it's that bad on this estate," Mrs Harrisford interjected.

"It is as I explained. It's my hope that the new rules, if adopted by Mr Harrisford, reduce the pain and hopefully all other barons will do the same."

"Victoria, I am in awe of your knowledge and your use of language. May you find peace within yourself to forgive us for that which you feel has hurt the illiterate and downtrodden."

"You need not ask for forgiveness because it is just the way it is, madam. Downtrodden, yes but illiterate, I doubt it; maybe in the English language and culture. India has changed the world. The many nations who invaded our country brought with them ideas to change India. India can incorporate new and unique ideas without dismantling her own culture and social structures. She withstood the might of nations from far and wide and surrendered to barbaric hordes, but she was never brought to her knees. Just as the flame dances to nature's beat, within our hearts flickers a tiny flame of freedom and, by the grace of our gods, it shall arise and burn eternal."

"My angel, our conversation has given me a lot to ponder."

"I hope you're not offended by my views and utterances."

"No, not in the least, dear. It was refreshing and educational. You have a gift for a person so young."

"Thank you, madam."

"Could you oblige me with an answer to a sensitive question?"

"Yes, madam. It would not offend me."

"Thank you. Do you feel you are Indian or British?"

"I am of two worlds – two cultures brought together by love – and I respect them both. I feel the British in me will prepare me for my future role in society, and it seems it will be my preferred choice, without neglecting my Indian heritage, unless fate intervenes."

"For now, it is a pragmatic and appropriate choice. I am overwhelmed by your maturity, dear."

The two women sat together without a word being spoken for a few minutes. Mrs Harrisford finally got up to douse the lamps.

"May I please take leave now, madam?"

"Sure, dear! Mr Harrisford and I have much to plan for your future."

"Thank you."

"The pleasure will be all ours, my dear," Mrs Harrisford replied as she closed the door.

Wisps of the white clouds that veiled the fields of green began drifting westwards and in the beautifully manicured garden, bees attracted by the fragrance, buzzed from flower to flower. The sun broke through and lit up beds of amaryllis, arum lilies, daisies and carnations. In contrast to this bright and beautiful scene, just a short distance away workers, weighed down by implements, marched in a single file to begin a new day.

Victoria and Sushila stepped out onto the porch to a beautiful dawn.

"Mr Harrisford would like you to meet him at the Madras-South[1] Estate's shed, Miss," a servant informed Victoria.

[1] Note: Most Estates were divided into Madras or Calcutta Sections to simplify communication with workers due to linguistic and cultural differences."

"Thank you, Arvin," Victoria replied.

Wiping away perspiration, they reached a group of workers, looking nervous and very restless as the morning warmed up.

"Are all the managers and sirdars here?"

"Yes, sir," Sirdar Murugappa confirmed.

"Sorry for being late, sir," Sushila apologised.

"It's alright, Mrs Payton."

"Gentlemen and ladies, it has been brought to my attention that rules must be changed to improve the working conditions."

Mr Harrisford paused as Sushila translated.

"It has also been brought to my attention that managers and sirdars are imposing corporal punishment on workers. As of this morning, any sirdar using any act of punishment on a worker will be called up by his manager for an investigation. There shall be no reason whatsoever for corporal punishment.

"If a worker is found guilty of any wrongdoing, an appropriate sanction will be instituted by the sirdar and the manager. If a sirdar is found guilty, the manager shall be responsible for taking the corrective action and if the manager is responsible for an error of judgement, then I will investigate the matter. Do I make myself clear?"

The group nodded as Sushila translated.

"Now, Miss Victoria will read out the rules that I have written down. These rules have benefits for both the workers and the estate. You must thank Mrs Payton for bringing this matter to me."

"Thank you, sir."

Mr Harrisford spent a few minutes listening to Victoria translating into Tamil as she read from the page, then he called for his horse, mounted it and rode towards the beach. Once the last few instructions were read out, Sushila waited for questions, which she responded to firmly.

"It's simple," Sushila clarified. "If a worker breaks the rule, the sirdar will be responsible. If a sirdar is guilty, the manager must act and when the manager is wrong, then Mr Harrisford will investigate."

The mid-morning sun beat down as the group dispersed.

It was Sunday morning and Victoria answered a knock on their door. Venkat stood a few feet away. She grabbed him by his hand and pulled him into the house.

"Mother, we have a visitor!" Victoria shouted excitedly.

"Well, it has been a long time, son," Sushila reprimanded a bemused Venkat.

"We work on some Sundays, but I'm happy to be here now."

Victoria rushed into the main house and excitedly asked Arvin for biscuits and a pot of tea. He couldn't pretend to refuse as her excitement was infectious. Rushing back, she spread out a tablecloth and waited. Arvin placed the pot, three cups and a plate of biscuits on the table.

"Will that be all?"

"Yes, thank you." Turning around, she invited Venkat to sit.

"Now let us talk about the past few months," Victoria suggested, inviting her mother to join in.

"I will after I prepare a picnic basket for you two for a trip to the beach. It's a beautiful day to be out."

"Thank you, Mother!"

Wave after wave tumbled, rolled and flattened out on the gritty shoreline and further along the coast thousands of crabs raced to where the water met the dunes. Gulls floated above the blue ocean and dipped into the water to scoop up their favourite prey.

A few feet away from the water's edge, beneath a colourful umbrella on the sun-bleached pearly sand, Victoria slept on a blanket, blissful and happy, challenges of the recent past, forgotten. Venkat walked along the waterline, bagging shells.

Waking Victoria, Venkat dropped the shells next to her.

"I'm hungry."

"Me too," Venkat agreed as Victoria prepared a late lunch.

"Did you bring your books?"

"No, Princess, I have not. Did you want me to carry them all the way here?"

"Yes, it will be good for you. Education will set you free," she replied firmly.

"They call me Madras now," Venkat tried to distract her from the topic of his studies.

"I enjoy being with you. It has been a long while; I wondered whether I would ever see you again."

"I prayed that we would see each other again. There are so many things to talk about and memories are special. The sadness of the recent past is fading away day by day. Now my greatest yearning is to meet my father. There is no greater love than what exists between a daughter and a father, so I await his return."

"Princess, he will return to carry you on a horse and take you back home."

"It would be quite difficult, as we have an ocean in between," Victoria teased.

"Our childhood was fun. I remember spending time with my grandfather. Every Sunday he would visit us. Having walked many miles, he would rest on a bench, beneath the banyan tree. He would prop me and my brother on his knees and feed us my grandmother's delicious French biscuits and sweets. On one such visit he cut off a section of a bark of the banyan tree trunk and told us that whenever the shadow of the roof touches the mark that he had cut, he would be sitting here with us. He kept his promise for many months. Then one Sunday we waited for him and he did not come. A few weeks later, my grandmother paid us a visit and brought news that he was very ill. He had stepped on a rusty nail and his foot swelled and was unable to walk. Later that month, he passed away. As his body burnt on the pyre, we prayed for guidance and although we moved from place to place, I always felt his presence."

"Princess, can I quote from the book you gave me to read?"

"Please do."

"Enter into your temple – into your heart – fill it with good thoughts and therein shall dwell the images for eternity."

Victoria, dumbstruck by the fluency of Venkat's quotation, sat silent for a few minutes.

"I'm really impressed and excited that you have learnt so much."

"I read every minute I have available and memsahib helps me when she can."

"Lunch is ready."

"This food is fit for royalty, Princess Victoria."

"Thank you, kind sir, it's an honour serving you. I accept your appreciation on behalf of my mother."

Nervous sea birds fought each other for the bits of food thrown by Victoria. Venkat was about to bag the shells which he had sorted into different groups according to their size and shapes, when Victoria stopped him.

"Can you place the small shells on the sand to make a letter 'V'?" Victoria asks.

"I can. It's easy."

"Very confident, I see."

"I will learn much more. You are a good teacher," he said as he formed the letter with the shells.

"Brilliant. I will do another 'V' next to it."

"Now tell me what letter you see on the sand?"

Hesitating, and quite embarrassed, Venkat looked at Victoria and said, "You will laugh if I'm wrong."

"I will not," Victoria promised.

"Then it is a double 'V'. I read sentences better."

Victoria looked away to hide her grin.

"You promised you would not laugh."

"Okay, you tried. It's a 'W'. One day you will be better than I am," Victoria assured him. Venkat's literacy only included written and oral lessons in Tamil and now faced English as a new, surmountable challenge.

"Princess, we need to leave now as I have a long walk back home," Venkat said as he began to fold up the blanket.

"I think so too. I hope I don't have to wait for another few months to see you again."

"Princess, I will visit you on the Sundays that I'm free."

Tucking the umbrella under his arm, Venkat picked up the basket and followed a path through coastal vegetation that eventually spread out onto newlyprepared cane fields.

A few hundred yards away, Rosehill Manor stood majestic as the afternoon sun glistened off its windows.

"Home at last," Victoria sighed as she dropped onto the porch's floor.

Venkat spent a few minutes with Sushila. Promising her that he would visit again soon, he bowed and wished her well. Victoria, who waited outside, held Venkat's hands and wished him a safe walk back to the Nessfields. He crossed the cane field, ran along a firebreak and from atop a mound, he waved back to the ladies standing side by side, happy that they could be part of his life.

Nessfield Manor

The following morning, refreshed by an unbroken sleep, Venkat eagerly entered the house to begin another day. Gertrude informed him that the memsahib was not well. The captain left home early and advised Gertrude that he would send a doctor to examine Nancy before he set out on military duties. Venkat tiptoed as he went about his chores and dared not enter the main bedchamber. However, as he passed the open door, Mrs Nessfield called out feebly to Gertrude.

"Gertrude, where are Patrick and Madras?"

"I will call Patrick for you," Venkat answered.

Venkat followed Patrick closely as they entered the bedroom.

"Memsahib, it's Patrick," Patrick whispered.

"Patrick, Agatha is arriving tomorrow by ship. Bring her home. Take the carriage. The captain's mother will be coming as well. She is tall and always wears a pink bonnet," as she spoke, she gasped for breath.

As Patrick and Venkat walked to the stables to clean the carriage, Venkat wanted to know; "How will we know who Mrs Emily Nessfield is?"

"The ship will be full of British and they all look alike," Patrick shared his opinion.

"We can look for a small girl and an old lady or we can ask the administration officers on the docks."

"How would they know?"

"On arrival, all passengers are listed in books."

"You could be right. We will leave very early in the morning, then."

The scene on the pier was very different from when Venkat had disembarked. Chairs were laid out around tables. Ladies walked around under tiny parasols while others sat and sipped tea from delicate bone china cups. Thin, tall crystal glasses stood next to jugs of freshlysqueezed orange juice and plates of biscuits. Officers in their military uniforms occupied themselves by reading newspapers and tucking into the refreshments. Some engaged in animated discussions about the recent skirmish with the Zulus, which was a major talking point. Some men peered into the horizon with binoculars to spot the dull plume of smoke.

"I see a ship!" a soldier shouted. It was the signal they were all waiting for and the crowds turned towards the indicated direction as the ship came into view from behind the bluff.

"I hope it is not a coolie ship. It will be at least an hour before we find out," an army officer told his companions.

"Is Patrick your real name?" asked Venkat.

"No, the ladies at the missionary gave me the name. My real name is Dingaan, after a great Zulu king."

"There are tales from our districts in the south of India of ancient generations going far and wide, over many seas, using boats driven by wind, finding new land and settling there and taking with them our religion and culture and bringing back gold, tin and other goods. Wherever they went, they lived and mixed with the local people who shared their lives."

"How do you know?" Patrick asked.

"Fireside tales told by fathers to sons for many hundreds of years."

The ship slid into port. The gangplank was lowered, and the passengers streamed out, waving to people as they walked down.

"A tall woman in a pink hat... there are so many! Let us rather look for a lady with a little girl," Patrick suggested.

It was hours before they spotted a likely pair. The woman, beautifully dressed and her skirt pulled tightly around her stomach so that it created a bustle behind her, led a little girl by her white-gloved hand. Behind them, two crew members wobbled under the weight of many bags.

"I think that's them," Venkat pointed.

Finally, the last of the stragglers stepped onto the quay and entered the administration offices. A bit later, small groups gathered outside saying their farewell as they departed into waiting carriages, leaving behind the soldiers who still milled around.

Patrick led the way towards the lady in pink.

"Are you Mrs Emily Nessfield?"

"Who might you be?" she sneered.

"I work for Mrs Nessfield. We were sent by her as she is not in the best of health. She appointed us to welcome you and to escort you to Nessfield Manor, your ladyship," Patrick relished this demonstration of his understanding of the English language.

"Your carriage awaits, madam. We will carry your bags," Patrick pointed towards the carriage, hoping that she would climb in, for she seemed to be very suspicious of them already.

"Lady…ship," Venkat repeated softly, resisting an urge to crack into laughter.

"Respect, my dear chap, respect!" Patrick snuffed a grin.

"Where is my son?"

"Chasing Zulus or truth be told, fleeing from them, madam."

Mrs Nessfield almost yanked Agatha's arm out of its socket as she pulled her towards the carriage. Venkat and Patrick followed, struggling under the weight of the luggage. Once the bags were loaded, Venkat placed a small wooden box on the ground as a step.

As Patrick picked Agatha up to put her into the carriage, Emily Nessfield shrieked. "Don't touch her!" She jumped down. In doing so, she missed the box and fell in a heap, her skirt completely covering her head.

On seeing this, two soldiers ran to help her. Raging tempers suddenly exploded and they ploughed into Patrick and Venkat.

The pair rolled on the ground, shielding their faces from the kicks that thud into them. They had no chance to explain and those few moments illustrated the prevailing emotional state of the British soldiers.

Finally, Emily said, "I fell."

The soldiers stopped the beating and calmly walked away through the crowd that had built up, relieved of some of their anger. Both men sat up groggily, stunned by the ferocity of the attack.

Onlookers passed contemptuous glances and ridiculed the defenceless, bruised men as they wobbled to their feet. Dusting themselves, they walked to the carriage. Patrick's ripped right sleeve dangled by his side. Some of the fellow travellers helped Emily and Agatha into the carriage. Venkat joined Patrick in the driver's seat as he cracked the whip.

"You need a new shirt!" Venkat grimaced.

"I think you need a new body," Patrick countered.

Patrick guided the team into the yard. Nancy, who was waiting for their arrival, waved eagerly. Agatha jumped off and ran to hug her mother, whom she had not seen in years. Emily Nessfield walked over to Nancy and kissed her on her cheek, greeted her and sat down on the rocking chair.

"What happened to you?" Nancy asked Patrick, concerned.

"Ask the madam."

Nancy turned around and looked at Emily.

"It was a misunderstanding!" Emily shook her head.

Gertrude touched Patrick's swollen lips.

"Patrick and Madras, get cleaned up. We will talk later."

"It is rather hot. How is James?" Emily enquired.

"He is well, I hope. He's away on military duties. I am not certain how much longer he will be gone for," Nancy told her aristocratic-looking mother-in-law.

"Is there a war going on?"

"There is always a war or something near enough."

Venkat and Patrick carried the bags into the entrance hall, placed them on the floor, turned around and left. It was mid-afternoon and there were still chores to be done. Gertrude offered Agatha a glass of fresh orange juice. "Hello, I'm Gertrude," Gertrude introduced herself. Agatha thanked her with a delightful smile.

On the patio, the two women chatted, updating each other on the events in the colony and in England. The conversation continued until early evening when Gertrude moved a small table close to them and placed snacks on it.

"Supper will be ready soon," Gertrude informed Nancy.

"I see you have a coolie, as well," Emily observed.

Taken aback by her tone, Nancy sat silent for a while, then replied snappily, "His name is Madras, and he does the housework and the gardens."

"Have you lost any valuables?" Emily asked, lowering her voice and leaning towards Nancy. On hearing the question, Venkat slipped away with the kitchen waste to the compost heap in the garden.

"We lost nothing," Nancy replied sharply.

Two days after Emily's arrival, the captain came home from yet another Zulu expedition, tired and dishevelled. He hugged his mother and picked up Agatha. He threw her up into the air and lovingly held her close as she fell into his outstretched arms and then, in turn, he fell playfully onto the ground.

"You are such a big girl now and heavy as well!" he told his beautiful, giggling daughter. He kissed Nancy and walked into the bathroom to wash away the dust and grime of the past few days.

"He looks terrible. Is he being cared for properly?" asked Emily.

"He has been away for almost a week and has been living in the wilds of Africa; what do you expect, Mother?" Nancy responded, frustrated and showing it.

Venkat's new home was almost complete and Patrick helped him to nail shelves onto the inner wall as he placed small bottles on the middle rack. The top shelf was reserved for his marble carving.

"I have faith that this bird shall one day fly," he told Patrick as he reached up to place the bird on the shelf.

"When are you going to finish it?"

"Very soon, I hope!"

"I'm going to visit Guru Sundrum. Do you want to come?"

"Oh, yes! Yes, please! I would like to," replied Madras excitedly.

Once Patrick had left, Venkat removed the traditional hollow brass oil lamp from the small sack and washed and polished it with a clean cloth He carefully fashioned a cotton wick, placed it on the curved lip, poured oil into its hollow-cup and lit it. The small flame filled the room with a dull orange glow and in his heart, it was as brilliant as the mid-morning sun. He raised his hands in prayer, thanked his parents and then god, for his wellbeing. Lighting the lamp every evening just before sunset was a cultural practice, and sometimes Patrick would join him in prayer.

A few months since the voyage had passed and Venkat had not seen Guru Sundrum. He had been preoccupied with his new responsibilities since he had arrived in Port Natal, but now, he thought of home, his dreams and the promises he had made. He needed someone to take money home to his mother, preferably on the next ship sailing to India.

"Guru will find someone," he told himself.

The sun was slipping behind the tall trees and darkness settled in rapidly. The chorus of sounds made by the insects and animals reminded him of nights spent in the open wilds of India. Back home in wild pastures, once the goats had been herded into a safe area away from the jackals, the group of young boys would kindle a fire and chat until sleep ended their day.

In the backyard, a fire burnt brightly as Venkat fed it with dry sticks. Sensing the presence of someone else, he turned around. He was startled by an angelic figure staring at him, her face shining orange, lit up by the rising flames, and he shifted nervously in his seat. "You should not come here. Your father would not be happy."

All Agatha did was to shield her face from the brightness of the flame and remain where she was. Venkat ran into the stable, knocked on the wooden wall and called out to Patrick.

"Uncle, we have a problem!"

"What is it?" Patrick asked worriedly.

They walked out to find Agatha sitting on the stool that he had just vacated.

"Ah yes, we do have a problem." He called Gertrude.

Gertrude walked up to Agatha and led her away as they sat on opposite sides of the flames, warming their hands.

"So, she cannot talk …" Patrick told Venkat. They waited for Gertrude to return. "When she went back to England after her last visit, she fell sick and has not spoken since. Can it be god's wish?"

"If it is god's wish, then god is the only one that can make her talk again," Venkat predicted.

"It is possible."

"Uncle, she will talk again."

"Maybe," Patrick replied.

The flames died down and the embers glowed. Patrick got up from the bench and followed Gertrude into the house, closing the door behind him.

A week went by and Agatha's condition bothered Venkat.

"We will talk to Guru Sundrum on Saturday," he mumbled to himself as he polished the living room floor.

"What did you say, Coolie?" Captain Nessfield demanded.

"Nothing of importance. I was just thinking about my work."

"You work – not think. Coolies are paid to work and leave the thinking to us!" the captain shouted as he walked onto the patio to sit next to his mother.

"There are thousands of them here already and many thousands more are expected to come over."

"Do we need that many?"

"We enjoy the fruits of their toil, Mother."

Saturday finally arrived. Gertrude prepared food parcels and filled two canteens with orange juice for the long walk to the plantations. It was a threehour walk and a difficult one, through thickets, over rivers, and the appearance of snakes an everpresent threat. They chose to walk along the beach and then head inland after about two hours.

Dark green thickets of shrubs covered most of the sandy dunes and amid the thorns were cherry-red, juicy, plum-like fruits. They collected a bagful, then continued.

"Will you be able to find Guru's house?"

"Yes, I'm sure I will."

The rain clouds sailed westwards and once again the sun shone brightly. Perspiration ran down their faces. They rested in the shade of a large tree and drank from the canteens.

"Let's go, otherwise we will fall asleep," Patrick got up to his feet and lent a hand to Venkat who, still exhausted by the long walk and weighed down by the heavy bag of fruit, struggled to get up.

An hour after leaving the beach, Patrick pointed towards two white cottages ahead of them, nestled in a field of dark green cane swaying in the breeze that blew in from the sea. They reached the compound and knocked on the first door. Guru Sundrum answered and stepped out to welcome them heartily.

"This is Madras," Patrick jokingly introduced Venkat.

"I am called Madras now," he told Guru.

TYPICAL PLANTATION COTTAGES

"Madras … Oh, well! You're still the same man." He gestured, leading them into his tiny room.

The visitors were surprised by the conditions of the room. It was very small, windowless, cramped and dingy. Cooking was done in an earthen stove; blackened pots sat on iron rods and all worldly possessions were packed against the walls; clothes cooking utensils were on open shelves; firewood and farm implements lay on the floor. The rain dampened the floor and walls; mould grew from cracks that looked as if they might split the walls from roof to floor.

Guru suggested that they sit under the shade of a syringa tree and continue the conversation. The rest of the afternoon was spent chatting and sharing thoughts on various topics. Others came in from the plantation and dropping their implements, joined the group. Amid the drudgery, the indentured labourers found time for prayer, rest and recreation. Guru's wife brought a floral tray with tin cups of tea and a bowl of freshlycooked dumplings. Patrick emptied the bag of fruit into a small bucket.

"How was the day?" Guru Sundrum asked the newcomers.

"Not much better. Madhu, the pregnant girl, had to carry out her punishment for not being at work yesterday," one man replied as he bent down to take a fruit.

"What was it?"

"She had to stand the entire day on a box outside in the scorching heat."

On the outer fringes of the fire, the wives sat, engaged in their own conversation.

"Will India ever be free again?" Abdul Rahiman asked.

"Two centuries or more has passed and how long subservience will continue is unknown, yet we must believe that it will end. How many of you know the life cycle of the sacred lotus flower?"

A few seconds of silence followed.

"The lotus flower lives and thrives in murky ponds. Every night it sinks into the dark depths to re-emerge the next morning, refreshed and more beautiful than the day before, untouched by the dirt around it…so is our life."

"I am concerned, like so many of us here, about our family's future under the British rule and the effects of famine on our people."

AMAALU MOODLEY WITH SONS DORASAMY & MANIKUM

CONSTRUCTING A RAIL LINE

"Baboo, let us carry thoughts of those we left behind and pray for their health. Once again, we raise the issue of British rule in India. Raising painful memories at times weakens our resolve, but if it helps us to find ways to remove the hurt that we carry, then we must talk about it. In many ways, the famine is nature's phenomenon and generation after generation will find ways to cope. Death is always inevitable; in our case, it is worsened by unnatural causes. New ways were found to best use the effects of the famine to create the proposition that some of us were forced to accept. Our harvests were taken away; our craftsmen could not find work; our lands became barren, monsoons disappeared as if nature colluded with forces, unbeknown to us to add further pain. Children starved and yet no rations relieved their hunger. We will survive and we shall wait. In times gone by, conquests and colonisation by other empires also devastated our country when they pillaged and left. Even our ancestors sailed to remote lands and established themselves and prospered, contributing to the development of trade, cultural and religious growth."

The Guru, stopped, answered his wife and continued.

"Sorry… the only difference is that our ancestors did not destroy the people or the country. Our history, as well, is of dynasties and kingdoms, with rules that also subjugated the people and imposed laws as they decreed. Many of those conditions that permeated aspects of everyday life exist even today. To progress, we must organise ourselves because there is a need for religious centres, schools, medical facilities and businesses to support the people who will be looking for work. As more of our people come, there have to be work on the plantations; and other businesses must grow to employ the many recruits. Those who terminate their girmit must actively participate in the skills that we left behind. We can change our own lives. Use those skills to grow. We, as a community, must bear the responsibility as it is our future."

"Thank you, Guru. One question, please."

"Yes, Baboo, go on."

"We are here as one united group, yet we are differentiated by religion, languages and customs. How did we change?

"We should know that Saint Thomas brought Christianity to our land and spread it far and wide. The Sultans spread the word of the Koran. Some of our people chose a home for their faith in Islam and Christianity, but we are all of one distinct culture, irrespective of newfound faiths. Secondly our religious and linguistic differences have its foundations in one of the oldest practising religions in the world."

"Thank you, Guru."

"This is my third girmit. Each time I return, I come back with more images of home and it saddens me. However, we made our decision to come here because of a multitude of reasons. We left behind fathers, brothers and mothers to care for those we love, and we hope that when to go back home they will welcome us. The images I carry in my heart and mind is of mothers crying as fathers and sons carry away the dead, on frames made of tree branches, draped in white sheets, sadly, without garlands of jasmine, chrysanthemums or marigold. The pyres burn and the smoke darkens the sky.

"Above the smoke vultures circle, dawn till dusk, afloat on ill wind, watchful, patiently waiting for the death of gaunt animals that litter parched riverbeds, dusty plains and dried farm canals. Every feeble breath signals the inevitable and when death prevails, on silent, gentle wings they swoop, dropping around the carcass, satisfied that their patience has paid off. When the feeding frenzy is over, heavy with the spoils, the vultures one by one take flight. Perched on rocky cliffs and tall lifeless trees, eyes peeled, they scan the countryside for another bounty. These birds clean up our land of the dead beasts; only bare, bleached skeletons, mark the landscape as stark reminders of the catastrophe. The vultures, it seems, were a divination of an imminent tragedy that affected both man and nature. Year after year the famine annihilates our people. For those who survive, there will be other challenges to overcome."

"Can I say a few words," Singaram requested.

"Yes, yes, please," Guru urged him.

"We are here, brought together by circumstances and together we shall progress. As Guru and others explained, we will be given choices. Whichever option we choose must be well thought out and let it be the correct one. For now, let us enjoy whatever pleasures we can seek out of our life, pray and support one another."

Abdul Rahiman raised his hand.

"This land is a place grown out of imagination. We are caught between the British and the British. Back home, our ability to find work were destroyed, even our skills were strangled and here we are given the opportunity by the British to earn money, but at the cost of human dignity. We are far from the centre of our faith and we all live in the teachings of our ancestors and the words written in religious books. My faith is in the teachings of the Koran, so is Baboo's, Hussain's and Gafoor Kader's; Gabriel Anthony and Thomas Joshua believe in the Bible and the rest of us, in gods worshipped for thousands of years, but we must know that we all live in the shadow of Mother India and our roots run deep. We are resilient and this chapter of our lives is a challenge we will win. Thank you."

"Wise words, Abdul," Guru thanked him.

"Old order changes, giving way to a new. I am older than most of you and I am the past, and you the young, are the future. I see the world in wonder, filled with joy and happiness and all of us are a few steps away from a new life we strive for. When the smoke clears, we will find peace and happiness." Guru Sundrum was summing up when his wife gestured to him.

"Can I tell you about a folklore?"

"Yes, Thomas."

"Old tales from my parents as told to them by their parents. There was a scorpion wanting to cross a river. He crawled over to a wild duck and asked whether he can carry him across the water. The duck said, 'I am afraid you will sting me, and I will die.' The scorpion replied that he would not. So, the duck accepted. Mid-way through the river, the scorpion stung the duck. The duck asked, 'Why did you do that?' and the scorpion replied, 'That's what we do.' Both the duck and the scorpion drowned."

"Is there a meaning to the story?" Guru asked.

"I think that the actions of people and nature are one of predictability. We, therefore, before we act must think of possible consequences."

"Thank you, Thomas, very appropriate indeed. Trust is very difficult to explain or understand. Though desperation sometimes could cloud judgement and others are convincing enough to camouflage true intent, and when an honest man speaks, we listen to his heart."

"It's getting late and our guests must be tired," his wife suggested politely.

"In a few minutes," Guru Sundrum promised.

"We have not changed who we are and never will. Finally, when you are hungry, you look for food. When the wells run dry, you think about water. When family members die, we ask why. In truth, we are caught up in a web; like insects and trying to free ourselves only worsens the problem. When you are faced with a problem, think first and then act with dignity and stick to our moral code and hold on to the possibilities," Guru advised.

"We shall sleep here by the fire," Patrick decided. "It's a warm night."

"Before we go to sleep, let us sing in praise of our gods," Guru suggested. He sang the solo parts and even Patrick joined the chorus, while the women hummed the verses.

Guru Sundrum dropped a reed mat, two cotton bags stuffed with dried cane leaves for pillows and a thin cotton sheet.

"That is all we can give you, I'm afraid."

Abdul Rahiman offered a blanket in exchange for the sheet.

"I will use the sheet tonight."

Venkat crawled in next to Patrick and settled down to sleep. Thankfully it was a warm, dry night.

A chilly morning breeze woke Patrick. He pulled the blanket close to his chin and shook Venkat awake. They washed up and for breakfast had tea and pancakes.

Agatha's condition was discussed at length.

"It's difficult to say, but faith and God work in mysterious ways. You will help her, I hope."

"Yes. We will do the best we can."

"Son, I will make arrangements for you to send your money home."

They bid the guru farewell and started their walk back home. Venkat broke off a thick piece of sugarcane, bit off the hard outer skin and chewed the softer inner core as the sweet juice ran down the sides of his mouth.

"Our Guru really is a man of god."

"I think he is more god than man and I think one better is yet to be born," Patrick confirmed.

Pointing to the sugar cane, Patrick said, "This is the reason why you are here and maybe it will keep you here for a very long time."

"Perhaps …" Venkat replied, chewing another piece of cane.

CHAPTER 7

Nessfield Manor

"The little girl had been waiting for you for hours," Gertrude told the two exhausted men as they dropped onto the workbench.

"Where is she now?" Patrick asked.

"She is asleep."

After resting for an hour on the bench, they got up and accepted food from Gertrude. Venkat showered, changed into fresh clothes and, on completing his afternoon prayer, sat down to meditate.

Agatha, who had succumbed to sleep, woke up and marched towards the backyard. She pushed aside the tarpaulin sheet that hung over Venkat's door and poked her head in. Assuming Venkat was asleep, she stepped into the dim light and shook him. He jumped up, surprised and afraid.

"What do you want?" he asked, for a moment forgetting that she could not answer him. Agatha sat on his bed and wrote on a piece of paper that she had brought along with her. He stood by nervously and once she handed him the note, he rushed off to Patrick.

"She wants to go to the beach."

"It could be bad for us if we take her," Venkat whispered.

Gertrude took Agatha by her hand and led her back to the house. She gave Agatha's note to Nancy.

"Call them."

"We could be in trouble tonight if Emily is at home," Patrick warned Venkat of the possible consequences as they stepped onto the patio.

"Wait here. I will tell her you are here," Gertrude instructed as she entered the house. Nancy dropped her knitting on the table and called them in.

"Thank you for coming. Agatha wants to go and spend some time on the beach. I think it's a good idea. I have been stuck in this bed for far too long!"

"What about the captain and his mother?"

"The captain is away for two days or more and his mother is staying with friends."

"We could get into big trouble, memsahib," Venkat stammered.

"It will be alright. We will go on Saturday morning," Nancy decided for them.

Saturday dawned. Agatha waited outside the stable and clapped when Venkat pushed aside the door cover and stepped out.

Patrick, with a basket in one hand and a beach umbrella in the other, joined the excited group. "It will be very hot today."

Agatha skipped and jumped as they headed to the front of the house. Nancy sat waiting in the rocking chair.

"It is a beautiful day, memsahib."

"It is. Let us go then, Patrick," she called out to Gertrude as well, who was laden with two picnic baskets and a big cloth bag. Venkat took the bag and a basket from Gertrude and they set off to the beach.

Agatha ran excitedly ahead of the group and then ran back to urge them on. The beach was a few hundred yards from the house and the path that led to the shore was narrow and covered by a canopy of branches and cascading streams of colourful flowers.

"Mrs Nessfield is looking better," Patrick nudged his wife.

"She is looking like a queen."

As they passed shallow tidal pools, tiny crabs darted into muddy holes and slimy mudskippers foraged among dead leaves. The sound of the ebb and flow of the waves joined in the chorus with the gulls as they flit just above the water. The beach fanned out on both sides of the calm sea. Patrick chose a spot with shade provided by a tall rocky outcrop. The men planted the umbrella and Gertrude laid out the blanket, placing the baskets at the edge. Agatha was already having fun as the waves chased her back and forth on the long sandy shore. Nancy's face lit up and it made a wonderful change from the forlorn look that she had carried for as long as they could remember.

Patrick and Venkat sat on the sun-soaked sand.

Agatha ran to them carrying a conch.

"We use these in our temples to summon the god within us," Venkat said, as he palmed the shell.

Nancy hugged Agatha and held on to her for a while. She then picked her up Agatha, settled her on her hip, and walked along the beach.

"If only this day could last forever," Gertrude said to the two hungry men as she handed each a glass of juice and a plate of food.

"Thank you, Mrs Cele, this is a feast," Patrick complimented his wife.

Between bites of food, Patrick scanned the horizon, shading his eyes as he did so, ensuring that Nancy and Agatha remained within sight.

The day wore on and as the sun began its descent, tall palms cast long shadows on the white sand. Nancy and Agatha arrived back in time for the snacks that Gertrude had taken great pains to prepare. She complemented a beautiful day with the finest food she had ever prepared.

When white horses began to run the length of the waves, racing one another, each time edging further up the sandy beach, the happy group packed up and headed back home. Dusk was descending and Agatha was tired. Venkat carried her on his back; with her arms encircling his neck and her head on his shoulder, she fell asleep. Patrick led the way onto the green lawn of the manor. Emily, who was sitting on the rocking chair, fanning away the heat of the evening, jumped up and screamed, "Put her down, coolie!"

"She is asleep," Nancy said firmly and instructed Venkat to put her to bed.

He sat on the edge of the bed and gently turned Agatha on her side as he pulled a thin sheet over her.

Nancy thanked him as he came out of the house to join Patrick and Gertrude.

"Mother, ever since you've been here, you've treated the servants unkindly. Christianity teaches us that we're all children of God. Treat them as equals, and if you cannot, we'll have a problem."

Taken aback by Nancy's vehement reaction, Emily immediately got up and marched into the house. The others jumped into action. Gertrude went into the house and Patrick and Venkat vanished, taking the baskets and umbrellas with them. Darkness set in and each one was cocooned in thought as they parted for the night. Venkat lit the brass lamp and a candle and was about to begin his evening meditation when the sack covering the entrance to his room flew off the nails that pinned it. Captain Nessfield stood in the doorway, slapping his army belt against his left palm.

"You are not supposed to touch my girl, you heathen," he fumed as froth appeared at the corners of his mouth. The next few minutes turned wild. Venkat was at the receiving end of a flailing belt and heavy army boots pounded into his small frame. In the confined space he tried vainly to shield his face. More insults poured out. Satisfied, the captain eventually stalked out, knocking his head on the low overhang of the roof, and swearing as he walked away.

As he straightened the tilted candle, drops of hot wax ran down Venkat's fingers. Patrick and Gertrude tiptoed in and placed a lantern on the floor. They righted the overturned bamboo bed, picked Venkat up and propped him against a wall. Parts of the broken bed and shelves, clothing and utensils littered the room.

Gertrude went back into the house and returned with a bowl of hot water and a cloth. She was about to wipe away the small beads of blood that popped up around the swellings and cuts on Venkat's face and arms when Agatha walked in. Taking the cloth from Gertrude, she wiped off the wetness around his eyes and then bathed the swellings. Patrick and Gertrude spent a few minutes cleaning up the floor.

"We will repair and rebuild everything tomorrow," Patrick promised as he and his wife slipped out. Agatha sneaked out a few minutes later.

Left on his own, the lonely, battered boy picked up a letter from home which he had already read a few times. He leant on one elbow to get the best of the dim light from the lamp and read it again.

'My son, we are all together as I write this letter to you. We are proud of you for the sacrifices you are making for the sake of the family and we are truly blessed to have you as our son. We have met other families who also have brothers, uncles and fathers in Port Natal. The news is that you work in difficult conditions. We shall pray for you all. Your friends want to join you in Port Natal, but they are waiting for the right time. We will write again soon.'

Dousing the flame, Venkat placed the letter on the broken shelf, sat back and began to meditate for the second time that night.

It was sunrise when Patrick called him. "Memsahib wants to see you."

"I am embarrassed to see her."

"Why?" Patrick asked.

"I look like an injured dog."

Agatha entered his room and took him by the hand. Venkat hesitated, but Agatha tugged vigorously. He gave in and went with her. Nancy and Emily Nessfield were sitting on the patio. Venkat stood in front of Nancy whose face mirrored her concern.

"Are you hurt? I see you are bruised and swollen."

"Not much physically, memsahib."

"We are sorry."

"We cannot blame the master for momentarily losing self-control, being a soldier in troubling times cannot be easy," Venkat offered his understanding of the incident. "Memsahib, can I miss work today? I must rebuild my room," he asked, glancing at the older woman.

"You may, Madras. I apologise, on behalf of the captain, once again."

"These coolies should never have been brought here!" Emily screamed, spewing venom as she rushed into the house. Nancy's gaze followed her.

Rosehill Estates

On a beautiful Sunday morning, Victoria asked her mother, "Mother, you have been silent for the past few days; is anything wrong?"

"Today is the anniversary of my meeting your father. Eighteen long years and the dreams he had for us had been taken away by the army. And now we are nowhere near uniting as a family."

"Oh, Mother, we have much more than when we left India. Mr and Mrs Harrisford gave us the stability we need. We have money, and as Passenger Indians, we have freedom of thought and movement."

"I'm concerned about you. You are beautiful, intelligent and mature enough and being here stifles your future. The world awaits you. Your father has planned your future and he will be annoyed with me if I don't put the plans in place."

"Mother, I'm convinced Father will find us. One day he will knock on our door to rebuild the lost years. He promised."

"I guess you are right… and existing in a world of dreams and possibilities is not an ideal life as we go in search of a brighter future."

"Mother, you shall be a queen soon."

Victoria answered a knock on the door. Excited, she embraced a blushing Venkat. "It has been a long wait for your second visit," Victoria complained. "I need to have a talk with Mrs Nessfield. It isn't fair."

"Well, I am here now," Venkat said, smiling. "How is Mother?"

She led Venkat by the hand to greet her mother.

"It has been a long time," Sushila echoed Victoria's sentiments as he unpacked the flowers, bread and biscuits from the bamboo basket.

"We would enjoy more frequent visits, my son."

"Mother, as I explained to Victoria, we work on most Sundays. I also eagerly await my time off to visit you."

"We should visit you then."

"Memsahib will gladly welcome you," Venkat said.

"And you?" Victoria tested.

"I will enjoy your visit as well."

Victoria went into the kitchen and requested tea and biscuits, which Arvin set on the balcony.

"Princess, you have liberties here."

"We have. Mr and Mrs Harrisford treat me as their daughter and Mrs Harrisford teaches me about all things British. I love them both."

"It would be difficult for anyone to treat you any different."

"I am fortunate," Victoria responded, blushing.

Tea was followed by an early, long lunch in the shadow of a huge tree. Their friendship, born out of a common purpose, now spread into a deep mutual appreciation of the time spent together. Close as they were, Venkat did not cross the boundary out of respect for Victoria; her social standing would always be a reminder of their differences.

Battle of Isandhlwana - January 1879

The frontier stretched far into the interior as the British prepared to instigate a war with the Zulus. A simmering tension existed between the Zulu king Cetshwayo and Sir Bartle Frere, High Commissioner for the British Empire. He took it upon himself to invade Zululand. The stage was set to pit battlehardened troops, equipped with modern firearms, artillery and supplemented by local allies, against the Zulus whose numbers far exceeded that of the British forces.

Increased tension made the British forces wary and lookouts posted at high points scanned through binoculars for enemy movements. The Zulu armies were unique as a fighting machine and used strategies like those used by Napoleon, yet they possessed no weapons like the French or even the British. Their main weapons were the cowhide shield and a short stabbing spear or at times, a long throwing spear.

The oppressive heat and humidity from the recent rains made the task of the lookout difficult as mirages from the wavering thermals hindered identification.

Below, on the valley floor, the Zulu war machine was gathering, priming the deadly force for battle. Their scouts had seen the British positions and they were waiting for the right moment to strike.

A British scout scanning the horizon adjusted his binoculars as he did so. The sun was just climbing over the rolling hills and suddenly, close to where he stood, quails exploded into flight from the tall grass. The scout fell to the ground with a spear tip protruding from his back, hands still clutching his binoculars, arching his back in agony. A lone Zulu warrior stood over him, raised his short spear and ended the soldier's young life. Then he waved his spear high in the air, giving a signal.

On seeing the attack on the scout, other members of the group gave chase and followed the warrior into the valley and headlong into a trap. A 20,000-strong Zulu army was awaiting their arrival and its commanders pressed the trigger that catapulted the mighty army into battle, falling into attack formation on the run.

Lord Chelmsford, the Commander of the British Force, had underestimated the disciplined, well-led, motivated and confident Zulu. His failure to secure an effective position, the poor intelligence and the Zulus' tactical exploitation of the terrain, plus the weakness of the British formation, all combined to catastrophic consequences for the troops. The retreating scouts fired their rifles as they raced to their camp and the Zulus, in hot pursuit.

During the next few hours, the disciplined British guns pinned down the Zulus, who fell back behind the hills until noon, when they made another assault on the camp. However, the left horn of the Zulu advance was moving to outflank the British right flank position and smother it – a true Shaka strategy.

The carnage that followed would be the worst the British Empire had ever experienced in their quest to expand their colonial dominance over the proclaimed territories. Under strict instructions from their leaders, the Zulu warriors were ordered to disembowel the dead soldiers to cleanse their souls for the afterlife and to take pieces of their clothing for their own rituals.

When the sun finally set, the bodies of both victor and vanquished lay side-by-side, darkening the ground they had fallen on. It has been said that many who visited the battlefield days later could still hear the sounds of rifle fire, the thuds of bullets into flesh and the screams of the injured horses, the terrified shouts of men as spears pierced their bodies – as they sacrificed their last moments to the annals of history in the name of the Crown and country. An officer from Lord Chelmsford's force gave this eyewitness account of the final stage of the battle at about 3 p.m.:

"In a few seconds we distinctly saw the guns fired again, one after the other, sharp. This was done several times – a pause, then a flash-flash! The sun was shining on the camp at that time, and then the camp looked dark, just as if a shadow was passing over it. The guns did not fire after that, and in a few minutes all the tents disappeared."

Nessfield Manor

It was a Saturday and, with all the chores completed, Patrick and Venkat sat on the bench enjoying a drink. Gertrude appeared in the backyard to announce that Venkat had a visitor.

"Who is it?"

"A young British girl with an Indian boy."

"Oh! Is the memsahib here?"

"No," Gertrude told him.

"Please, please, can you ask them to wait? I need to change."

Venkat disappeared into the bath cubicle, poured half a bucket of water over his head, lathered feverishly, poured the remaining water over him and dried himself. Racing into his room, he jumped into his pants and pulled a cotton shirt over his head, all in a matter of minutes.

"That was quick," Patrick grinned.

"My arms are sore."

Venkat stepped onto the patio and Victoria jumped up to hug him. She held him for a while.

"If you cannot visit me, I will come to you."

"You are welcome, but I promise to visit you soon."

"I missed you. It has been a long time," Victoria complained.

"We are busy planting; it is midsummer."

Arvin, Venkat and Victoria sat down to enjoy Gertrude's tea and fine biscuits.

"This is a beautiful home and Gertrude is very sweet."

"She is, and so is Uncle Patrick, whom I shall introduce you to."

"We met on the day we arrived, but I would like to see him again. Can we go for a walk? I want to talk to you about something."

"Am I in trouble?" Venkat joked. "Okay, after greeting Uncle Patrick and a visit to our gardens."

Patrick was delighted to see Victoria again. He bowed and held her hand, "You are even prettier than when I first saw you."

"You embarrass me," Victoria giggled, blushing.

Visiting each flower bed, Victoria knelt and caressed the beautiful carnations, asters, marigold and the perfect red roses.

"Can I help you to plant?"

"Yes, not today though, Princess. What do you need to talk to me about?"

"I am troubled, and I need your help," Victoria began.

"I hope I can."

"A few weeks ago, my visit with Mrs Harrisford ended a bit early. The guest house door was locked. I knocked and waited. There were voices inside and it took a few minutes to open and when it did, Mr Ogilvy stepped out, looking sheepish. He wished me goodnight and rode off. Well, I was surprised and went to bed without speaking to Mother. Thoughts of my father haunted me, yet the sacrifices my mother made overwhelmed all other assumptions that ran through my mind. Who was I to judge my father or my mother?"

"I think you acted correctly, not to judge your wonderful mother. Only she can clarify the visit. Is Mr Ogilvy a regular visitor to Rosehill Manor?" Venkat asked.

He felt uneasy as he was in a position that was completely new, and he felt unprepared to help Victoria overcome her emotions and doubts about her mother's fidelity.

"He has meetings with Mr Harrisford and sometimes my mother joins them."

"Princess, what is your opinion?"

"I don't know. I think I will wait for her to tell me about it."

"You are young and resilient – and wise to not think much of it."

"I have a second matter for which I need your honest opinion.

"Is it also difficult?" Venkat asked.

"Mrs Harrisford and I have become very close and she is teaching me to dance. It is great fun. However, she asked me to join her to a ball and she has even designed and sewn my gown. I have waited weeks to talk to you about it."

"I know what a ball is, but the ball you talk about is as confusing as the English are."

"It is where men and women attend a dinner. Once dinner is over, people dance to music. The guests are wealthy estate owners, friends, businessmen, their families and military personnel."

"Did you ask Mother?'

"Not yet. I want your opinion first."

"Why me, Princess?"

"I just thought you could help me decide ... Mother hasn't been invited."

"I think you must go as Mrs Harrisford would be very disappointed if you do not attend."

"How do you feel about me attending the ball?' Victoria asked.

"I am happy for you. Remember that you are more British in many ways and should get used to their way of life before you go to Britain. Meet young people who share the same lifestyle."

Back at the house, Victoria joined Arvin on the patio. Venkat disappeared to the backyard and when he returned, he had a beautiful bunch of flowers.

"This is for Mother."

"I am disappointed. I came here for your opinion on whether I must attend the ball or not. All you say is yes, Princess, no, Princess," Victoria chastised Venkat.

"You must have fun. Mrs Harrisford loves you. Why disappoint her?"

"Are you sure?" Victoria sought confirmation.

"Definitely, Princess."

"Thank you then."

Mrs Nessfield rode in and Patrick took hold of the reins and held the horse firmly as Nancy jumped off.

"Madam, this is Victoria Payton of Rosehill Estates and Arvin. Victoria and I met on the voyage from India," Venkat introduced them.

"I'm pleased to meet you, Victoria."

"Thank you, madam."

"Call me Nancy, dear girl, and do not make this your last visit."

"Thank you. I'll visit again."

Venkat walked with Victoria and Arvin to the carriage and rushed back to complete the planting before nightfall.

During dinner, Venkat explained the complexities of Victoria and her mother's past to a curious Gertrude.

"It's a sad tale, indeed!" Then Gertrude said, "She loves you very much."

"I love them both as well."

"I mean she *loves* you," Gertrude insisted.

"Well, then I cannot differentiate the love I have for family and friends from the special love which you claim Victoria has for me. She's very important to me and I will forever love her and take care of her as I would take care of my sisters."

"You have much to learn, dear boy," Patrick chipped in.

CHAPTER 8

Madras (India)

Across the ocean in the burning cauldron of oppressive Madras, just a short distance from Fort St. George, Colonel Alexander Payton wiped away the perspiration that poured down his face. It had been six hours since he visited the last of every known address of his missing family. His horse swished his tail to keep away the everpresent flies that buzzed around the salty residue on its rump. Around him, there was a constant milling of people and animals. He was desperate to find his beloved daughter, Victoria, and his wife, Sushila.

Drawing in the reins, he turned his horse and entered the last place that might offer him a clue to the whereabouts of his family. It had been four years of hell. Unrelenting British autocratic orders passed on by deskbound stodgy old men decimated millions, and he was caught between the povertyridden people of South India and the huge quantities of food that were rotting in the stockades on the beaches of Madras. Having been re-commissioned and sent to Australia, Colonel Payton was in no position to intervene as a new set of officers were now in control. His only objective now was to find the location of his family. At every address he went to, the answer was the same: "They lived here for a few months but moved out."

He tied the horse to a fence post and entered the military offices. The officers saluted him and offered him refreshments. They directed him to a small room to rest and an officer followed him in. "How can we help you, sir?"

"I'm looking for my family. It has been four years since I last saw them."

"Sir, if your searches were unsuccessful so far, the only option left is to visit the emigration administration office."

"God forbid, why?" the colonel wanted to know.

"Sir, we received orders to increase the awareness of the possibility of a smallscale uprising. People are dying in the millions all over the presidency. Families of officers moved out to safer places, and some to other colonies."

"I regret the hardships we put them through."

"I'm sure you tried your best, sir."

"Thank you, officer. I must push on now to find them."

"Sir, according to dispatches received, you have three days before your departure to Australia. The ship has docked, sir."

"Blasted orders! Thank you, officer."

Tipping his cap, the colonel walked out. Night fell.

The very next morning the colonel, refreshed from a night's rest, walked through the emigration office gates and returned the salute of uniformed guards.

A clerk immediately saluted and offered him help.

"Sir, how can I be of service?"

"I have been searching for my family without any luck."

"Do you have any details that may assist me in finding them for you, sir?"

Captain Payton explained the events of the past four years.

"Sir, every person who emigrated or posted to another location – be it Indian or British – were catalogued in two separate books of departure. February of 1878, or a bit earlier, could be a starting point as there were a number of British nationals leaving around that time."

"I value your help and thank you."

"It is my duty, sir."

Standing alone in the tiny room, Colonel Payton prayed that this thread of a lead could be fruitful. Taking out his leather pouch, he gently pulled out a picture and stared at it. He ran his fingers through his matted brown hair.

"Sir, you can start with these books."

The colonel turned the thick cover and began the search.

Month by month, page by page, he searched. A clerk placed a plate of snacks and a glass of mango juice next to him. Just as he was about to take the second book, he shouted, "I have found them. I found them. God in Heaven!" He pointed to the page.

"I think you did indeed, sir. We'll get in touch with the authorities in Port Natal to find out their location and other relevant details."

Colonel Payton wrote down his details and promised the clerk a medal and rushed out, relieved of the tension that cowed him for so long.

Nessfield Manor

As the sun broke from behind the morning clouds, Nancy went to the stables in search of Patrick and was surprised to see the gardens that Venkat cultivated. They were thick with succulent beans, cabbages, carrots, spinach and strawberries. Beds of big, colourful marigolds shone brightly as the sun's rays touched the soft petals. She picked a few stems and walked to the front of the house, where she stopped abruptly. Two soldiers rode up the path towards her.

"We bring news. Can we go somewhere we can talk, madam?" one of the officers requested, removing his helmet.

"Y-yes, certainly," she stammered and supported by the wall she walked, ashenfaced into the house. Sliding onto a sofa she gestured for them to sit on the couch opposite her. Agatha came into the room, smiling at the officers.

"We have tragic news, Mrs Nessfield," the lieutenant said, looking at his dusty boots. His fellow officer sat next to him.

"The captain was a very brave man and his soldiers engaged an entire army. They lost their lives and the battle, but we will enjoy victory soon."

The lieutenant faltered as he spoke, ill-prepared to carry a message as tragic as the one he had just conveyed. The officers sat silently as Nancy tried to come to terms with the news.

"There will be a memorial service at the church the day after tomorrow," the lieutenant informed her.

"How … how many died?"

"Eight-hundred-and-fifty and about 450 of the Zulus who had joined the British army," the lieutenant replied.

"We are deeply sorry, madam!" the officers offered their condolences, left the house, mounted their horses and without looking back, headed for the fort.

Nancy sat there, trying to make sense of the painful news, then burst into tears when Gertrude and Emily came into the room.

"Put this in water," Nancy sobbed, giving the marigolds to Gertrude.

"What happened?" Emily asked.

"Your son has died in combat, Mother. Your son has died in combat," Nancy repeated.

Emily reached for the couch and slid tearfully into it. "It is a tragedy indeed … Oh! My son," she sobbed.

Venkat and Patrick came in through the gate as the soldiers were leaving.

"All is not well," Patrick sensed.

Agatha ran up to them, tugging at Patrick's hand. He picked her up and walked into the house. When Gertrude gave them the terrible news, he gently let Agatha slip down to the floor. She ran to her mother who held her close while shedding many tears.

"It is a sad day indeed," Patrick commented.

"There is no death, only a passing from one world to another," Venkat whispered as they walked out of the house.

They sat on the workbench in the stable, stunned by the death of the captain.

Wives of military personnel and friends visited Nancy for the remainder of the day and Gertrude was kept busy well into the night.

"Let's prepare our supper."

"Good idea," Venkat agreed.

Patrick prepared the ingredients for the stew while Venkat started the fire, placed a pot over the iron rods, knelt and blew into the heart of the fire. Patrick dropped the contents of the bowl into the pot and went into the kitchen for chunks of bread.

"It should take at least an hour."

Gertrude, having finished her chores, joined them and apologised for not preparing supper.

"How is the memsahib?"

"She is strong and brave," Gertrude replied as she disappeared into the house.

Patrick called out to Gertrude, letting her know that supper was ready. She dished out three plates of steaming stew and sat down to enjoy Patrick's first attempt at preparing supper.

"It is good!" Gertrude complimented the cook.

Agatha joined them at the fire and sat between Gertrude and Patrick on the bench. Venkat was afraid to offer her food, but Gertrude asked her whether she would like to eat, and to their surprise, she accepted by nodding. Gertrude brought the best plate and spoon from her own kitchen, ladled stew onto the plate and passed it to her. The dainty spoon shone in the firelight as Agatha tucked in and cleaned out the plate. Gertrude hurriedly gathered up the empty plate and spoon, dusted her dress and took her back to the house, where she changed her into her pyjamas and tucked her into bed. Venkat was about to douse the fire when Nancy appeared.

"Madras," Nancy spoke softly. "The day after tomorrow the army is holding a memorial service for the soldiers at the church. You all can come."

"As much as we would like to be there, we cannot attend, memsahib, but I will tell Patrick of your invitation," Venkat replied apologetically.

"Why not?"

"Memsahib, it is a difficult time for all. There is anger about the loss of so many lives and if we are at the service, it will create more problems for you. Our thoughts will be with you and your family."

"Thank you," Nancy stood for a minute then walked away.

Most of the next day was spent in silence. Agatha made frequent trips to the stables with Emily overseeing these visits. Gertrude was, as usual, engrossed in her daily chores. The men spent the day cleaning the stables and sheds. Later Venkat cut large bunches of fresh flowers for the service and for the home. Nancy sat on the patio looking out to sea, breakfast and lunch untouched.

At dawn the next morning, a special carriage arrived to take the Nessfields to the service. The ladies were dressed in black and thin black veils covered their faces. Agatha followed her mother into the carriage. Emily was the last to get in. The three servants watched from the patio as the carriage pulled away.

They watched until the carriage was out of sight and went back to their daily tasks. "We should talk to the British and find out where they are buried," Venkat suggested.

"Why, Madras?" Gertrude asked.

"The memsahib should visit the burial site."

"Do you feel that she should?" Patrick asked.

"Yes, it would be good for her and Agatha – and even Mrs Emily – to pay their last respects to the captain."

"It will be dangerous for them to go there," Gertrude raised her concerns.

Nancy, Agatha and Emily returned from the church. Lieutenant Croydon and two officers accompanied them. Nancy ushered them into the living room. Gertrude had prepared supper and sat waiting for further instructions.

"We will be fine, now," Nancy thanked Gertrude, who then slipped out through the back door.

The tragedy seemed to have changed Emily – her appearance at the stable was indeed a surprise to both Patrick and Venkat. Agatha joined the men in the shed and tinkered with the gardening tools. They looked at Emily, waiting for a comment of some kind. When there was none, they looked at one another and continued with their chores.

"The strawberries look wonderful. Patrick, can we pick a few?" she eventually asked.

"Yes, you may – as many as you want, memsahib," Patrick offered.

Venkat picked them for her. He dropped a few leaves into the bottom of Agatha's small doll's basket and put in the succulent fruit one by one, being careful not to damage any. Emily thanked them and they made their way back to the house.

"Are we going to the fort?" Venkat asked Patrick.

"Yes, we will go after I fix the saddle. Memsahib wanted to go for a ride on the beach."

"Will she be okay? Memsahib has not allowed herself to grieve, and she may need to be with someone."

"Maybe she needs to be alone to work through her pain," Patrick suggested.

Patrick hesitated to enter the fort for many reasons, but once there, they resolutely approached the door, Venkat a few steps behind.

"What do you want?" growled an officer dressed in the familiar red coat of the British troops.

"We are here to find out where the soldiers are buried."

"Why?"

"Captain Nessfield's wife wants to visit the gravesite," Patrick offered a polite and courteous response. The officer called a colleague whose bearded face frowned on seeing them. He spoke English in an accent which Patrick found difficult to understand.

"It is a long way out, but we can give you a map of how to get there. There is a war going on and she wants to make this dangerous trip?" he coughed, spraying tobacco juice blended with alcohol as he did so. Patrick took a step back but was too late to avoid the spray.

"Alright, come back later and we will give you a map," his sober colleague told them.

They sat outside the fort for rest of the afternoon waiting for the map, which they eventually received.

"Where is the memsahib?" Patrick asked Gertrude on his return.

"She hasn't yet returned from her ride."

It was supper time when Nancy led the grey into the stables. Patrick unsaddled the mare, dropping fodder into the feed box and shut the door.

"Memsahib, Patrick and Madras would like to speak to you when you feel it is comfortable for you," Gertrude told Nancy as she served supper.

"Call them once supper is over."

Gertrude set out three chairs onto the patio, arranging them around the table.

Patrick and Venkat waited nervously for Nancy to join them. The flame of the lamp flickered in the chilly breeze.

CHAPTER 9

Nessfield Manor

Patrick pulled back a chair for Nancy and took his seat once more.

"How are you, memsahib?" Patrick broke the silence.

"I'm confused and afraid of the future."

"We can come back later or tomorrow if you prefer, memsahib."

"No, it is fine."

"Memsahib, we are deeply sorry for the loss of the captain. Gertrude, Madras and I share your grief," Patrick paid his condolences. He then nodded and nudged Venkat.

"You, Agatha, Uncle Patrick and Auntie Gertrude are my family, and I call this home," Venkat began.

"I am glad to have you all around me," Nancy responded immediately.

"Death is not the end of life as we know it to be. Beyond death exists an eternal life of migration and transformation of the soul. It is a sacred journey and a touchstone of our belief in reincarnation and our understanding of life and death. The captain's passing is tragic and his last moments would have been with those whom he loved. His body rests and the journey of his soul begins and will be judged by god."

Venkat paused for a moment and took a sip of water from a tin cup. Nancy looked blankly and him. Venkat changed his approach.

"You prayed for all those who lost their lives and the captain served his country and kingdom with his life and with honour. It is, therefore, a fitting tribute for you, Agatha and Mrs Emily Nessfield to visit the burial site to pay homage to a husband, father and a son."

"We have received directions to the burial site, and we will find the safest and best possible way to get there," Patrick added.

"Memsahib, for the living, time softens pain and sorrow but there has to be a spiritual response to pacify the souls of those who tragically depart."

Patrick shifted nervously, passing a sideways glance, then addressed Nancy, "The ground where the captain's body lies shall be consecrated by our faith and prayers, memsahib."

"Thank you, Patrick."

"It is a strange suggestion we make, memsahib, knowing the pain you are in, but as a member of this family I'm bound by ancient laws to perform a ritual that shall create an avenue for the captain to pass through the various stages before he stands in front of god on the sixteenth day of his passing."

"Patrick, I understand very little of what has been said, but I feel Madras gives credence to his firm belief. I am intrigued by his commitment to us as his family. We shall go."

"Memsahib, lastly, the first step you need to take is to allow your emotions to express themselves freely and not to be restricted by how society wants you to act," Venkat concluded.

"We need a plan and money for the journey," Patrick suggested.

Nancy left the patio and returned a few minutes later with a biscuit tin. "You can use this, Patrick."

Patrick's jaw dropped at the sight of a tin full of money.

"You two, our lives are in your hands."

"Madam, we will protect you at the cost of our own lives," Patrick promised.

It took Venkat, Patrick and Gertrude almost a week to prepare for the long journey, knowing little of the challenges that lay ahead.

CHAPTER 10

Port Natal

A chilly breeze blew in from the ocean as black clouds floated westwards. The rain of the previous night filled hollows in the traffichardened streets. Workers drifted by as the morning sun still lay hidden behind the grey horizon. Store owners, making an early start, swept wooden floors. In the corner café, a young man stacked fresh fruit onto shelves while next door a Zulu woman cleaned large showcases. Venkat watched as the prelude to the day ahead began to take shape. The last of the wispy white clouds began to disappear, heralding a clear new day.

Agatha and Nancy huddled together in the foul-smelling waiting room of the Perseverance Stagecoach Company. Patrick and Venkat blew into their hands as the breeze flowing in from the ocean, cold and moist, wafted in between the buildings. At their feet were five large canvas bags, about another ten smaller ones and a roped bundle of bedding. The sun eventually topped the golden ocean as a stagecoach, driven by a wiry, unshaven man, pulled up next to the station.

The clerk stepped onto the street, handed the driver small packages and then inspected the empty coach. It was 7 a.m. and time to board the stagecoach for a day's trip to Pietermaritzburg. Vapour rose from the wet rooftop of the coach under the heat of the midsummer sun. The uniformed clerk ordered the ladies to get in while Patrick lifted the big bags onto the roof. Venkat perched gingerly on the load box and pulled the bags up; running thick ropes across, trussing the heavy luggage. Some of the remaining smaller bags and cone-shaped bamboo baskets were pushed into a net covered box at the back of the coach and the others in any small spaces found within the coach itself. Finally, Patrick and Venkat entered the coach as the driver cracked his whip, cursing the day that lay ahead.

The team of six horses strained their bulging muscles as their hind legs pushed hard to gather momentum for a slow trot. Guiding his responsive team, the driver led them out of town.

Agatha lifted the stained curtain and waved to the people on the street. Passing the toll gate at Berea Ridge, the whip snaked out and cracked once more as the team began to canter and the passengers endured a bumpy ride. A few hours into the journey the scenery of the landscape changed.

The rolling hills, divided by tree-filled valleys, were covered in carpets of green and rivers wound their way over the rock-strewn beds. Small clusters of homesteads were chiselled into the green slopes and footpaths crisscrossed the landscape where cattle, heads down, grazed on the sweet grass.

The white settlers had taken most of the prime farming land and the local Zulus were given work by the farmers, who also offered them accommodation for which they were required to pay rent. Most chose to settle in places where they could practice their traditional way of life. Workers from the towns made their way back home to support any causes that offered them a way to regain their lost culture. Some of the more knowledgeable Zulus were able to arouse the emotional fervour of their people to a point where battle was the only solution and death was welcomed.

It was after midday when the driver pulled his team to a stop at a halfway station where the passengers could stretch their legs and enjoy a meal before the final ride to their destination.

Nestled among trees and huge rocks, a neat trading post made a welcome sight. The owner ran out to meet them. Nearby, corralled horses snorted and neighed boisterously.

Venkat filled the canteens from a nearby pond that was fed by a gurgling spring and Patrick helped the driver to feed the horses with freshlycut grass. The blazing sun passed its midday position. The intense heat and the humidity made conditions unbearable and the only respite was from the shade provided by the tall trees which separated the road from the station.

All around, undulating hills and valleys stretched for miles. Agatha and Nancy walked together admiring the beauty of the place, amid nature's paradise. Wild, colourful shrubs grew from earthen pots, sloping boughs of stubby trees were adorned with bright streams of flowers and Zulu maidens danced to the beat of drums. Venkat and Patrick eagerly put together a muchneeded lunch which was served with refreshing juice, to the delight of an unusually hungry mother and daughter.

An hour later, they set off again. The destination was many hours away and both Agatha and Nancy felt the effect of the journey, twisting and turning to find suitable positions on the stiff, studded seat of the coach, made uncomfortable by the bouncing monotony of the ride, wooden wheels rolling over stones and ruts baked hard by the relentless sun. Dust and grit streamed through the smallest of gaps to add to the discomfort of the clammy heat. Even for Patrick the journey seemed endless; he was filled with the fear that an accident or other incidents might occur before they reach their destination.

The duration of the journey itself, in the cramped space, was of great irritation. However, for Venkat it was different; he slept through it all, even when his head slumped from the wooden panel of the coach he rarely woke from his slumber. Agatha, and eventually Nancy herself, heads pressed against the shutter, fell asleep. Patrick took in the scenery as the coach rattled along. Looking at Nancy, he noticed tears running down from both her eyes and tiny drops emerged from her nostrils. He nudged Venkat awake. Removing the pillow that covered his head, Venkat looked in the direction of Nancy.

"She is crying. What do we do?" Patrick asked.

"Leave her for now," Venkat whispered. They sat and watched her for a short while to allow her to be awakened by the bouncing coach. When she was jerked out of her sleep, she sobbed for a few minutes.

"Patrick, I'm sorry," she apologised.

"There is no need to be, memsahib."

"Memsahib, the burden of your loss weighs heavily on you. You cry and we shall not question why. However, if you want to share your pain we will gladly listen and try to provide any support we can," Venkat comforted her.

Nancy thought for a moment and then adjusted the pillow that Agatha slept on. Taking a deep breath, she sobbed again and then looked at Patrick.

"In life, I drew strength from God, my parents and more recently, the captain. Now that we are alone, I'm afraid of the future and what it holds for Agatha and me."

The two men sat silent for a while, taken aback by the sudden realisation of the great responsibility they were faced with. It was indeed a responsibility beyond their capabilities to ensure the wellbeing of an employer and, more importantly, a newfound 'family'. Nonetheless, it was a task they were willing to undertake until nature took its course and provided Nancy with the direction and the focus she needed.

"Memsahib," Patrick began, "we shall be your strength; we shall be your family for the rest of our lives. Know that life is uncertain and filled with disappointments, joy and new beginnings. You will find that special moment that will change your life for the better as God shall provide you with a plan. You are not alone."

"Thank you, Patrick," Nancy responded. "Now I'm hungry."

Venkat immediately knelt on the coach floor, reached beneath the seat, pulled out two sacks and emptied the contents on the seat. In neatly wrapped parcels were biscuits, sweets, strawberries, cheese, fruits, water and a bottle of juice. After rinsing the cups and plates, Patrick helped him split the contents onto the plates and the juice into four cups. Agatha woke in time to accept her share. Happiness seemed to return, and a short while later, Nancy was sound asleep.

Dusk was approaching and with it the expectation of rain as thick, black clouds blocked out the setting sun.

"Are you expecting rain?" Patrick called out to the driver, poking his head out of the coach.

"Not till midnight; the clouds are far away," he shouted back.

When darkness set in, the driver relied on his instincts, the two lanterns caged on either side of the stagecoach. Millions of stars and a rising moon would guide him to the end of the journey. He coaxed his team to a gentle trot and then the curses suddenly erupted, supplemented by a steady flow of vulgarity, possibly induced by the gulps of alcohol he had been imbibing – a potion to dull the strain of his important responsibilities. Nancy tried to ignore the blasphemous outpouring but showed signs of real discomposure.

Sensing Nancy's unease, Patrick opened the coach door and asked the driver to stop. The passengers jumped off the coach for a few minutes to stretch their tight muscles and strained backs. The air was crisp and refreshing, blowing away the dust that covered their clothes. Patrick jumped into the space next to the driver, who welcomed his presence.

"How much longer?" Patrick asked as the driver urged the team forward.

"Time enough for two more swallows from this bottle here," he said, tapping his pocket. "Hold these reins. Just hold them straight," he instructed Patrick.

Reaching into his jacket pocket and uncorking the bottle, he swallowed a mouthful of alcohol, belching heartily. "One more time and then we're home," he coughed.

As the dull lights of Pietermaritzburg came into view, Patrick handed the reins back to the driver who slowed the pace of the team to a trot. The coach stopped just as the stagecoach clerk waved his lantern, signifying the end of the journey and relief for the weary passengers. Welcoming them, he placed a bench at the foot of the coach door.

Dim oil lamps lit up the station. Nancy and Agatha stepped down backwards onto the small bench as the tired horses snorted. Patrick and Venkat laboured under the weight of the bags which they stacked into the small waiting room.

"We should look for a place for the ladies to sleep," Patrick suggested. Nancy and Venkat ventured into the night while Agatha sat close to Patrick in the cold waiting room.

"There is room for the ladies only!" Venkat blew through cupped hands on his return.

"I'll take Agatha to her mother."

Carrying Agatha on one arm and hooking two bags over the other, he walked rather unsteadily towards the inn, disappearing into the black night. Upon his return to the waiting room, he found Patrick already asleep, wedged between bags to shield him from the knifing wind. Venkat wormed himself in next to Patrick and slept.

Thawed by the morning sun and awakened by the noise of a thousand chirping birds, they heaved themselves up and bathed with icy water collected from a rain tank. After changing into fresh clothes, they started breakfast. Patrick boiled water as Venkat laid a cloth on a big canvas bag and set out the biscuits and cakes which Nancy had purchased at the halfway stop. He then left the station to bring the ladies back from the village inn.

"We are so hungry!" Nancy exclaimed.

"Patrick has breakfast ready."

"Patrick, can we eat?" Nancy asked as they reached the station.

"We'll have to use tin cups again."

"We don't mind. It is a cup, nonetheless."

The four sat together enjoying every sip and crumb.

"We need to hire a wagon and six horses," Patrick suggested as he filled his cup.

"The clerk told me that there was a place nearby where we could rent them," Nancy replied as she slurped the hot tea. Looking up at Patrick, she smiled.

Once the cups were washed and packed away, Patrick followed Nancy. They were about to leave the station when they saw an old man coming towards them.

"Good morning, sir!" Nancy called out to him.

"Do you know where we might be able to rent a wagon and horses?"

"Walk a bit and turn left beyond the sheds and you will see some stables, Ma'am," he directed them, a half-chewed cigar dangling between his yellow teeth and tobacco juice dripping from the corner of his mouth that, over time, ran onto his alreadystained beard. She thanked him and walked towards the stables. Patrick followed.

"Good morning!" Nancy summoned the attention of a man hammering on a horseshoe. He dusted his hands on his leather apron and looked up.

"William Foxgate, madam. How can I be of service?"

"We would like to rent six horses and a wagon, please."

"How long do you need them for?"

"About five days, I think. We need to go to the site of the recent battle."

"Then seven days is what you need them for, madam," Mr Foxgate said. "The fee will be ten pounds, ten shillings, and ten pounds extra if a horse dies and costs to damages to the wagon or equipment will be extra. I will make an exception and not charge a guarantee fee. Payment for the extras as explained will be charged when you return, madam."

"Fair enough. We will take them," Nancy said, looking enquiringly at Patrick. Patrick nodded. Nancy paid Mr Foxgate and accepted the receipt – an oilstained slip of paper.

"Do you know how to get there?"

"We have an idea," Nancy replied.

"Help me with the harness, ole' chap." He then sketched a map and provided more details of the route they needed to follow.

Patrick agreed and led the horses around to the waiting room to tie them to a wooden post. He and Venkat then carried the bags to the wagon. With some of the contents of the bags they fashioned a bed for Agatha and a comfortable seat for Nancy. They drew a canvas sheet over the steel frame of the wagon and dropped another sheet over the back section. In front, the horses were keen as they pawed the ground restlessly. Patrick took the reins and Venkat positioned himself into the space next to him. The harness strained as the horses pulled and soon, they were trotting briskly, swishing their tails as they picked up speed.

"Do we have food for the ladies for seven days?" Venkat asked.

"I'm not sure, but we'll follow the wagon trail and there will probably be places where we could buy food if ours run out," Patrick replied.

"Memsahib, can you read these instructions?" Patrick requested, handing her the map. She unfolded the sketch across her lap.

"Follow the road that we are now on for a mile. You will arrive at a section where the trail meets another used by wagons heading north. Join up with a wagon train when you come across one, as it will provide safety. Travel with it and ask for directions from one of the train guards. Be careful when crossing rivers."

Patrick stopped the team when they reached the trail and they waited for about an hour. There were no wagon trains in sight. "Why don't we go on as we may meet them ahead? The signs show that wagons passed by a few hours ago and ox-drawn wagons are very slow, as you know," Patrick suggested after examining the ruts on the trail.

To their surprise, an hour into the trip a wagon train came into view just a few hundred yards ahead, laden with bags, large equipment and wooden crates tied down by sturdy ropes. There were three long wagon trains, each pulled by a team of at least sixteen muscular oxen, straining against the weight of the load. Riding next to the train were brawny, mean-looking men on majestic horses, black manes swishing, hearts wild as mustangs.

"Train guards," Patrick said.

Long leather whips snaked out, reaching the lead oxen and cracking around their rumps. Men toiled behind one of the wagons – pushing, and some turning the wooden wheels that were being swallowed by the muddy trail. Shouts and threats urged the oxen on, muscles taut as they stretched every sinew.

Patrick drew closer to the wagons. A guard wearing a stained hat and sunbleached coat spun his horse around and approached them.

"Where you heading to?" he asked, removing his hat as Nancy rose from her seat in the wagon.

"We're in need of your help. We are going to the burial site of the British soldiers. My husband lies buried there."

"Madam, my condolences. You have a long, long ride ahead. If you're able to go faster, I suggest you go on as there are other teams a few hours ahead. Join them when they pull over for the night. It's not safe for anyone in these parts after the recent events."

Nancy thanked him. The guard took up his horse's reigns and returned to his team.

Just before nightfall, Patrick chose to follow a wagon train that most likely would pull over for the night. The sun was sinking fast, and as expected, a burly, bearded man ordered the teams to stop for the night. The wagons were pulled off the trail and settled in a clearing. Patrick followed and guided their horses to a safe distance from the mean-looking bunch of alcohol-soaked men.

"We need their help, unfortunately," Nancy consoled Agatha, who stayed hidden in the wagon. Patrick unhitched the horses, rubbed them down with handfuls of grass and tethered them to sturdy tree branches. He cut more grass and heaped it near them. Venkat built a fireplace and placed pots on thin iron rods that he had taken from Patrick's tool shed. Agatha and Nancy left the wagon and sat on benches next to the fire, eagerly waiting for tea and biscuits while supper was being prepared.

Patrick filled the pot and the kettle with water from the containers they had brought and added a mixed variety of precut vegetables that Gertrude had sent along. Two men from the wagon train offered them a parcel of fresh impala meat to flavour the stew.

"Memsahib, can we add this to the stew? It looks very good."

"Yes, Patrick, that would be delicious."

Venkat handed Nancy a plate of biscuits and cooled Agatha's tea by transferring the contents from one cup to another a few times, then he handed it to her. Nancy blew into her cup and sipped.

"You make good tea, thank you."

"It's an art, memsahib," Venkat smiled.

Supper went down well, and the ladies changed into fresh pyjamas for bedtime. The men from the train also found spots next to their wagons and rested their tired bodies, swallowing mouthfuls of liquor and belching. Eventually, all fell asleep, except for those who stood guard.

Venkat and Patrick sat by the fire and fed it with dried twigs and small branches to keep away the biting cold. Inside the wagon, Agatha and Nancy were experiencing their first night in the wilderness, comfortably and cosily. Warming their hands, the two men took turns to stay awake, upholding the promise made to Nancy to protect them on this journey.

Morning broke with the noise of men barking orders. Energetic teamsters popped up between sedate oxen as they checked the harnesses, while others prepared the wagons for the long journey to the hinterland. The ladies washed and changed and sat waiting for the breakfast that Venkat was preparing. He served bread, tea and the remainder of the stew. With breakfast over, they packed the wagon and took their places. Patrick was ready to leave when the guard from the wagon train approached them.

"Go ahead as you're faster. You'll travel for another two days with the locals guiding you. Do not leave or detour far off the trails."

"Thank you," Patrick acknowledged the guard's help.

The African sun blazed as always, and the canvas covering increased the oppressive heat inside the wagon. Agatha and Nancy fanned themselves, stopping at times to rest their tired hands. Patrick stopped the team. They raised the side sections of the canvas and strapped it over the top to create a thicker roof, able to provide more shade for the ladies and allowing what little breeze there was to cool down the wagon. Around them stretched miles of open grassland, dotted by flattopped trees and domeshaped hills. Warthogs, disturbed from their sleep, broke into frantic dashes for their burrows, tails pointing skywards. Impala resting in the shade panting to keep cool. The wagon trail stretched ahead, disappearing into valleys and then resurfacing over rolling hills shining in the noonday sun. The travellers quenched their thirst from canteens and Nancy poured some water onto her neck to wash away the dust.

"I am sorry to put you through all this, memsahib," Venkat apologised.

"It's alright. It's a new experience, one that I did not expect to undertake."

"We will stop here for a while to rest the horses and have something to eat," Patrick told the weary group. He collected buckets of water which he put in front of the horses and splashed buckets onto their sweaty bodies. Venkat joined Patrick in the rock pool.

Agatha and Nancy also splashed themselves in the cool water of the pools. Patrick washed down the horses with more water and rubbed them down with grass as Venkat heaped more for them to feed on. The ladies came back refreshed and jumped into the wagon. They spent a few minutes sharing snacks before Patrick cracked his whip. The teams strained their muscles and picked up a trot.

Suddenly in front of them, blocking the trail, was a group of Zulu warriors dressed ready for battle, each with a spear in one hand and a cowhide shield in the other. Time stood still.

"Great warriors, carrying the blood of many kings, with the bravery of lions and the strength of elephants, we salute you!" Patrick spoke, collecting his thoughts, and bowed his head as he knelt on the ground. Venkat pushed Agatha back into the wagon as he also eased himself to the ground, petrified.

A potbellied warrior stepped forward, touched Venkat's hair and bellowed, "This is the first time I see a Zulu with straight hair!" He broke into laughter.

"Great one, he is not Zulu. He's an Indian from across the ocean."

The other Zulus followed the first warrior's example, taking turns to touch this strange phenomenon.

"He is no bigger than an iklwa (spear). He cannot be a warrior," they said, as they tested his arms and shook their heads.

"Great warriors, we want to visit the sacred grounds where the great king defeated the white soldiers," Patrick searched for the right words.

"Those were brave men to fight when they knew they would be killed. Their blood quenched our spears," their leader spoke as he sliced the air with his spear.

Patrick sensed that there was no danger yet and was thankful that Nancy didn't understand the language. Pointing to Nancy, he said, "Great leader, we request your permission for the wife of a dead soldier to pay her last respects to her husband who was killed by your mighty spears." Patrick spoke with his head bowed.

"Who is your king?" the potbellied warrior demanded.

"King Cetshwayo," Patrick answered softly.

"Go in peace and you," he said, pointing to Venkat, "eat meat." His belly bounced as he cracked up laughing again.

One lithe young warrior, gazelle-like, leapt onto the wagon wheel, removed a thin goatskin choker, reached out and handed it to Agatha.

"Give it to your king."

Agatha looked at Patrick who translated.

"Take it," he gestured to her. "It's a leopard's tooth."

Agatha tested the sharp point of the tooth and examined the sundried, rolled goatskin band.

"You were great." Nancy reached out and touched Patrick on his shoulder.

The war party melted into the tall grass as quickly as it had appeared, and the wagon creaked forward slowly.

Their uneasy calm broke when Patrick imitated the warrior: "Eat meat." He couldn't help breaking into a giggle as he finished translating the conversation to Nancy.

"Great warriors, carrying the blood of many kings," Venkat teased, and in trying to re-enact Patrick's kneeling stance, he fell off the wagon. Patrick leant over and helped Venkat scramble back onto his seat.

"He does weigh as much as a stick!" Patrick laughed.

The few moments of amusement were the tonic that was needed to cast aside the effects of the shock of meeting with the band of warriors.

Three days had passed since they left their home and it astounded both Patrick and Venkat that Nancy, face and exposed arms and legs browned by the sun, seemed to be getting stronger. Even her voice increased in strength and showed that she was adjusting to the rigours of the trip.

Patrick followed the wagon trails, crossing many rivers and streams, pitching camps, where travellers once camped on their way to new mining towns in Kimberley and the Witwatersrand. It was a monotonous, energysapping and exhausting journey. Passing small towns, and temporary fortifications that were used to fend off warring Zulu factions, the trail led them closer to the battle site. They were now in the heart of Zulu territory, where renegade bands roamed freely. Fortunately, any encounter would be less hostile as this area was Patrick's birthplace and he belonged to the chieftain's household. Knowing where and whom to approach, he bartered for pumpkin, sundried maize and millet to stock up for the return journey.

During some stopovers, Patrick set basket traps at strategic spots to catch quails or partridges that roamed the grasslands. This was done discreetly as it could have upset the ladies, killing such dainty birds.

Agatha and Nancy slept for most of the trip, only getting up to splash in rock pools or swim in rivers to bring relief from the dust and grime. When awake, Nancy read a lot without complaining – a sign of her resilience. For Agatha, the journey into the bush populated by animals never seen before was an adventure. She even tried to draw some of them.

At night Patrick and Venkat took turns to guard the campsite and they shared the chore of preparing breakfast and other meals. Venkat spent many hours reading the books Victoria gave him. Bringing laughter to all with his pronunciation of some words, Nancy guided him in his reading.

"I am trying," Venkat complained.

Before sunup on the fourth morning, Venkat had breakfast ready before the ladies awoke. Patrick collected water from a nearby stream, boiled it and later weaved branches together, creating a private space for the ladies to bathe.

Venkat emerged from the bushes, shivered and pulled on a cold shirt and wet pants. "It will dry soon," he responded to an enquiring look from Patrick.

The wagon was packed, and after breakfast, Patrick flicked his whip, urging the team forward.

"Memsahib, we should be there at about midday."

"Thank you, Patrick. I am afraid, nervous and impatient, all at the same time."

Patrick turned the team and slowed them to a trot. The terrain had become treacherous. Stones and soft muddy underfoot conditions made moving forward difficult, resulting in the horses moving cautiously, testing the ground for good footing. The wagon wheels rolled dangerously over loose stones. The continuous slippery conditions persisted for another hour until Patrick finally pulled the team to a stop, perspiration soaking his shirt. Wiping his face with his shirt sleeve, he pointed.

"We are here, memsahib."

The rains had washed the blood-soaked ground. Small pools of bronze-coloured water-filled hollows gouged out during the battle. Venkat supported Agatha as she clambered to the ground to join her mother.

Beneath the haphazard collection of stone-packed mounds lay the bodies of more than a thousand men, both British and Natives, united in death.

Patrick and Venkat walked around hoping to find clues that would identify the soldiers who were buried in mass graves, fearing that they would not be able to identify where the captain lay. Their fears were valid, as none of the stone-covered 'resting places' revealed any details. They spent a little more time continuing the fruitless search and finally walked back to where Agatha and her mother silently stood.

"Sorry, memsahib, we do not know which grave the master's body lies in," Patrick, head bowed, spoke softly.

BATTLEFIELD WAR MEMORIAL – ISANDWLANA, NATAL

A flock of wild ducks changed formation as they split the blue sky in search of their last feeding round before nightfall and all around the small group nature stood breathless, as the heat and humidity stifled them. Mother and daughter shared heart-wrenching moments.

Standing still, Nancy took in the scenery: the aftermath of a tragic campaign consuming hundreds of young men in the prime of their life, lying in shallow unmarked graves – a career choice gone horribly wrong. Tears welled and then rolled down her cheeks; it was a surreal experience for all. Agatha looked up into her mother's face and clung to her tightly, unable to share her feelings. Then she left her mother's side and calmly walked among the piles of stones, stopping at times, changing direction as if following a call. Venkat intended to follow her but was stopped by Patrick. "Leave her. She is safe."

Nancy looked on but didn't stop her either.

Beyond the graves, the knoll stood steadfast, guardian over the mortal remains of departed souls and it would, for eternity, hold the tragic details of the events that led to the bloodshed. A short distance on, Agatha stopped and pointed hesitantly towards a grave. Patrick was the first to reach her, followed by Venkat and Nancy. Agatha once again held on to her mother who was unable to hold back the tears. Even Patrick and Venkat openly shed tears.

At their feet in a stone-covered grave lay the bodies of brave men, whose lives were sacrificed by a leadership lazing in comfort in ornate offices, thousands of miles away. Yet a woman mourned her husband's death and an innocent daughter was unable to comprehend the full impact of her father's slaughter.

Patrick brought a wooden cross from the wagon and planted it on the grave. Beneath the mound of soft sand and stones was the resting place of the captain and his fellow soldiers, whose demise was just another step taken by colonialism in the new world.

A lone jackal that stood on a termite mound pointed its narrow face skywards and called out, announcing the intrusion into its domain. It probably was an eyewitness to the epic battle that had scarred that very ground two weeks earlier.

While in Britain plans were being made to counter the Zulu victory with an invasion of Zululand, Patrick and Venkat stood immersed in their own thoughts. Agatha held her mother's hand as they walked away from the grave. Patrick led the way back to the wagon.

The clouds were gathering, silhouetted by the setting sun beyond the ridge of mountains along the western frontier.

"Let's find a safe spot to camp," Patrick recommended.

Leaving the site, they drove around for a while searching for a safe campsite.

Patrick directed the horses towards a rocky outcrop and pulled on the reins, urging the horses backwards so that the back of the wagon faced the rock wall. He then attached a sheet of tarpaulin to the wall so that it could serve as a private space for Nancy and Agatha. The site was perfect for a camp. As he did the past few days, Patrick again chose a site near a stream fed by the gift of summer rains. On the one side, an outcrop of rocks washed down during storms provided a perfect protective wall, and on the opposite side, a thicket of thorny trees was equally reassuring. Patrick tied the six horses to stubby tree trunks.

They sat resting for a while, satisfied that they were safe. Taking a cane knife of the type used by the plantation workers, Patrick cut down branches from the thorn trees and encircled most of the open spaces around the camp, leaving a small area that served as a door. He then cut fresh grass for the horses as they had already eaten that which they were able to reach. Venkat started a fire and placed a water-filled pot on the metal rods. Nancy prepared the vegetables for the stew.

The bubbling pot and the bobbing lid of the kettle summoned Venkat to his recently-acquired skill of cooking. Stomachs growled in anticipation of the food that was simmering over the fire. When supper was over, the ladies washed, changed into clean clothes and were soon fast asleep.

Venkat, collecting water from the stream, shielded by a bed of reeds, undressed and poured bowls of water over his shivering frame, lathered himself a few times, emptied the bucket over his head and dried himself. He changed into a white shirt that fell easily over his shoulders and pushed his legs into thin cotton pants, pulled the string to tighten it around his waist and sat for a few minutes by the fire. Patrick looked at Venkat, questioning without speaking.

"We need to pray for the unknown warrior who lost his life in the battle, as well." Venkat stepped into the darkness, chose a spot, bunched long grass into a cushion, sat cross-legged, brought his hands together and raised them in prayer, silent and motionless, a hazy white reflection against a dark backdrop. Patrick sat by the fire and kept it alive.

"This boy," he mumbled, shaking his head.

The night was chilly. The sky adorned with millions of stars and beyond this spectacle, the darkness stretched far. Later, as the moon topped the eastern knoll, raising the curtain for nature's chorus to begin, a jackal cried out and the echoes bounced away into the night. Close by an owl hooted.

Crickets, frogs and scores of other insects joined in. The stream gurgled as it splashed over rockstrewn beds in the silvery surrounds.

Venkat appeared quite suddenly, disturbing Patrick who had been dozing. Sitting opposite Patrick, he fed the dying flames with tinder-dry wood.

"Are you finished?"

"Yes, I am for now. Tomorrow I will do the remainder."

The horses were restless, and Patrick instinctively picked up a burning stick and went to investigate. He swished the stick and hoped that whatever was out there took flight. He walked between the horses, calming them.

The two men sat under a clear night sky lit by the moon and the stars, drugged into sleep by the warmth of the fire. Stepping off the wagon, Nancy added sticks to the fire, crouched and blew into the ash-covered coals. Patrick woke up, surprised. He kicked out, spraying ash and sparks onto Nancy.

"Sorry, madam," he apologised.

"It's cold in the wagon."

Venkat was also awakened by the commotion. He recovered his composure and helped to rearrange the fire as the flames tasted the frigid air. He pulled a bench out of the wagon and placed it next to the fire.

With her shoulders covered with a blanket, Nancy sat and warmed her hands as Patrick threw the last bits of wood onto the fire. "I could not fall asleep. Can I have a cup of tea, please?" she asked Venkat.

He hurriedly filled the kettle, placed it over the fire and sat on the bench.

"Memsahib, I'm sorry for having suggested this trip. It was unfair of me to put you through such inconvenience," Venkat apologised.

"Last night, I finally understood your views on the subject of faith and the strength you draw from it," Nancy surprised them.

"Memsahib, we are guardians of our faith, and I'm a part of this family. If I ignore our traditions, it would make me an unworthy member. Faith lies embedded somewhere within us, founded on the spoken words of saints and sages, and just maybe this trip will bring clarity to our lives."

"Just as you and Patrick predicted, I'm already feeling stronger and I'm certain that today will be the beginning of the change you prayed for."

"We are very proud of you, memsahib," Patrick told her. "Also, what we witnessed yesterday with Agatha was a communion between her and God and I don't think she should be questioned about it."

"Agreed," Venkat and Nancy replied together.

"Your tea is ready, memsahib," Venkat said, handing her the cup. Nancy accepted it and climbed back into the wagon to wait for daylight.

Slanting rays of the rising sun filtered through the branches as breakfast was served. However, the mood was sombre. The ladies dressed without a word being spoken. Patrick packed the wagon and positioned a bench for Nancy who climbed in, pulling Agatha up. Venkat cleaned up the campsite and jumped onto his designated seat. Patrick urged the horses into a trot; being refreshed, they were eager to run, taking just under twenty minutes to reach the burial site. He stopped the wagon close to the gravesite. The men stood by the wagon and waited for the ladies to lead the way.

Walking in a single file, Nancy and Agatha reached the grave first. The group replaced a few stones that had rolled away from the grave. Nancy unfolded a page and began to read. Once finishing the reading, they stood for a few minutes, then Nancy knelt and put her hands together in prayer. Leaning forward, she touched the wooden cross. Agatha also knelt and placed the leopard-tooth choker over the cross. They then walked to the edge of the cemetery and sat at the edge of gravesite. A few minutes later, Patrick and Venkat stood on opposite sides of the grave, each engaged in prayer. Patrick recited a verse from the Bible, crossed his chest as Catholics do and walked over to the ladies.

Venkat walked three times around the grave, chanting a mantra, and at the end, he knelt next to the cross, filled a small tobacco pouch with sand and joined the others.

"I want to plant flowers on the graves," he told them. "We should put more stones on the captain's grave."

Helped by Agatha, they gathered stones and covered the edges of the grave. Venkat deposited seeds into all the small holes he had dug and covered them with soil. He then sprinkled the same seeds on a few of the other graves, softly chanting a prayer at each one. Finally, dusting his hands, he headed back to the wagon.

Patrick was ready for the journey home.

Bundles of flat-bottomed, white clouds floated eastwards, and the sea of tall, green grass swayed in the stiff breeze as the horses waited, patiently.

"Memsahib, there are fifteen steps from when one is conceived to death, with death being the fifteenth sacrament. Prayers are offered during the fifteen days and the sixteenth day is the final sacrament, accompanied by prayers and rituals to provide the soul to rest that dwells in a spiritual world, cleansed, awaiting a re-birth (reincarnation). Each sacrament washes off the sins the soul has gathered during the fifteen stages of life, and he'll attain a place, in our case, in the House of Lord Shiva. He shall be your guide for the remainder of your days," Venkat bowed to Nancy.

"Interesting! What is the sand for?" Patrick asked.

"I will explain it to you at home."

"Madras, Patrick, the wife of a soldier always lives with the possibility of losing her husband. Soldiers' wives prepare psychologically for the day, yet when it does happen, we are challenged to find answers. Great as the loss is, it is a life chosen, a career and loyalty to the Crown. We now seek solace in God's grace."

"We must leave now, memsahib. The storm is just a few hours away. We need to find shelter until the storm passes over," Patrick suggested.

Dark bulbous menacing clouds blew from beyond the pinnacles of the mountain range. Tall, dark peaks lit up as streaks of lightning blazed across the blackening sky with a thunderous roar.

Patrick steered the team into a long valley and pulled them up onto a flat, broad rocky floor just above a flood line. Flattopped trees circled the rim of the rocky outcrop and Patrick urged the team as close as possible to the trees so it could block the howling wind that was picking up its intensity. He hastily secured the canvas with ropes and Venkat tied the reins to a tree, hoping that the horses won't bolt with the wagon. Patrick placed sacks over the horses' heads to keep them calm and jumped into the wagon to wait for the onslaught of the storm. Agatha pressed against Nancy, fearful and anxious as she witnessed a storm of immense power while the acrid smell of ozone filled the plains and sheets of rain assaulted the canvas. Patrick observed the raging storm through a small tear in the canvas.

The wind howled and battered the wagon with a continuous onslaught of water. Tiny streams of water ran along the wagon floor. Nancy passed around a tin of biscuits. An hour went by and the storm began to ease.

"It will be over soon," Patrick lied. "The wind is pushing the clouds back over the mountains. Memsahib, we shall leave once the rain stops completely."

Patrick jumped out to help Venkat strap the wagon wheels with sacking and began the long journey back home.

CHAPTER 11

Port Natal

The Gailey family purchased a comfortable house south of the town centre from a businessman who had relocated to the Transvaal Republic. Rathna, Radha and their children were also provided with a neat little cottage on the same property, consisting of a kitchen, three bedrooms, a living room and a patio. The move from King Williams Town to Port Natal was quick and smooth, though, both Rathna and Radha had now had to rebuild their lives once again and for Rathna, it was a place that he always preferred.

The house was heaven on earth for Radha. Rathna was tasked with the responsibility to maintain the stables, horses and grounds while his wife took care of the household chores. Mrs Elizabeth Gailey treated them well, for the relationship between the two families spanned almost twenty-five years, going back to various military locations in India.

Major Garvey Gailey joined a team who analysed the events leading to the catastrophic Isandhlwana battle, then devised a strategic plan to launch attacks into the Zulu heartland. Hemmed in by protocol instituted by the War Office in Britain and a lack of intelligence, the incursions into Zulu territory stagnated. However, little did he realise that his participation in the Zulu Campaign would catapult him into the forefront of the bloody Anglo Boer War a few years later.

It's two weeks and a few days since Nancy's group returned from the gravesite and life was falling back into a routine again. Venkat had his household tasks, Patrick was in the stable as usual, engaged in some sort of noisy chore and Gertrude hung the washing to dry in the gentle sea breeze. Emily Nessfield had changed a little; she made more trips to the expanding vegetable patch, each time reducing the number of crimson red strawberries available for Patrick, Gertrude and Venkat.

Many months had passed since Venkat had first arrived in Port Natal. Working for the Nessfields provided him with a reliable income. However, the passing of the captain could change the circumstances of his employment. Just as Venkat was about to start off on his muchawaited visit to Rosehill Estates, Victoria and Arvin walked across the lawn.

"Welcome! This is a surprise. I was just about to visit you!" Venkat told Victoria.

"My mother and I came here a week ago to offer our condolences to Mrs Nessfield."

"We went on a trip, but she's here now. It's a tragedy for all, but she'll be happy to see you, Princess."

Gertrude waved from the patio. "Aunt Gertrude, will the memsahib accept visitors?" Venkat asked.

"Let me ask her."

Nancy embraced Victoria as she reached the top of the stairs.

"Mrs Nessfield, we are sorry for your loss. My mother and I cannot even comprehend how you feel."

"Thank you. It is tragic. However, the wives of military men always live in constant fear of news of such nature. Would you like to share breakfast with me?"

"Thank you, it will be a pleasure."

Leaving the ladies, Arvin and Venkat went to the backyard.

An hour or so later, Victoria joined Venkat and Arvin. "Can we spend some time alone? I have much to talk about. It has been a few weeks and I missed being with you."

"I did, as well."

"In my heart, I feel my father must be searching for us. I believe he loves us and didn't want to just disappear. I also know that he is not a casualty of war as we have contacted authorities in Britain."

"That's great news! From what you've told me, he is a wonderful father and I don't think he'll shy away from his responsibilities."

"Unlike many British officers and businessmen who solicited special favours from Indian females and then vanished, leaving behind disgraced women and children, scorned and tarnished by tradition and cultural beliefs, my father had planned for us to unite as a family when his duties ended. We are the first in his life. My British grandparents are waiting for us as well, I think. But for now, we have each other."

"Then why the sad and disappointed look?" Venkat asked.

"My mother and Mr Ogilvy are spending more time together. I hate to confront her about it."

"Unfortunately, parents are difficult to understand because so much of their thoughts, hopes and dreams are hidden from their children, so that they are not affected by all the complications. Their love never changes."

"I know, but how can I protect my father if their relationship goes beyond just friendship?"

"Princess, you first must be certain that a relationship beyond friendship exists. If you mistakenly perceive that it is more than pure friendship, you'll alienate your mother if you approach her with your opinion. You are the only pillar she has and I hate to see you or Mother hurt."

"Okay, I shall wait for a while."

"That will be the best," Venkat agreed.

"We need to speak to the memsahib about our future."

"About what, wise young one?" enquired Patrick, surprised.

"Where will the memsahib find the money to keep us employed?"

"Let us tell my wife to ask memsahib if we can speak to her," Patrick hesitated, considered and called out to Gertrude.

Nancy waited for them on the patio as it was much cooler there than inside the house. "You wanted to meet with me?"

"Yes, memsahib," Patrick began. "Now that you are alone, will you be able to keep us employed?"

"We can look for work elsewhere, memsahib, if it is a problem," Venkat offered, as he thought this was the best option.

Nancy thought for a while. "When the time comes and I feel that I cannot afford to keep you, I will tell you. For now, we must go on as usual."

Gertrude handed them tea and left. The shrill calls of gulls and the waves breaking on the sandy beach sounded louder in the silence that prevailed.

Relieved that their employment was safe for now, they went back to their usual tasks. As the months went by, income from the sale of vegetables to market hawkers exceeded all their expectations and the number of bottles filled with money increased. Even Gertrude joined in to establish new garden patches. The Celes and Venkat were now in business.

Venkat sent home all his wages and most of the money earned from fresh produce sales to his father. Now his thoughts turned to the time he had already spent in Africa and of his future.

Nancy approached Patrick who was hard at work in the stables.

"It's a beautiful day, Patrick."

"Yes, it is," he replied, surprised.

"Can we talk? All of us."

"I will get them."

"Where shall we sit?" Gertrude asked.

"Here is good enough," Nancy pointed to the bench. "We need to talk," Nancy addressed them.

Gertrude went to the main house and returned with a chair which she placed in front of the bench. Nancy sat down and faced the nervous trio, who were silent and looking rather confused.

"Why the sullen faces?" she asked. "I need to thank you all for supporting me during my difficult time."

Venkat shifted uneasily.

"*As a young girl and being the only child, I enjoyed many privileges. I had many dreams for the future. My parents had many plans for me. We enjoyed visits to museums and spent many evenings in theatres and music halls. Sometimes I still hear the beautiful sounds of the orchestra. Much of my time was spent playing the piano, which I miss dearly...*

"*I met the captain at one such concert. My parents were afraid because he was a soldier and it meant that there was a probability of him being shipped out to a distant colony. However, we were married about six months later in a small church. Another six months later, James was sent to India. I was devastated but compelled to accept the posting. My life changed and I indulged in simple pleasures to pass the time. Agatha was born and as a young mother, I immersed myself in the responsibility of raising a child. I fell ill when she was about a year old. We moved in with Mrs Nessfield as my parents had moved to America just after Agatha was born. Emily was good to us and we enjoyed the comforts she offered us and we, in turn, provided her with the companionship she needed, as the captain's father was based at a military garrison in Patna, as was his uncle who was a professor at the university.*

"When the captain suggested that I move to Port Natal, I agreed. The letters he wrote told of a young, exciting country and of a proud Zulu nation, well trained in the art of war. His letters described the native warriors in war as daring, cunning, ruthless, and in peace as just, generous, hospitable and modest.

"He also wrote of this house, which he had purchased from a retired army colonel and that he had retained the services of a husband and wife. At that time, I had no idea how good you were. During the voyage, however, apprehension set in. Leaving behind the world I knew so well, I was now embarking on a journey into the unknown. The accounts of Africa I heard from fellow passengers were of barbaric tribes, savagery and bloodshed. It was too late to change my mind. I prayed.

"Strangely, when we docked and after I took the first steps on dry land, much of the doubt I had imagined disappeared. After all, we were children of God, and furthermore, the captain would protect us. But all the way to the house, as I rode in the carriage with the captain, I felt fear.

"Now I have very few friends, mainly because my ill health does not contribute to interesting conversation. In the last few weeks, however, I feel that I have regained some of my strength and due to my responsibilities, it is important that I recover. Your knowledge of the simple but meaningful aspects of life itself has given me a new perspective.

"I was so wrong – we are so wrong in our perceptions of the people of Africa and even other colonies of the Empire. Patrick and Gertrude, you are wonderful as always and I thank you. Even more recently, Madras has provided me with a different set of views as well." Nancy was smiling as she spoke calmly.

"Memsahib, can I make you some tea? I think we all need tea and biscuits." Gertrude got up and left and while she was away, they spent the time in idle chat.

Gertrude placed the tray on the bench and served them each a cup. Patrick nervously drank the tea, still uncertain about the point of this meeting. Venkat was also anxiously awaiting the end of the meeting.

"I feel much better," Nancy continued. "I'm stronger and it's my responsibility to take care of my family now. Would you help me with the changes I need to make?" Nancy asked.

"Yes, we would gladly," Patrick replied, nodding to Venkat.

"First, I would like to refurnish the house, change the curtains and give the entire place a facelift. To do that I need all of you to help … you are my family now," she concluded to the relief of an anxious staff.

"Memsahib, our lives could not have been better, and we are here to serve you as long as you need us," Patrick promised.

"Thank you. We will start in a few days then," Nancy thanked them and left.

"I was afraid all the time. I thought we were going to be without work," Venkat heaved a sigh of relief.

Surprisingly, Nancy joined in to give the house a thorough clean. Piles of curtains were washed and hung again. Wooden floorboards were scrubbed and polished. Rugs hanging from low branches were thumped and dusted.

Nancy, after years of being ill, was now filled with enthusiasm and a newfound vigour, helping whenever a hand was needed, much to the delight of Gertrude who saw this change as being part of the recovery that she earnestly prayed for.

"Madras, I think we need Patrick to help us move this heavy dresser."

Approaching the stables as Patrick was pounding a red-hot metal rod, Venkat knelt, head bowed, addressed Patrick, "The honourable Dingaan, son of a great warrior, as brave as a lion with the strength of an elephant; descendant of great kings, I salute you, your lordship. The memsahib seeks your presence on a matter of utmost urgency, kind sir."

Patrick took a few strides, reached out and grabbed Venkat, tucked him under his arm and walked to the house.

"What is this?" Nancy smiled.

"These bones will make good soup, memsahib."

Venkat wriggled free and straightened up, adjusting his pants.

"Not very Christian, I must say," Nancy teased as Patrick moved the dresser.

It took two weeks for the team of four to complete the tasks, with Emily providing suggestions that Nancy mostly ignored as it conflicted with the plans she had. At the end of it all, Nancy celebrated with a specially prepared dinner.

Rosehill Estates

Rosehill Manor sat amidst a greenery of flowing fields of cane, scented flowers and draped tall trees. Colourful birds danced from branch to branch as insects buzzed around nectarfilled blooms.

Victoria and her mother sat in the shade on a blanket – at peace with themselves and the surroundings. A fresh breeze rushed up the valley and reached the top of the hill, cooling the gardens. Out on the sandy shoreline, families sat under umbrellas spending time away from the humdrum of life's labour. Children built sandcastles and others chased sea birds on the crunchy surface of the shore.

"Victoria, I have arranged this picnic because you seem to be preoccupied and distant. Do you want to discuss anything?"

"I'm fine, Mother."

"You must have heard gossip about Mr Ogilvy and I."

"Mother, without being disrespectful, is it really gossip?"

Sushila hesitated and took a breath: "I've waited every day for your father to step into our lives again. Every morning I hope to find him in the kitchen preparing breakfast. Every day the memory fades. I go to sleep disappointed. My life is barren, and the daily routine adds to the monotony."

"Does that allow you to replace the memory of Father?"

"I'm not replacing the love I have for your father. Just as you enjoy the companionship of children of your age, I too need to be with someone whose friendship helps me to get through day by day."

"Mother, I am in no position to decide whether the friendship is right or wrong."

"My friendship with Mr Ogilvy is just that, and I promise that it will not change my love for your father or you and Jasper."

Port Natal

Many more thousands of contract labourers arrived. Among them were traders, artisans, tailors, barbers, priests and others who provided a service, not only to those employed on the sugar plantations but also to those working in other businesses that were flourishing in the colony. New buildings were springing up all over town and small settlements were growing into villages.

The British influence was spreading well into the interior and the nature of the war with the Zulus was changing. The establishment of forts in Zulu territory quelled sporadic uprisings. The consolidation of treaties with the kings allowed British settlements to expand and in the forefront were the Indians, who accepted the option to settle in the colony permanently.

Two years and a few months after Venkat first set foot in Africa he found that he missed his motherland, family and friends more as the time passed. Life was much easier and comfortable now. Happily, he addressed Nancy and Lt Croydon, "Memsahib, can I put up this sign above the gate? Patrick and I worked on this for a day."

"Show me the sign."

It read: 'Where there is darkness, there is light.'

"It is what I have learnt from you, memsahib, and it's written in your language."

"How delightful – and yes!"

"Whatever does it mean?" asked Lt Croydon.

"Lieutenant, you need an education in cultural differences," Nancy suggested.

"Memsahib knows."

"We need to know the people: their culture, beliefs, fears and their hopes and dreams before we decide who and what they are," Nancy told Lt Croydon.

"Both Madras and Patrick could teach us much more than we can teach them."

"We are civilising a demonic band of heathens and ingrates who know only blasphemy," Emily chipped in as she walked out on the patio.

"Goodbye, Mrs Nessfield, Nancy," Lt Croydon hastily swung onto his horse, tipped his hat and rode off.

"You have certainly lost your mind, girl, and I'm disappointed with your recent behaviour!" the older lady chastised Nancy, who did not respond as she calmly walked into the house.

It was the start of the third summer for Venkat and he had seen many changes since he first arrived. The colony had expanded; many small towns were created to cater for the increasing numbers of settlers and many more Indians accepted indenture and sought employment in emerging businesses, mills as well as plantations. Many went to Kimberley and sought employment in businesses that were springing up on the back of the diamond industry.

Venkat sat on a bench and wished that he could visit his family as he had enough money for the return trip, but he needed Nancy's permission to allow him to go for a few months.

"Why don't you come with me to India?" Venkat asked Patrick.

"When are you going?" Patrick asked, surprised.

"It's just a thought. Memsahib must agree first. I would like her to come with us, as well. You could experience India – you're always talking about it."

"Maybe I will ask Gertrude and the memsahib. But I must admit I'm afraid of travelling by ship."

"The ship is like a big house filled with strangers who would soon become your friends with everyone packed in tightly with very little to do, so it's an experience that I'm afraid of as well."

"Why go then?" Patrick questioned the wisdom of making such a difficult trip.

"I would love to see my family. I would love you to enjoy India, and the memsahib to experience the power of faith."

"I will think about it," Patrick promised.

Memsahib, do you believe Agatha will talk again?" Venkat posed the question to Nancy.

"Why, I'm not sure – we tried in England."

"She will talk again. Our faith will help her. If you come to India, she will talk again, because we must believe and have faith that she will. India has much to offer, memsahib. You would experience centuries-old culture and learn to understand the people and their perceptions."

"It would be a difficult trip – and where would we stay?"

"If India was not a land of opportunity and great comfort, then Britain would not still enjoy being there, memsahib! You could tell the world about us as well once you experience the life in India," Venkat spoke after much deliberation.

"What is India really like?" Nancy questioned hesitantly.

"India is majestic to us and mysterious to Europeans. I would give you a biased picture. It's best for you to see her for yourself – through the eyes of her people."

"You speak with clarity and with much emotion," Nancy observed.

"Thank Victoria for her lessons, memsahib."

"Stop wiping the floor and let's talk about it," Nancy ordered.

He pulled himself up and stood silent for a few moments, searching for the best way to express his feelings to a person whom he respected highly. He needed to dispel a sentiment that had been tormenting his very being. It was a gnawing irritation that had to be removed in order to open his mind and body to the enlightenment of meditation.

"Memsahib, what I have to say is being said without malice and I hope you will not be offended by it," Venkat spoke with conviction.

"You tell it as you see fit."

Venkat sat on a chair and began, "I feel a great urge to tell the world that we are all the same. As happy as I'm here, we all have different dreams. Though I may not be able to achieve mine in this lifetime, circumstances have changed, even for you. You pray that Agatha will regain the ability to speak."

"Agatha's condition concerns me."

"My promise to you is Agatha will regain the ability to speak."

"Are you convinced of that?"

"Yes, memsahib."

"Will we be safe?"

"Your safety is assured, and it will be the death of me to protect you and Agatha. The British have destroyed the free spirit of millions, pauperised millions more, starved to death countless others, yet we carry no resentment in our hearts."

"I did not know you felt that way about the British."

"It is not about the British people, memsahib, the edicts of colonisation permit and promotes the pillage and plunder of our lives, our nation, our country."

"You are very young to carry such feelings. Do you dislike us?"

"Memsahib, we do not measure age in years but in wisdom and the way in which we conduct ourselves within the family. We grow to share adult responsibilities, much earlier than most. I owe you a debt, and when Agatha speaks again, it will go a long way to reduce the weight of the burden of dislike that accumulated due to a few incidents, which I need to remove to cleanse my mind. You were an innocent bystander and I misread your actions as being like those who hated us, yet you cared for us, therefore, my wish is that the trip will fulfil both intentions."

Nancy sat for a few minutes thinking about Venkat's suggestions.

"We still have a lot to do here," she hesitated.

On the opposite side of town, Rathna Pillayiar – also known as Pillay – takes a refreshing bath after a long day of cleaning stables. He sat in the living room and wrote his first letter to Guru Sundrum.

CHAPTER 12

Rosehill Estates

Victoria sat on the porch, enjoying the breeze blowing past her as she sipped from a glass of pressed cane juice.

"Hello, dear," Mrs Harrisford broke the silence.

"Oh! Hello, madam."

"A penny for your thoughts … Being young has problems as well. What, may I ask, is bothering you?"

"I really do not know."

"Victoria, I can help if you want me to."

Arvin stepped onto the porch and placed a tray on the table.

"Memsahib, if that is all, can I leave now?"

"Yes, Arvin. Please do and thank you."

"Madam Harrisford, you might know that my mother and Mr Ogilvy are more than just friends," Victoria hesitantly resumed their conversation.

"I've heard a murmur or two."

"So, do you think she is being dishonest to my father who just might be tearing himself up searching for us? Military life is not ideal for a happy family," Victoria complained.

"Dear, I gathered from your mother that your father has been away for many years."

"Yes, about six years."

"Darling, that is a very long time. Men and women are not cast in stone but are born with a gift of thought and feeling. Your mother is resilient, warm and beautiful and you are her source of strength. She has fought for you in the past and still fights every day to overcome the obstacles in her path. I love you as much as I would have loved a daughter if I had one and, therefore, what I have to say is important..."

"Yes, madam."

"Being an adult or a parent in these difficult times is not the easiest of tasks. So, give your mother time and she'll soon find a solution that will please you."

"Do you believe that?"

"Yes, most certainly, my child."

"Madam, my father is my life. When I was eleven, I painted a picture of my family. Before he left for Britain, he cut out my and my mother's part of the picture and placed it in his book. He promised me that we would always be with him and in his heart and that when he reunited the family, he would put the two parts of my painting back together to complete the picture."

"You have made many new friends since the ball, I gather?" Mrs Harrisford navigated a new course.

"There are a few, but they will always be just friends."

"Anyone I know?"

"Remmy Dagg and George Hasp."

"Do they know about your parentage?" Mrs Harrisford hesitatingly asked.

"It didn't come up."

"Have you given thought about your future?"

"When Father takes us to Britain, I aim to study. On completion, I will go back home to India and work hard at changing the perceptions of both the British and Indian because there is a chasm that separates the two. Only by knowing, associating with and understanding each other will there be peace. Instilling this sense of responsible behaviour on both sides may work to reduce violence as a solution.

"That's indeed an admirable vocation."

"Madam, there's a mistaken philosophy that the more you beat a beast, the faster it will pull the plough. Here, except at Rosehill Estates, by a strange act of fate, the indentured are beaten, whipped and insulted. The opposite works better. Why is it the norm and do they deserve such treatment?"

"It's difficult to say why this is happening."

"We need compassion and integrity because they are human. Can I demonstrate?"

"Please do."

Victoria went into the house and returned. Facing Mrs Harrisford, she put on a hat and, with a bent tobacco pipe between her teeth, she reenacted Mr Harrisford's manner of addressing the plantation workers, complete with tapping the ash off the pipe and with his hand gestures.

"Hello, managers, sirdars, and workers. We have reached a point where we need to rethink how we must run our affairs at Rosehill Estates. The bundles of harvested cane we send to the mills have increased beyond my expectations. The price of sugar we are getting at auctions have also increased – showing me that every person on this estate contributes towards such successes.

"Everyone, irrespective of the work they do, is entitled to benefits. In the next few weeks, management will have a meeting and discuss the compensation that befits your commitment. We have abandoned corporal punishment long ago and have improved safety and health matters. It is my hope that other barons would follow our example. The British have an economic tie to the Crown and must, therefore, follow our obligations as best we can, but we also have a moral principle to the people we employ. To thank you for your accomplishments, we've decided that from next weekend onwards there will be no work from one o'clock on Saturday afternoon until Monday morning. All employees are free to engage in prayer and family pleasures. Thank you."

Mr Harrisford, who had been listening in, clapped and Mrs Harrisford joined in the applause.

"I'm sorry, sir."

"We could use your motivational ideas, dear. I think you should deliver my talks from now on."

Nessfield Manor

Victoria became a regular visitor to the Nessfields. Nancy always welcomed her presence and they spent many hours sharing views, opinions and lighthearted humour. Saturday shopping with Nancy, who regarded herself as Victoria's big sister, always brought a gift for Sushila whom she had met once.

"Nancy, my mother loves every gift and she has no way of thanking you personally, therefore on her behalf, I thank you."

"You are welcome, my dear."

After lunch, Victoria found Venkat in his favourite spot and sat next to him.

"When were you going to tell me about the trip to India?"

"Are we going?"

"You look so surprised!" Victoria chided, punching him on his knee.

"It was only a plan," Venkat responded immediately.

"Had I known, I would have joined you to search for Father."

"Princess, I apologise, because it was only a suggestion and I had no idea that Mrs Nessfield would agree. I promised her that Agatha would regain her speech on performing a sacred ritual with Guru Nagar. You can give me a list of all the places you stayed; my friends and I will not rest until we find information about your father. We will visit garrisons, army posts, officials and officers' homes to confirm if he had been searching for you."

"I will miss you more than you think."

Venkat gave a questioning sideways glance. "Princess, the time will pass quickly and when I return, I will visit you every chance I get."

"I will be waiting. Please promise you will come back."

"I will. I promise."

Port Natal - A Voyage Back Home

A few months later, Venkat, Patrick, Nancy and Agatha waved goodbye to Lt Croydon, Gertrude and a tearful Victoria who remained standing on the pier as the ship embarked on its voyage to India.

Venkat and Patrick could only meet up with Agatha and Nancy a few times during the voyage as the upper decks were exclusively for British nationals, senior officers and military personnel. However, whenever the chance arose, Nancy and Agatha visited them on the lower decks, which were crammed with people returning home.

To find Patrick and Venkat among the immigrant plantation workers would normally have been difficult, but as soon as they set foot on the lower deck, Venkat and Patrick were virtually carried by their fellow passengers to meet their visitors. Nancy and Agatha's arrival were of public interest and a source of immense excitement.

Every meeting was pure pleasure for Agatha and even Nancy looked forward to getting together, but Patrick was not enjoying the trip. He was the picture of despair as the swaying ship turned him green with seasickness and fear.

"I'm going to walk back home," he burped, as he braved another dip into a huge trough.

Thousands flocked to the quayside as the ship entered the port of Madras. People came to welcome brothers, uncles, fathers and cousins, excited at the prospect of the reunion. Patrick and Venkat waited for the ship to empty before they joined Nancy and Agatha. After disembarking, they sat with their luggage and planned to wait for Ramu for about an hour. If he failed to arrive, alternate plans would have to be made. He was notified of the trip by a letter sent a few months earlier.

A ragged looking Ramu showed up, leading an ox pulling a two-wheeled cart. Once the introductions were over, the luggage was loaded, and they set out.

"It is my third week waiting for your ship to arrive," Ramu complained, grinning from ear to ear. "I have notified the officials at the fort about the lady and her daughter."

"We will leave you at the army post for two nights and then come back for you," Venkat told Nancy.

When they reached the fort, a uniformed guard in clothing meant for a person twice his size pushed open the cast-iron gate and welcomed them. He helped to carry the bags in and directed Nancy to the colonel's office.

"Mrs Nessfield, I presume! Welcome," Colonel Robert Andrew Halifax greeted Nancy. "Sincere condolences to you and your family on your husband's passing. He was a fine soldier, just like his father. As privates we served to end the 1857 war, the first war of independence, most times, misguidedly referred to as the Sepoy Mutiny of Lucknow," he said as he puffed out a cloud of smoke.

"Thank you, Colonel."

"I received the news from the War Office in London."

He called out to the servants.

"What would you like to drink, madam?" he asked Nancy. "And you, young lady?"

Agatha looked up and presented him with her usual delightful smile.

"I would love a cup of tea and juice for Agatha," Nancy replied, thanking the colonel. The servant vanished through one of the many doors.

"Would mango and coconut milk be to her liking?

"Yes, sounds delicious."

Blowing another huge puff of smoke, he looked at Nancy, shaking his head. "Now, what brings you to this part of the world? Sorry for the smoke; I just cannot live without it," he said, shaking his curved pipe. Nancy explained about Agatha's condition and Madras's suggestion.

"Madras, the young man who works for me, suggested that my daughter Agatha can be cured and regain her speech once we attend a special prayer ceremony at a temple here. Why I accepted to come on this trip is still a mystery."

"You are here, are you not? Your decision to come on this trip was orchestrated by their faith. A gift that lies dormant in all us, it does surface when called upon."

"Yes, I am here and strangely, I now realise that I accepted the suggestion without really questioning the outcome."

"What prompted you to travel thousands of miles to India?"

"I do not really know."

"It's the power of their universe that lies embedded in their faith. I think that's what brought you here."

"Good god. It could be so true, sir. This is the second trip I made at Madras's suggestion."

"I have had the pleasure of engaging both young, and wizened, old men about religion and its role and surprisingly, all carry knowledge and wisdom, some beyond their years. Coming back to your question… to be honest, I have witnessed miracles here," the colonel elaborated as he accepted the tray from the servant.

Nancy and Agatha bit into nutty biscuits as they sipped their drinks. The colonel apologised to them as he poured brandy into a tall, silver tumbler. "It relieves my throat – the dust, you know," he explained. "An appropriate remedy for a chronic discomfort, I must add." The colonel justified his action by clearing his throat once more.

"The rooms are ready, sir," a young servant informed the colonel and he picked up the bags as Nancy and Agatha followed him out of the office.

"Enjoy your stay here, Miss!"

Meanwhile, Patrick and Venkat joined a convoy of people heading in the direction of Ayepakkum. It took them a day and a night to get there and the group became smaller and smaller as its members parted company along the way. Only Ramu, Venkat and Patrick were left to complete the final stretch of the journey.

The route they took was shorter than that which Venkat had taken previously, as it connected Madras directly to his home village. The ox seemed to know the way home and the three tired men fell asleep during the trip. They reached the village as the sun rose and Venkat cleared his eyes – the homestead looked different, but the ox seemed to know it was home. It stopped and shook its dewlapped neck, ringing the bell.

The houses had been rebuilt with bricks and then painted. The roofs were made of tin sheets, and there were wooden window frames. Neat flower beds lined the edges of front yards. Many more houses in the village had been rebuilt after the fire and signs of prosperity were evident everywhere.

Venkat jumped off the cart as the front door of the house opened and his mother came to meet him. She hugged Venkat and kissed him on both cheeks. He bowed down and touched her feet and she held him by the shoulders as he straightens up.

"Mother, this is Patrick I wrote about in the letters."

Patrick repeated the same greeting to Venkat's mother. Taking his hand, she spoke softly. "You have been every person that my son needed, and I thank you."

Patrick spoke to her in Tamil, which touched her deeply.

"He can sing and dance as well!" Venkat told his family as they gathered around. Muthangu, Venkat's father, was the last to greet them. He held his eldest son close for a few minutes then led him around the homestead showing him the fruits of his labour.

"We have done all this with your money. As you can see, the house is built according to the drawings you have sent us."

"It was not my money, Father, it was ours."

"Your sisters have their own room, your brother has his and we have ours as well," Muthangu was proud of what they had accomplished. Venkat sat with Patrick in the kitchen, drinking the best tea he had tasted in years. The room was much larger than the house he had lived in as a boy.

In the fields goldenbrown ripened rice, tied into bunches with rough ropes, stood, steadfast against the morning breeze. Little water-filled potholes littered the course of the riverbed. Later, alone at the river, Venkat sat on a rock and was awash with memories of the past and the reasons he had to leave home.

Venkat's thoughts were interrupted by the voice of his sister.

"Mother would like to talk to you!" Saraswathie called out.

Venkat picked a few stems of marigold and returned to the house. There he stood in prayer in front of the oil lamp that burnt brightly and thanked god for the gifts he had been rewarded with. He placed the flowers at the base of the lamp and joined the family. In the shade of tall palms, Venkat sat by his mother's side and told her about the reasons for making this trip. Firstly, he explained, it was to see them and secondly to bring Patrick to see India, its people and to experience the culture. Then he explained the third reason.

"Mother, you have read about Mrs Nessfield, the kind lady I have written about. She has a daughter who is about six years old and cannot speak. How can we change that?" He explained Agatha's condition and his own feelings about it to her. "Mrs Nessfield finally agreed to make the journey with us, and she has brought her here. They are staying at the fort awaiting your decision. I want to help the little girl and pray that she can be cured."

"If you feel strongly that through prayer the girl will regain her ability to talk, we shall believe that she will," his mother responded. "We must take them to the temple in Guru Nagar. We should make the trip on Wednesday as it is an auspicious day. Would Mrs Nessfield agree to such a visit?"

"I think she would," said Patrick, who joined them.

"Then you have three days to get her there."

CHAPTER 13

Madras, India

Nancy was sitting under the shade of a huge, flamboyant tree. Accompanied by a guard, Venkat approached her. He thanked the guard as he sat down, facing her.

"How are you finding India?"

"Different from what I expected. The people seem much happier and it always seems busy here, although I have not been outside the fort yet."

"We've discussed Agatha's condition and my mother assured us that she will be able to talk again!" he said, confirming his mother's belief. "We want to take you to Guru Nagar on Wednesday. We must leave tomorrow. The trip is not easy, but it is important."

At that moment Agatha saw Venkat and excitedly ran up to him.

"She insists that I take her out, but the trip has made me tired and I don't know where to go or what to do."

"Shall I take her out?"

"Yes, please," Nancy thanked him.

Venkat popped Agatha up on his shoulders and as he walked past the guardhouse, he threw a stone into the stagnant water that filled the moat encircling Fort St. George. The road he chose took them past the emigration depot where he had spent time a few years ago. The structure was just as he had remembered it, but now blackened by use and neglect. Men stood guard at the crumbling gates and inside throngs of emigrants eagerly awaited embarkation to escape from the realities of a stifling existence. They had walked from all corners of India just as thousands did before them, driven by their expectations, undaunted by tales of brutality – every one of them willing to shed blood to achieve their dreams.

The threat of rebellion against British rule in India was gathering momentum and scattered skirmishes broke out, bursting fragile sentiment, providing officers and sepoys with valid reasons to subdue any uprising with brutal force. Brothers killed brothers, each bearing no malice, no malicious intent. One to preserve the life once known and the other to protect the sovereignty of a distant kingdom. On hallowed ground, their souls unite to share a new spiritual world as their mortal remains return to dust.

They were away for a few hours and Nancy sat alone relaxing and enjoying the attention that was lavished on her as she mulled over the events that led to her being in India and the proposed trip to Guru Nagar. She sat there fanned by waves of cool air flowing in from the ocean.

"Very little has changed," Venkat told Agatha.

He walked through the crowded streets chatting to people who were curious about the little British girl. A vendor sliced away the tops of two coconuts and offered both to them. Venkat let Agatha slide off his back and held her coconut to her lips, tilting the fruit as she sipped the tasty liquid. Then he wiped her chin and drank the milk from his own coconut. Refreshed, they started back to the fort.

"I will take her," Nancy lifted Agatha from her perch. "I think she enjoyed her outing."

"I must go now," Venkat said. "I will come back in the morning to take you to my family's home."

Venkat looked back at them, waved as he passed through the open gate and walked towards a small food stall a few hundred yards down the road.

Rosehill Estates

With Venkat, Patrick, Nancy and Agatha in India, Emily staying with friends for the duration of Nancy's absence, Victoria and Gertrude enjoyed each other's company and Sushila also spent a lot more time with Mr and Mrs Harrisford.

"When will Victoria be back?" Mr Harrisford asked Sushila.

"Sir, I think she will be in and out until Mrs Nessfield returns from India in three months or so," Sushila replied.

"I miss the young lady. She is good to have around the manor."

"We all do," Mrs Harrisford agreed.

"We are grateful that Mr Ogilvy recommended you to Rosehill. Your commitment to the workers and to us is commendable and it is a rare trait in a person," Mr Harrisford spoke as he puffed out small clouds of smoke.

"Thank you, sir."

"We were influenced by Mr Ogilvy to appoint you, but your skills were the determining factor. Victoria's charm and her British lineage added a bit of sway as well."

"We are blessed by your kindness, sir," Sushila responded.

Over the next few weeks, while Victoria helped Gertrude at Nessfield Manor, Mr Ogilvy and Sushila spent more time together. It was an opportunity for Sushila and Mr Ogilvy to go on picnics and long walks without being wary of Victoria's questioning looks. Her and Victoria's bond, which had grown through the turbulence of a torrid stage in their lives, was balancing on a thread that was threatened to breaking point by her growing admiration for Mr Ogilvy and the uncertainty of her family ever reuniting.

They became a couple in every sense of the word as daily visits progressed to weekend stays. Mr and Mrs Harrisford shied away from any conversations about the relationship.

Every second Sunday, Mrs Harrisford sent Arvin with the carriage driver to pick up Victoria for lunch or early dinner. It was special as Victoria's exuberance enhanced the occasion.

"How are you enjoying being away from Rosehill?"

"Madam, there is no place better than home. But as much as I miss home, I enjoy teaching English to the labourers."

"How in god's name did you come up with that idea?" Mrs Harrisford asked.

"During our voyage, Guru Sundrum encouraged me to teach English whenever the opportunity arose. Venkat was my first student, and now I have four young women whom I'm helping."

"That's fascinating. Is it fulfilling?"

"Yes, madam, very much. I'm learning more about myself as well. Most young females have accepted roles in the emerging society, and at times, male dominance overshadows their importance. So, I play a small part in their emancipation."

"Quite a leader we have here," Mrs Harrisford smiled at Sushila.

"You are a perfect tutor, madam."

Over strawberries and cream for dessert, the idle chat drew long into the sunset.

"Mother, you look radiant."

"Indeed, she does," Mrs Harrisford agreed.

"Do I?" Sushila sought confirmation.

"Yes, Mother, you do."

"Well, thank you."

As darkness descended, Arvin lit the lanterns and set a tray for the evening tea. Mr Harrisford, pipe dangling from his lips, was engrossed in the dealings of the sugar auction. Victoria joined Mrs Harrisford in the living room to discuss the complexities of a Shakespearian Classic.

"Madam, can I leave in the morning?"

"It pleases me greatly, my girl."

Madras (India)

It was 8 a.m., and Venkat arrived with the cart at the gates of the fort. He sent the guard to tell Nancy that he was waiting.

"She will be here shortly," the guard told him on his return.

Patrick and Venkat had prepared the cart to be as comfortable as possible for the trip. They covered the floor with a thick cotton sheet placed over a bed of dried straw, and the small bench at the front of the cart had been cushioned with a soft cloth. Patrick had used his expertise to bend saplings to create a frame and had covered it with canvas to provide shade. The sides of the cart were draped with marigold garlands and a bell dangled around the thick neck of the ox.

Venkat picked up the bags and a basket packed with food – a gift from the colonel – stacked them on the floor of the cart and ran a rope around them to tie them down firmly. Nancy climbed into the cart and pulled Agatha up after her. The ox edged forward and gradually trotted at a speed that would get them home a little quicker. It was a bumpy ride and Agatha eventually joined Venkat on Patrick's modified driver's seat. They slept that night on the roadside beneath millions of stars and awoke just before dawn to continue.

"I think I'm getting used to these wagon trips!" Nancy said, her voice jarred by the bumpy ride.

"Sorry for the rough ride! When we reach the village, you can rest comfortably for the rest of the day."

"How is Patrick?"

"He is enjoying himself very much. It looks as if he will be Indian before he leaves here!" Venkat joked.

Surprisingly, the entire village had gathered to meet them. It was rare to find a British person in their midst and his parents outdid themselves to welcome Nancy and Agatha. A table was already set under the shade of tall trees. It was covered with the best table cloth that the villagers could find and laid out on the table was a spread fit for royalty. Glass jugs were filled with crushed mango juice, coconut milk and store-bought biscuits adorned tiny trays, silver bowls brimmed with strawberries and fresh stems of marigolds and carnations were displayed in dainty vases. Cotton sheets were draped over new wooden chairs.

"You are welcome to our home," Muthangu addressed Nancy. Agatha was a bit taken aback by all the attention and held on tightly to her mother's hand as they were directed towards the table. Patrick introduced Nancy to them, one by one. His head was shaven, and he was dressed in a long white shirt with equally white pants.

"This place is beautiful!" Nancy looked at Venkat.

"It is because of you it is so, memsahib."

The village's girls lavished their attention on Agatha and examined her from hair to her shoes. Venkat's parents thanked Nancy for her generosity and kindness in taking care of their son and promised her that Agatha would be a normal little girl again.

"We must leave early tomorrow, so you need to rest," Venkat's mother suggested, as Patrick translated.

The bedroom in which Nancy slept was sparsely furnished compared to her own, but that was more than made up for by the kindness, effort and cost she knew must have gone into making her stay as comfortable as possible. Nancy was sound asleep when Venkat sneaked Agatha into the room and dropped the curtain.

In the morning, Nancy was awakened by a noise outside. She sat on the bed for a while, gathering her thoughts before she went outside. The yard was abuzz with activity and the cart was ready, brightly decorated with flowers and small twigs of syringa. On seeing her, Venkat's mother pointed her towards a makeshift shower – more of Patrick's handiwork. Fresh clothes hung from a wooden rail and Nancy was told to use them for the visit to the temple. Next to Nancy's clothes was another set for Agatha. All were hand-sewn from store-purchased fabric.

Refreshed by the long sleep and a hot shower, both mother and daughter were ready for the day. Patrick and Venkat jumped into the driver's seat as Nancy and Agatha made themselves comfortable in the decorated box. The road ran parallel to the river course, passing through small villages, drying riverbeds and maturing rice and wheat fields. Buffaloes and goats moved aside as the carts trundled along the stony and dusty path. Behind them, following in another cart, were Venkat's parents.

"I am afraid …" Nancy spoke of her fears to Venkat.

"We all are – I too am afraid of the outcome of this visit. Though I have faith that Agatha will talk, I can't help but wonder what if she does not. My faith would then be tested and the promise my parents made to you would not have been fulfilled."

They swayed and bumped their way for another two hours when the road suddenly levelled out into a flat clearing. Cut into a granite rock face was the beautiful façade of a temple and beyond it, the inside of the temple stretched into the bowels of the mountain. Entire walls were decorated with majestic carvings of deities. The columns that rose from the floor to the roof were works of art depicting their faith. Agatha anxiously held onto her mother's hand. The group assembled, washed their feet in a flat pan at the temple entrance, wiped them with a white cotton cloth and stepped inside. Venkat's mother instructed them to wait while she went in to summon the priest.

"It is beautiful here," Patrick commented.

Followed by Venkat's mother, the priest – a slightly hunched elderly man – stepped out of the shadows to meet them. An assisting priest took a big bowl of red powder, drew two circles on the floor, and then encircled them with a larger one. The priest sat in the first circle and asked Nancy and Agatha to sit in the other small circle facing him. Venkat's mother and Patrick, who interpreted for Nancy, sat within the big circle. They all had to sit cross-legged. Nancy winced; the journey had made her muscles sore.

"The small circles are our own private sanctum, and the big circle is the universe we all belong to," the priest explained. "Today we must pray so that our wishes will be answered. We must be aware that god is a conscious being."

He raised his hands in prayer and chanted hymns in Sanskrit. Mother and daughter also raised their hands and closed their eyes. Venkat's mother gently touched her middle finger into a brass tray containing red powder and dotted Nancy's and Agatha's foreheads. A slight breeze picked up and gradually, the small circles of powder began to blow away. Soon they were all sitting within the big circle.

"We are one both in spirit and body. Peace and spirituality rest in the heart of the faithful. Now we shall begin," Patrick translated.

Under the sweltering sun, the call of an eagle broke the oppressive silence as it floated on the updrafts that rose from the valley floor. Parched vegetation crackled as Venkat and his father waited in the shade of the huge wild fig.

"Father, memsahib has promised to tell the new world of our traditions, beliefs, aspirations and dreams." Venkat elaborated on the conversation he had with Nancy just before embarking on this trip to India.

"I pray that she will succeed. We are an age-old people steeped in tradition, culture and we're god-fearing. How will she tell the world about all that we are in one lifetime and in a world ignorant of our values and a life of Dharma? We are ridiculed and mocked. Will the new world accept the truth when she tells them about it?"

"It's difficult to say, the British do have skills which we don't."

"Son, she may crack the spark that starts the fire."

It was just past noon when the others emerged from the temple and joined them. They all shared in the offering of milk, honey and fruits. Thanking the priest, they walked to the carts and started their trip back home. After some time on the road, the silence was broken when Nancy asked Venkat, "Madras, will she be okay?"

"I am sure she will be."

The silence resumed and persisted for the remainder of the journey.

It had been a profound experience for Nancy, and Venkat and Patrick's faith that Agatha would regain her ability to speak carried her. She was filled with hope and expectation – her dream that her daughter's speech would return had been paramount in her decision to make this trip. She understood very little of what had taken place in the temple, yet she had closed her eyes and prayed for a miracle in the way that she knew.

Once back at the homestead, everyone who had been inside the temple showered and changed back into their regular clothes. The cool breeze rushed along the valley floor creating little whirlwinds. Dust, feathers and dirt rose, twisted and disappeared over the trees. Small plumes of dust rose as silver arrows pierced the dry ground. Gradually more followed and grew in intensity. The first rains of the monsoon season blessed the valley.

Sitting down for an afternoon snack, Nancy told Venkat and his father, "I would like to know about the many gods that decorate the temples."

After moments of careful thought, Venkat's father replied, "Our religion is as profound as yours and others. The images of our gods are created in the minds of the believers. The thousands of images that are found in the temples are the products of the imagination. Our belief transcends reality and takes on forms or shapes the mind sees, each one signifying an aspect of existence. God is in everything you imagine, see or touch; therefore, those forms are part of our worship. They are the medium through which we experience divine enlightenment, but we hope they will not be revered as god."

The patter of raindrops began to ease, and the clouds were thinning out.

"My son has an allegiance with god. I am sure he has filled your mind with aspects of our culture and traditions," Muthangu continued.

"Yes, he has. I have had the benefit of his knowledge, even though he is so young. I am proud of him and surprised by his knowledge and wisdom," Nancy replied.

"Age is an assumption that the soul within a body is the same age as the body. I think that the soul which is the spiritual life that has travelled through many forms and it just may be that a fortunate few are gifted with the ability to reach into that inner sanctum of absolute faith."

"Do you feel that there is one god for me and different gods for others?"

"Saints and sages believe that god is a power existing within us. Everyone can find that inner source of our being. Getting to the state of being one with god differs from religion to religion. When one reaches out to pray and how one does it may also differ, yet we're united in one aspect – that there exists one force that is supreme. God has given us all the very same energy to find that source of power. How then are we different? Remember that in all of us there is a measure of faith. We must learn to harness that power."

"Memsahib, can I simplify my thoughts?" Muthangu asked.

"Please do," Nancy requested.

"You have seen the sun from three different countries, yet it is the only sun, the energy of which we all share. Humanity and nature use its energy in their own unique ways to ensure physical survival. Similarly, all of humanity has only one source of spiritual energy.

"How apt," Nancy replied.

"India is a land where spiritualism is the foundation of life itself and where Mother is god. India is our Mother. In the recent past, she cries, and my son is trying to wipe away the tears. Even though she laments the death of millions, she clothes herself with the promise of a brighter future. We have very little opportunity for a discourse of any kind. He hopes that you can try to express India's situation without creating trouble for yourself. Life consists of commitments, selfsacrifice and values which are different for every one of us, but with the strength of religious belief and the power that lies within each of us, we shall in time experience the understanding of freedom and free thought," he concluded.

Muthangu, with palms held together, thanked Nancy, wished her a good night's rest and left. The rain was just a drizzle and Venkat led Nancy to her room, holding a lopsided umbrella over her head.

It was bright and sunny the next morning and the excitement was palpable. The overnight rains had arrived on time and it seemed even the birds celebrated this event.

Nancy was having tea and snacks when Venkat walked up to her. "I must take you back to the fort today. The colonel ordered this."

"Can't I stay for another day? I love it here," she requested.

"Will you tell the colonel on your return to the fort that it was your decision to stay longer?"

"I will!"

"Tonight, we shall sing in your honour and pray for your daughter," Muthangu told Nancy as he passed her on his way to the rice fields. It was time to harvest and it had to be brought in to avoid the effects of the rain.

"Madras, can I join in harvesting the rice?"

"You are welcome, but I must impress on you that it is not an easy task – it can cause lots of cuts and bruises."

"I'll take the chance."

Nancy worked as hard as anyone that day, swishing the sickle at the base of bunched bundles of rice, carrying them to the carts, loading them and then helping to push the carts out of muddy drains. It was an unusual sight for Venkat and Patrick who pulled their weight as well. When the day was over, there was very little energy left even to talk, so they simply showered, ate and went to bed.

Venkat dropped Nancy and Agatha off at the fort the next day and spent a few minutes discussing the schedule of the ships sailing to Port Natal.

"There is one sailing a week from today and the next one will probably be two weeks after that," Venkat said. "Could we spend an extra two weeks here, memsahib?"

Nancy thought for a while, then said, "Wait here."

She returned to the gate with the colonel at her heels.

"The colonel has offered us accommodation for another two weeks. I want to see as much of India as possible. So, we shall return home together."

"Wonderful! We will meet you here on the Sunday two weeks from next Sunday," Patrick confirmed.

"We will have a few days to take you around our town."

"Good idea," Nancy thanked Venkat.

The colonel led Nancy back through the gates.

"How was the trip?"

"Astounding! How did they build the temples?"

"I don't think we'll ever find out. I want to bore you with the experiences I had in this country."

"Boring, I doubt it, but yes."

"A few years ago, I spent a week at a retreat in the Northern Territories. It was life in a bubble, challenges a distant memory. I spent most afternoons on the balcony, gazing at nature's splendour."

The colonel's eyes glazed over as he remembered the time spent there.

"If I were an artist, I could have painted a masterpiece but now shall resort to putting it into words. It was all the most beautiful things found in nature. Before me, scenes so resplendent played out; on the placid lake, ducks and their broods zigzagged on a glassy surface; cormorants, perched on protruding twisted branches, stretched their wings to catch the heat of the sun; along the waters' edge, dappled lilies and lotus blossomed; white-, pink- and red-tinged petals covered in pearly droplets of dew…

"Jade green leaves spread over the lake. Long-legged birds walked on flat round leaves in search of their favourite morsels. The banks were a carpet of gold, brown and orange leaves and further up the slopes more autumn shades added to the ambience. Peacocks danced, and speckled deer tiptoed in search of green grass. Above, tall snowcapped peaks glistened as the sun stroked its softness and the blue of the sky stretched to eternity. Mountain streams dropped into the lake, bordered by showers of cascading flowers. Cool and majestic, the sun set behind the mountains as the bird's announced imminent nightfall. When silence prevailed, divine melodies from deep within the bowels of the mountain temple wafted in with the evening breeze. I sat long into the night, too captivated to leave."

"Beautiful setting for a temple."

"Miss, it could have been Eden, or the Gardens of Babylon put together. The night before I left for Madras, I invited the priest to the retreat. He came, just a wisp of man, simple-looking, yet he had an aura of mystery."

"I think most of the religious persons here have an aura about them," Nancy confirmed.

"He and two servants from the retreat sat on a carpet and played an enchanting rendition of a verse from one of the ancient texts. Joining them was a girl, a picture of an Indian princess, elegant, extremely beautiful, dainty golden jewellery adorning her wrists and ankles. She danced and each movement interpreted events in their lives. A second girl joined her, just as elegant, just as beautiful. The dance could have had a thousand meanings, but to me, it told of a journey through the turmoil of their existence and their struggle to untangle the chains of bondage and in the end, they knelt, dropped their heads between outstretched arms and touched the feet of their god. Getting up, the two girls took three steps, placed golden trinkets in my palms, brushed away their tears, turned around and left the room. The temple priest, placing a lotus flower in my right palm, whispered, 'From the dark depths of the lake grows the lotus that perfumes the land and its people.' He joined the dancers, their anklets jingled as they walked away. That image will be with me for a very long time."

"It was a dance for the gods," Nancy remarked.

"My interpretation of the sequences is based upon the knowledge that I was fortunate to gain from a revered guru. The repertoire, as in all cases here are deeply god centred."

"Quite a challenge to interpret such an art form!" Nancy commented.

"It was mesmerising, the beauty unblemished, the movements dramatic and enchanting, flowing from one sequence to another. It told a story of how the creator (Brahma) had blessed the land with beauty and sprayed the heavens with stars, to join the moon and the sun. He flew on a snow-white swan; silken white cloak, pluming, along a rainbow and bringing colour to the world, and blessed the people with love, kindness and humility. We promised him to care of the world that he created and rule over all the lands and live as he wanted us to… (Life of Dharma)."

"Today, we nurture the god or goddess that lies deep within our soul. We will pay attention to the spirits within us that dance with spirit, body and mind. We will awaken ourselves to this deep stillness in our hearts and will carry the spirit forth to eternity. Now, the stars of heaven do not send us their light; the sun is subdued when it fills the day and the moon does not shed its glow. Dark clouds gather, more and more, but bringing forth no rain, the rivers run dry and no tears shall fill the wells in our hearts. We shall beg for forgiveness at His feet, for we have not kept our promise… we will give the last of Mother's gold, to those who can bring forth the purity of the stars, the brightness of the moon and the sun, once more."

"The moment the dance ended, misty-eyed, I made up my mind to celebrate my being here and open my mind and my eyes, to reflect on our history. We have acted with impunity, we persevere with all that is wrong, without for one moment ever seeing the inhumanity we have inflicted on such gentlefolk. We came here to trade and took over the country, pillaging their land and their wealth, shipping away priceless artefacts, gems; enslaving a nation, perpetuating famine, all in the name of the Crown and country, a far cry from the façade we portray."

Colonel Halifax called the servants to bring in refreshments and to prepare the rooms for Nancy and Agatha.

"You like this country."

"Most certainly, I do, I think when this country is sapped of all its riches, Britain will walk away, and give India its sovereignty, under the pretence of it being a noble and humane gesture. When or if we seek forgiveness for the atrocities we committed in this land, it would be a cynical rhetoric."

A young servant placed a tray on the table, bowed and left. The colonel poured juice into the glasses, leaned back in his chair and brushed an insect off his jacket.

"At the moment my loyalty is to the Crown and I am bound by duty to perform as ordered. I believe there will come a time when my services will no longer be required. I will then stay here and explore this mystical land. Maybe I will write a book and try to capture some of its beauty and the people's beliefs, wisdom and traditions."

"I am fascinated with their devotion to god," Nancy interjected.

"Before I left home to come here, we were schooled on preconceived ideas and images of the people, but having spent years here, every one of those ideas is contradicted by all that we see here. I have indulged in reading ancients' texts, I've tried to comprehend the verses in the Mahābhārata, the Gita and the Manava-Dharma-Shastra. I would like to dig deeper, much deeper. The mythology may be real, and I will visit Nepal and Tibet."

Colonel invited the professor in, who had knocked and waited.

"Sorry, am I interrupting?" the professor asked apologetically.

"No, not in the least, come in. This is Ms Nessfield of Port Natal. We are honoured to have her in our midst and by her visit."

"A pleasure, mam."

"Thank you."

"Welcome, professor, how are you?"

"Colonel, in the worst shape of my life and yet tremendously elated. I have two chests full of treasures, waiting to be whittled down into two volumes for the planned reform adjudication. Now, I need to sink into a bath, saturate myself with a sack and brandy (sherry) and a bottle of whisky or gin."

"Is that all?" the colonel joked.

"Thankfully, I am protected and safe from prosecution, therefore shall report my findings succinctly, expressing the combined views of the natives and our own to chart the best way forward. I shall talk freely."

"Quite a shift from those who were here in the past. It is a task so important the future of the nation rests upon your shoulders," the colonel replied.

"I wish my work holds some of the answers in pursuing a just course. Sir, now, I will rattle on like a runaway steam locomotive."

"Matter of urgency, professor?" Nancy chipped in.

"Mam, I have a few layers of dust to wash off and also to quench the great thirst."

"You surely look in need of both. Your enthusiasm has grabbed our undivided attention," Colonel Halifax agreed.

"Sir, British, we are. Patriotic? Definitely, yes, and we are a nation devoutly insular. I am wedged between lion and lotus. Most of all, a conundrum is at hand. In short, the natives are being ostracised in the country of their birth and the rules that we set to govern them directly or through the British Raj is flawed. The locals are ageless, proud and their affection for their history have linked them to their gods themselves. They have lived here for so long and they are part of the land as much as the land is part of them and they own the right to live on it as they please. India afforded us and other nations the privilege to trade and live in it."

"Yet, we seem to have savaged the *lion's* share," the colonel said.

"Unashamedly, without doubt, Colonel. This is a country made up of a collection of stories, with individuals, demonstrating the highest value of heroism and we, the lowest form of guile and cruelty. Our Crown goes further to write chapters of their own to make up an indelible story. India is land of sacred realities, monumental shrines to their gods, temples, intricate and infinitely carved into rock by simple tools and ingenuity, their significance yet to be unravelled.

"You are in awe, Professor!" Nancy said while the professor downed his drink.

"Awe does not fully describe my feelings, mam. It all seems a myth, an elusive freedom and we as colonisers carved a new country and its ruin. India has a power of attraction. We tripped over other nations to claim it. India is not only of one commodity but a broad canvas, with limitless rewards which, for us and many others, were there to be taken. Taxation smothered the people and sapped their energy to live; famished, they perished. Many looked on in indignation, without a minute possibility of recourse. It is also a land of mighty, sacred rivers—Ganges, Brahmaputra, Yamuna, Indus and many more—and we, it seems, are being washed downstream."

"How did you cope with communicating with villagers?"

"Colonel, linguists, interpreters, historians and mystics provided us the insight we needed."

"I wish I was in your team."

"Colonel, it was fascinating and at times incomprehensible. When looked at from India's origins, catalogued texts, people and ageless stories, it all fell into perspective. Stories told of settlements on river banks, once home to pre-historic kingdoms, giving rise to languages, writing and spirituality that spread far and wide. It will be difficult to portray the present, as it is of pride and of competing promises, conquests and the vanquished, competing visions of a contrasting future. Many played a part in occupying it, but in the end, only one nation will fight fervently, a new struggle will begin, to be themselves once more, be entitled to it, share in its abundance and claim it and in the end, it will discover itself through its people."

"Very emotive, descriptive and true," Colonel Halifax sighed.

"Is that who we really are? Are we a nation so bent on destroying the colonised countries?" Nancy questioned.

MAMALLAPURAM – PARABLE OF FAITH

"More the people than the country. Greed, lust for power, indiscriminate pillaging, a powerless nation, deception and conquests yield great rewards, mam. Easy pickings and rich rewards."

"Colonel, I am infuriated."

"Mam, euphemism and deviance will embellish discussions and debates till the candles burn out. Will vanity allow for a fair and just outcome?" Professor Robert Milford questioned.

"Professor, we are at the cross-roads," the colonel suggested.

"Sir, indeed we are. Mam, I believe that a few decades hence, the British Parliament will introduce reforms in this country."

"Decades, why?"

"Colonel, the banquet is far from over, the bones are not yet picked clean. The greatest injustice inflicted on the natives has roots in the British socio-cultural belief systems with proprietorship over life and limb. Many may just fear dropping the golden goblet. Our kingdom and its subjects look at it in terms of wealth, power and expansionist ideals and layers of bureaucracy, whereas the native culture transcends all that we endear. They value the salvation and transition of the soul, simplicity and clarity of the essences of life. The natives understand the working of the cosmos and the science of the human mind and body that could astound the most perverse critics. Their daily lives are coded in ancient texts, discipline upheld by allegiance and governance, punishable by decree, thus maintaining strict principles in all aspects of their lives, unheard of in anthropology."

"Mesmerising, indeed," Nancy said.

"Mam, when the British East India Company established themselves in Madraspatnam in the 1600s, it was a precursor to deception and intrigue, thinly veiled and the catalyst being the abundance of plunder at arm's length. There should have been a sharing of socio-cultural processes, where common ideas could have greatly reduced the exploitation that we orchestrate; not diminishing the atrocities that we inflict with the assumption that we are civilising a backward race. It is farthest from the truth. We are not as polite as we claim to be compared to those here and other nations in the East. Our findings, if used fully in the reform process, could create a radicle shift in governing India. The native races tried to close the barn door after horses bolted."

"We already see signs of an impatient nation," Colonel Halifax mumbled.

"You could have your hands full, Colonel. Fortunately, the natives are not prone to uncontrolled large-scale violence. There has to be a unifying force to bring together the fragmented groups to thrash out any possible reforms."

"Professor, the resolution we seek is easier found when you walk amongst the people who need salvation, and there has to be unbiased and objective review for you to be able to distinguish between kingdom and subjects: the oppressor and the subservient," Colonel Halifax advised.

"Thankfully, my report will be presented to persons who seem to favour liberal tendencies and even then, I fear interference from the aristocrats with vested interest."

"Professor. Let us hope that your efforts in completing the tasks yield the outcome you desire," Nancy supported the colonel's wishes.

"Colonel, there seems to be a clear pattern when one looks at the history of the European colonisation of the new world. A metamorphosis occurs within invading colonisers, transforming from being a visitor or a trading partner and later emerging as vicious, bloodthirsty monstrosities, hitherto cloaked in a pristine garment, now at liberty to destroy nations, annihilating cultures and looting the wealth."

"Callous, calculating and cruel?" Nancy questioned.

"Indeed, mam, a bitter pill. Central to colonisation was a firm belief that it is there to be taken using deadly means, where necessary, without considering the value of the contributions made by the conquered nations in their self-development and of their cultures. In North and South America, the British, French and the Spanish, were responsible for much of the humanitarian tragedy. The Spanish, by far, were responsible for one of the greatest genocides ever witnessed. It has been written that almost eight out of ten indigenous people of South-East North America, Central and South America and the Philippines lost their lives, compounded by diseases carried by civilised invaders. In Africa, it was the same, with Italy, Belgium, Germany, Portugal and the Dutch scrambling for new territories and the rewards it brought with it. Asian nations were not unscathed by the scourge."

"Professor, this biological transformation may, in some way, bring revolutionary changes in developing new lands as part of modernisation plan, which did improve certain aspects, but the sinister factor was that it provided justification to strengthen psychological posture.

"It certainly did. The industrialisation founded in Europe spread far and wide. The revolution advanced the introduction of modernisation to remote areas. The rural and urban folk were disenchanted with rapid changes and rules that were enforced upon them. Beleaguered, unemployed and entrenched livelihood lost, their spirit, destroyed and unable to overcome effects of famine, millions died," Professor Milford confirmed.

"Did Christianity have any influence on the people?" Nancy asked.

"Mam, Christianity did its best and went against the grain in some quarters and to many priests and members of the church who enforced conversions from pagan belief, it was just, in my view, for peace of mind to relieve them of the Christian guilt for the inhumanity perpetrated. Missionaries were the harbingers of a new faith, yet for those who live by its word, driven by innate greed, it is a mere inconvenience, sacrificed in the face of the extraordinarily rich rewards," Professor Milford told a bewildered Nancy.

"Professor, mam, the influence of Christianity in a new world could be measured by the foothold that it has established in India, and I am sure it has in other places, as well. It seems that Christianity is more directed at the poor who are searching for answers to their plight, the aristocracy, without precluding the bastions of English faith, and those who swear allegiance to colonialism. If one measures past and present actions so far, then religion holds no or very little sway. However, many missionaries sacrificed their lives so that their teachings prevail to define the power of faith."

"The professor's room is ready and a new set of clothes, as requested, sir," a servant knocked, bowed and announced.

"Oh, Lazarus, what do you think about the British being in India?" the colonel tested the servant.

"Be honest and do not be afraid," the professor insisted.

"Sir, I am thankful to the British for the income that saves my family from poverty and famine. The life we lead seems an illusion and we hope that we shall receive the keys to our freedom. Time is a destroyer and a creator and has the wisdom to determine our future and our fate. To find out who we have become, I think we both must look in a mirror and reflect on whom we see," Lazarus responded.

"Thank you, Lazarus. That will be all."

"Sir, mam, this land and its people have a profound effect on those who see beyond what they look at and listen to what they hear. Generally, most of what takes place here are not a random occurrence but plans coordinated to suppress the people, bludgeoning into submission any perceived provocation to gain total control of the masses, which seems to be an intrinsic trait on the part of colonialists. I have changed and hope to provide ingredients to change the future of the natives. Their struggles, humility, a constant search for salvation, the emptiness of their physical existence are by no means a measure of the completeness of their spiritual world. I was once told that there is life in every breath you take, and many are willing to sacrifice their last breath to free India." The professor thanked them and followed the servant.

"Sorry for that, mam. I hope you did not mind. The professor and his team spent years in the far-flung regions gathering facts and I am glad that he has not lost his enthusiasm," the colonel apologised.

"Not at all, a fleeting but very interesting insight."

"Where were we?," the colonel asked.

"Oh, yes! Are you not afraid to go to Tibet and Nepal?" Nancy reminded the colonel.

"Not in the least. I have listened to saintly sages, all of whom carry the wisdom of ancient beliefs and teachings that span thousands of years. The concept of god exists among all of them. In the beginning, it was difficult for holy men to pass down the word of god, because how do you connect with a god who has no physical form. Saints and sages, through teachings of ancient texts, created symbols that even today provide the medium necessary to link their faith with god. My interest may be regarded as blasphemy. I probably could be tied to a stake and burnt or beheaded, but I have an overpowering desire to find out more."

"What would that be?"

"Ma'am, there are tales that our Saviour may have spent most of His teenage and adult life in India, Nepal and Tibet, taking in aspects of the Eastern culture, teaching and learning from monks on his journey to gain greater knowledge. In monasteries, I was told there could be written scripts of His stay. My aim is to do some research and quench my thirst to understand what the new world may ignore, yet ancient beliefs and possibly other texts may hold a secret. These secrets are hidden for us to find out. It's a burning desire to prove to myself and others that there may be much more than we are told or taught."

"It's fascinating. I'm surprised."

"Even at that tender age, it is said that He was revered as a prophet. Thousands attended his gatherings."

"Colonel, that is quite astounding – Him being here, I mean."

"Did you know that almost all the major religions can be found in this country? Christianity, Buddhism, Hinduism, Jainism, Islam and a few others. Yet in truth, as diverse as they are, the binding thread is their faith in god and in themselves," the colonel added.

"A spiritual guide once quoted: 'Happy are those whose equilibrium is found in uniting with god in their heart'. Outside ideology, they remain free in their way of thinking and acting."

"Am I as a Christian permitted to look for a solution outside the teachings of the Bible?"

Colonel Halifax tapped his pipe on the edge of the table, thought for a while and quoted: "There is no lesser religion, only lesser men and women afraid to go beyond their belief. You are in the land of the gods and the opportunity will change you."

The colonel pressed tobacco into his pipe, struck a match and inhaled deeply. Blowing out a puff of smoke, he coughed. "Is the trip as you expected it to be?" Drawing on his pipe, he turned to Nancy who replied, "I'm confused about everything that I have been brought up to believe in. When I sat in the temple opposite the priest, it seemed as if we were in a different world, but strangely, I loved being in it."

"I believe you. I have had many such experiences myself."

The colonel got up from his chair. "Sorry, I must go now. Enjoy your stay, mam. We shall talk more before you leave." He walked across to his office to tinker with the bottles containing the appropriate medication for his allergic reaction to the dust – and probably to British rule in India.

CHAPTER 14

Nessfield Manor

As the weeks dragged on, Victoria grew impatient. At dinner, she toyed with her food, and afterwards, she sat for hours on the patio, watching the distant dull lights of the town.

Gertrude recognised the behaviour, and on some nights, she joined Victoria on her vigil.

"Are you alright?"

"Auntie, it has been so long. I wonder if they've found information about my father."

"Is that all?"

"Yes. No."

"Madras will do as he promised."

"Yes, but will he come back?"

"My darling, he will do as he promised."

Crickets, frogs and a call of an owl broke the silence. Gertrude served a late snack of tea and biscuits.

"You miss Madras, don't you?"

"Yes, Auntie, I do, very much."

"Why?"

"Just the thought of him not being here unsettles me."

"Do you have faith?"

"Yes, in buckets."

"So, why then do you agonise? He will come back," Gertrude assured Victoria.

Above the din of the persistent frog-song chorus, the sound of horses blowing, and the creaking of carriage wheels brought the ladies out onto the veranda.

"It's them!" Gertrude shouted.

"Yes! Yes!" Victoria raced to meet them.

Patrick stepped off the carriage, carrying the sleeping Agatha. Nancy, and then Venkat followed.

"I thought you were not coming back."

"Why would I not come back?"

Once the excitement of the reunion was over, they sat on the patio in idle chat.

Gertrude took Agatha from Patrick. Nancy entered the house, conducted a quick tour and then she joined the others on the patio. The drizzle grew heavier and the earthy smell of rain and the freshness of the breeze were a welcome homecoming gift.

"I think we need to rest. We will meet at dawn," Nancy suggested. "Thank you all. Gertrude, I need some hot water and a fresh towel, please."

Patrick and Venkat dragged themselves to the backyard. Victoria followed.

"Princess, I have news that would make you very happy."

"Fantastic, I would like to hear all about it."

"We have many days ahead of us. I want to light the lamp and then go to bed. I am tired."

"I guess I have no option but to wait."

"Yes, Princess."

"Yes, Princess," Victoria shook her head a few times, chuckled and left. Venkat doused the exterior oil lamps and closed the door.

Lt Croydon paid a visit the next morning. "You have a guest!" Emily Nessfield summoned Nancy.

"How was the trip?"

"Wonderful. India is an amazing place."

"I will go there someday."

Taking her by the arm, he led her towards the beach.

Rosehill Estates

The friendship between Sushila and Mr Ogilvy reached a point where it was common knowledge among all at the manor, so Sushila approached Mrs Harrisford.

"Mrs Harrisford, I hope I can trust you on a confidential matter that I would like you to help me with. Victoria loves you dearly ... Could you be there to pick up the pieces of her fragile mind when I make it known to her of my conundrum?"

"I will, dear."

"Mr Ogilvy and I have spent much time together. He has become part of my life and I have succumbed to a weakness that shall forever change my life."

"Dear, Victoria is a bright girl and she must by now have recognised your condition and deduced the inevitable. In fact, it has been quite evident recently. Mr Harrisford and I shall not hold it against you as it is not fair for us to judge your actions. It is something that could happen to the best of us."

"Thank you, Mrs Harrisford."

"Does Mr Ogilvy accept the responsibilities and is he prepared to commit to fatherhood?"

"Yes, absolutely."

"Do you know that Victoria prays for her father's return?"

"It's a dream I cherish as well."

"How would this affect your living arrangement?"

"Mr Ogilvy and I have discussed it and hope to meet you and Mr Harrisford to request permission for me to move in with him."

"It could shatter Victoria's ambition to reunite the family, considering her love for you, her father and brother."

"I have committed a sin and shall pay for it till eternity and the lives hereafter."

"You are not the first, nor shall you be the last. Sushila, my dear, we do not live in a perfect world. I love Victoria as much as you do, and I promise I will help her through this traumatic period."

"Thank you, madam. God bless you."

Nessfield Manor

Venkat was busy polishing his stone bird when Agatha knocked on the wooden panel. Calmly covering the bird with the cloth, he welcomed her in. She smiled and showed him her drawing. It resembled the façade of the temple they had visited in India.

It had been almost six months since Agatha's visit to the priest, but she hadn't spoken a word yet. Venkat shared his concerns with Patrick one afternoon.

"We must wait," Patrick encouraged him.

"You have a letter from home," Gertrude told Venkat.

"Thank you. I will read it later."

That evening, just after putting the final touches to the stone bird, he opened the letter. Reading a letter from home was an event and he enjoyed every moment, completely immersed in its contents.

My son, your visit home was a gift from god. We have planted all the crops in time and there should be a good harvest. Your mother fell sick and we had to take her to the doctor in Madras. We all send you blessings and hope that you accomplish all your dreams. Give our regards to Patrick and his wife, and Nancy and her child.

He placed the letter with the others and went to visit Patrick.

"My mother is sick."

"I'm sorry to hear that. What is wrong with her?"

"The letter doesn't say."

The number of letters between Madras and Port Natal increased over the next few months. One afternoon, Madras handed an unopened letter to Patrick. The orange moon cast an eerie glow. Patrick read the letter because, for some reason, Venkat was afraid to open it.

"She passed away peacefully in her sleep and was holding one of your letters at the time," Patrick consoled Venkat. "Young man, you are very brave." Patrick felt the loss as well and thought about the warmth and compassion Parvati had shown him when he was in India.

The next morning Nancy and Agatha met Venkat.

"I am so sorry," Nancy sympathised.

"I'm sorry, too, Maddy."

Nancy and Venkat didn't immediately take in what had just happened as they were so caught up with their grieving. Then suddenly they both realised that Agatha had just spoken. Venkat leapt up and carried Agatha, Nancy, in her nearhysterical excitement, grabbed Agatha from Venkat and ran into the house, repeating continuously, "She can talk! She can talk!"

Patrick galloped out of the stables, a worried look creasing his face.

"Agatha spoke!"

Venkat tried to explain as Patrick rushed to the main house where Gertrude and Emily smothered the beaming little girl with attention.

Later, Nancy returned and sat on the bench next to Venkat.

"The funeral and the Kariyam Prayer will be over now, and I have missed both," he said.

"But she will be with you forever," Nancy consoled him as she held his hand. "Madras, I promised your mother that I would take care of you and tomorrow I want you to go with me to the market."

"Memsahib, the life we led is now in pictures, committed to memory and shall be viewed when days are dark or when her lamp glows in my house. Our lives back home were not measured by the hours in a day or the days of the week but by seasons. When the monsoons quench nature's thirst, we celebrate as one and when the dry spell turns to drought, we sit in the scant shade and watch the life's work swirl into dust storms, turning afternoons into crimson sunsets. A prolonged drought brings with it the seasons of famine, then survival. In a search to provide children with sustenance, our parents ignored their own hunger, giving us handfuls of boiled rice. I think my mother won many battles but the last one ended in neither defeat nor victory. In passing her soul would join the spiritual world. It is inescapable, memsahib, that that which dies is reborn and that that which lives dies."

Venkat found a measure of comfort in expressing his feelings to Nancy.

"We can all find comfort in the knowledge that she is with God," Nancy offered her condolences.

"During the past few months, on a few occasions, I felt her presence and I thought I heard her voice in the wind. I was at peace and felt moments of strange, warm embrace-like feelings. Memsahib, her last breath was taken by the god she worshipped, her body is gone back from whence it came and her soul, departed, free of worldly possessions, as god intended, leaving behind a legacy that I shall uphold."

"Madras, it could have been her. She is a god no less."

The next morning Nancy and Agatha waited for him. "We will walk to the market as it will give us time to talk."

Agatha loved the walk, picking flowers and chasing butterflies with carefree abandon but she spoke very little. She picked a small bunch of wildflowers and gave it to her mother.

"I love you, Mother."

"She has much to learn," Venkat offered his thoughts. Nancy agreed.

"Your mother told me about what she was made to do when her mother died." Nancy handed Venkat two small bowls.

"We are going to go to the people in the market to ask for rice and vegetables to cook your supper."

"Memsahib, you have not been to the market before. I am afraid."

"Afraid? Why?" She was puzzled.

"You and Agatha with me… in town!"

"I'm not afraid. We will be safe," she assured him.

When they reached the market, the first stop was Mr Patel's seed shop. They sat on chairs that he borrowed from his neighbour.

"What would you like to drink?"

"I would like a cup of tea and Agatha would like juice," Nancy thanked him.

"Madras's mother passed away."

"How very sad," he expressed his sympathy and chatted for a while. They thanked him for his hospitality and left for the market.

"Home now is a distant memory. I am far away from home, yet I feel I walk with her."

"But you have us," Nancy reminded him.

"Now, you must ask the people for rice, beans or other vegetables and you can only accept the offering from a person who has not lost a member of his or her family."

Venkat nodded and they meandered through the crowd in search of Singaram, a well-known hawker.

"Could you please give me some rice and vegetables? Memsahib would like to cook for me," he asked politely, showing him the bowls.

Singaram scooped rice from a bag and was about to pour it into a bowl when Venkat told him he could only accept it if none of his family members had passed on. Singaram looked at him. "My brother passed away a few months ago."

"Sorry," Venkat apologised and went to the next person he knew well.

Having spent the next hour going from person to person, Venkat understood the lesson of the entire exercise and returned the empty bowls to Nancy.

"So, you see, Madras, great as the loss in death is, it is part of our life and we need to be strong. We should head back home now."

They were tired, so they rested for a while. Agatha dozed off and they waited for an hour or so while she slept. Venkat and Nancy took the time to enjoy the beauty of their surroundings. Just above the trees, the wide, blue ocean stretched away into the horizon and gulls scanned the waves for food.

"Madras, I will always remember your father's words when I talked to him about the death of the captain. He told me that life and death are like two sides of the same page and that every book has more than one page..."

"Well, I am at peace, as my mother experienced, for a short while at least, the joys that she always dreamt of."

"I think we must go now."

Agatha was tired, so she rode back home on Venkat's back.

"It's okay. Don't be afraid of Emily."

When they reached home, Gertrude was outside, polishing silver on the patio.

"The lieutenant was here to visit, memsahib."

"When was he here?"

"Just after you left."

"Why the smile, Gertrude?"

"I think he likes memsahib very much!"

"Memsahib, she did that to me as well – with Victoria," Venkat smiled at Nancy.

"What on earth are you talking about?" Nancy asked and walked into the house with Agatha in her arms. She put Agatha on her bed, took off her hat and shoes, and kissed her as she turned her onto her side. Agatha immediately fell asleep.

Venkat got up, went to his room and brought out a small wooden box. He asked Gertrude to give it to Agatha.

"I will put it next to her bed now."

"Is it not too late?" Patrick asked.

"No, the back door is still open. I will go in quickly."

"Mother, see what I've found next to my bed!" Agatha woke her mother the next morning.

"What is it?"

Agatha handed her mother the box. Nancy looked at a beautifully polished white marble dove nestled in a bed of shredded paper.

"Who gave you this?"

"I don't know. It was next to the bed!"

"I will ask Gertrude when she comes in."

"It is Madras's gift to Agatha," Gertrude informed Nancy.

Venkat was cleaning a window when Nancy walked up to him.

"It's a beautiful bird. Did you make it?"

Venkat looked down. "At first, when I started it, it was an escape from the hunger and the realities of famine. Today it is a symbol dedicated to the human spirit in its quest for peace and freedom. Victoria painted the eyes. She believes that the eyes are a window to the heart."

"Freedom."

"Yes, memsahib. We all seek it – or something close to it – but obstacles are part of life. Agatha has her 'freedom' for which you prayed."

CHAPTER 15

Rosehill Estates

It was a balmy afternoon. Victoria waited for Mrs Harrisford on the patio. Three o'clock arrived and Arvin set the table with a delicious spread of cakes, biscuits and Egyptian dates.

"Do you know what Mrs Harrisford wants to discuss with me?"

"Sorry, no," Arvin shook his head.

Mrs Harrisford joined Victoria.

"Madam, you are spoiling me."

"That's the intention, dear."

Feeling edgy, Victoria bit into a biscuit and picked up a cup. Mrs Harrisford also seemed uneasy. Before her sat a young girl, innocent and committed to uniting her family. Now she had to face a different reality.

"How are you, dear? Did your friends find any information on your father's whereabouts?"

"My father had been searching for us in Madras. As to when he will come to us, I don't know. But I know he will do as he had promised."

Hundreds of white crests adorned the rolling waves and the crisp sea breeze provided a welcoming coolness. It was the time of day that plantation workers complained as being the hottest. Large heaps of harvested cane littered the blackened grounds where once green fields flowed like the waves of an ocean. The ladies took in the beauty of the manor gardens; birds called out and hopped between the twisted branches.

"Victoria, have you spoken to your mother recently?"

"Madam, I think she has finally broken the sacred bond that held my family together."

"Can you elaborate, dear?" Mrs Harrisford walked around the table and sat next to Victoria.

"She has ruined my father's dream and a promise of reuniting the family. She is pregnant."

Taking Victoria's hands in hers, Mrs Harrisford hugged her. Teardrops wet Mrs Harrisford's blouse.

"I am disappointed, madam," Victoria sobbed.

"Yes, my dear. It is a difficult time for all."

"The last few months I hoped and prayed that Father would return to prevent the situation we're now in."

"You are a young lady with gifts unseen or unheard of in many of your age. I know you will consider the situation your mother was in. I am by no means a judge nor do I condone her actions but know that since the dawn of time and man, there existed an attraction between men and women and it shall be there till the end of life as we know it. Your mother is attractive and intelligent. She was alone for many years and in a moment of sheer thoughtlessness, she yielded to a temptation with a man who has been part of her life since you both landed here. So, let us not judge them, as all of us are prone to fallibility. A solution will present itself."

"Mother has committed her life to ensure our safety and father's wellbeing, she fought for recognition from my grandparents, friends, society, but she succumbed to a weakness that shall forever break the family. How am I to explain this to Father?"

"Dear, look on the outside of your cup … There! There is a world waiting for you. You will soon be holding a brother or sister. That would be delightful, I am certain of that."

"Yes, I think it might. But it's also complicated."

The afternoon ticked away, and they sat deep in their own thoughts, finishing the last cup of tea.

"Madam, my brother or sister will be part British, part Indian and French, just as I am."

"My dear, let us change the subject and talk about you, the heart of my existence."

"I think it's okay. Expressing my feelings to you has helped. Thank you, madam."

"May I ask if you have a special friend in your life?"

"Maybe... I think so."

"Anyone I have met?"

"No. He is the poorest of the poor having nothing to his name. Yet, since our first meeting, as castaways floundering on life's ocean, both he and the guru gave us their hands, which I shall never let go unless nature breaks us apart. Young as he is, he has wisdom that surpasses his age. He is polite, caring and when I am with him, I am free – free from all the clutter of my past."

"It sounds like love, dear."

"No. I don't know what it is, madam."

"Does he feel the same way about you?"

"No. I don't think so. Venkat calls me a princess, though."

"Could he be the proverbial frog?" Mrs Harrisford joked.

"I guess. He is charismatic and has an insight into the things in life that matter to me. He is, however, of the opinion that purity of action is grounded in clarity of thought. I have, therefore, not mentioned my feelings to him, though I assumed that he would read into my thoughts and actions."

"He is young and naïve, my love, and may still one day understand your feelings," Mrs Harrisford consoled her.

"He is quite intuitive, with the exception of my feelings towards him, mam."

"My dear, he has very little or nothing to offer you, or are you forgetting the plans you have for your future?" Mrs Harrisford pointed out. "Is your affection for this boy out of pity?"

"No, madam, I don't think pity had anything to do with it. In him I find everything I value in life. We both broke the shackles that categorised us into caste and race and built a bond that will withstand anything life throws at us. Growing up was not easy and I did not understand the reasons; I was one of them, yet I couldn't join the children at play."

"It's indeed sad, dear."

"It was, madam. I found comfort in books."

"You have gained immense knowledge and wisdom, dear."

"For Venkat it was different. Colonialism broke them into little bits and when life itself in India was at threat, the British offered them a way out."

"So much to bear at your age. But you have us now to carry some of the burden," Mrs Harrisford consoled.

"I am blessed, madam. My guru provided us the stepping stones, you and Mr Harrisford gave me completeness of a family, Venkat and I brought all the pieces of both of our lives together. We are one and yet, there sits in me a hollow, depressive feeling that my future will not be as I expect it to."

"Why so, dear?"

"If I pick up the courage to tell him how I feel he will definitely say, 'Princess, you have the world at your feet. Don't let me be the cause of you not achieving your dreams'."

"Young lady, my darling, let us hope all ends well for you. What would be your reaction if he openly reveals his true feelings?"

"Delighted. Night will become day, madam. The stars will shine brighter and the flowers prettier than they ever been."

"Quite an interesting description."

"Madam, when the moment comes when we break apart the years it took to build a union and to say goodbye to all, the absence of Venkat in my life shall be a void for the rest of my life."

"Dear, uncertainties pervade life itself, but there is always a solution, and here we sit, beholden to those whom we love. Life does get complicated but for now, let's take life as it unfolds." Mrs Harrisford embraced Victoria and suggested that a shopping trip would be a welcome distraction.

"I love you, madam."

"I am fortunate," Mrs Harrisford replied as she closed the door.

Nessfield Manor

Venkat answered the door. Victoria stood there shivering from the morning's chill, a white shawl covering her shoulders.

"Come in, please. How did you get here?'

"I walked."

"Alone? It's a long walk."

"Yes, I left before sunup. I'm depressed and confused."

Venkat waited as Victoria, hands raised, prayed silently in front of the glowing lamp. "Thank you. I feel better now."

"How is Mother?"

"Oh, I could have a baby sister or brother soon."

"You should be excited, Princess."

"I'm worried about my father. He adores Mother." Victoria looked away to hide the tears.

"Have you spoken to the Harrisfords?"

"Yes, they are supportive. Mrs Harrisford is taking me shopping for the baby a week from today."

Victoria followed Venkat outside to their favourite bench.

"I have had sad news from home."

"What was it, please tell."

"My mother passed away a few months ago," Venkat broke the news.

Saddened by tragic the news, Victoria walked through the flower beds, crying. The sun's rays formed a halo above her head. The shawl slid off Victoria's shoulders and her pearl necklace sparkled.

From behind him, Venkat heard Patrick's urgent whisper: "Boy, what is it with you? Talk to her, comfort her!"

"Uncle, I think Auntie Gertrude is better at it than I am."

Gertrude immediately ploughed over to Victoria, leaving behind a trail of pulped flowers and soft leaves. Holding her close, she wiped away Victoria's tears and comforted her. Joining them, Nancy picked up the shawl and invited Victoria to spend the afternoon with her. They sat holding hands. "I'm sorry. I'm so embarrassed."

"It's only natural. You are a compassionate girl," Nancy replied.

"Mrs Nessfield..."

"Nancy, please."

"I saw Venkat's parents before we left India. They stood before him. They were exhausted and dustyfaced from the journey from their home village and they looked hungry. When it was time for them to leave to go back to their village, he knelt before them, touched his mother's feet, rose, wiped away her tears and walked through the gates of the emigration depot. I wanted to go to his parents to tell them 'we are sorry'. I could not do it. I would have been British to them and my words would not have been worthy of the misery that had befallen them and a million others."

"It's tragic. The loss of a loved one does reflect the transience of human life and our own mortality."

"Back home, in recent years, boys willingly accepted responsibilities at an early age as famine killed the aged and the weak. Knowing very little of the reality that awaited them. Venkat undertook a journey to achieve the solitary goal of supporting his family. Little did I know that he would become so important to me! Branding people by who they are or what they look like is against the will of god."

"I agree totally. All of them, Madras, Patrick and even Gertrude and I had opinions, fears and doubts but today they are my family. Can I ask Gertrude to prepare lunch?"

"Yes. Thank you."

"He only has us now."

Having recovered and looking refreshed and as though the clouds had lifted and the sun was shining once more, Victoria approached Venkat.

Venkat avoided any conversation regarding his mother and wiped the bench for Victoria to sit on.

"I have chores to finish and later Uncle Patrick and I need to run an errand for Lt Croydon."

"Can I join you?"

"I would need to ask Uncle Patrick, but I'm sure he wouldn't mind."

"Do you think I could spend the weekend here? Will Mrs Nessfield accept my visit?"

"Will she refuse? I doubt it very much!" Venkat replied. "Princess, we all undergo sadness and the inevitably of death. Therefore, although one cannot prepare for it, we need to find a way to accept it."

"You're an inspiration to me."

Victoria followed him to discuss her stay.

CHAPTER 16

Years passed and there had been many changes. Emily and Agatha were away in England and Nancy married Lt Croydon. Patrick, Venkat and Gertrude were still employed by Nancy and enjoyed the stability and good nature of the lieutenant.

The conflict between the British and the Zulus had stopped, and the colony was rapidly developing its economy.

Durban became the hub for the Indian settlers where businesses, religion, culture and aspirations flourished. Many families had relocated there, and Springfield provided most of the vegetables sold at the market. The market itself was governed by a new set of rules and taxation was introduced to control the traders who operated the stalls. A new road ran along the front boundary of Nancy's property; this provided easy access for the traffic entering the city from the north and it ran parallel to the coastline.

Venkat and Patrick were the proud owners of new houses built on plots given to them by Nancy. The two houses were completed in three months with the help of Sundrum and many of his friends, and with expert guidance from Lt Croydon and Nancy. Gertrude and Nancy volunteered to make the bedding and curtaining while Patrick made many trips to town to collect furniture, stoves and other utensils bought from Bhana's Trading Store.

Patrick, Gertrude and Venkat sat on the front steps of Patrick's house, resting after spending the day moving furniture.

"Madras, I'm grateful to you for a lot of things," Gertrude interrupted the silence. "I'm grateful to you as well," Patrick replied.

"Don't thank me. You've shared your lives with me, taught me much more than I thought I could ever learn, and you've been my family. For that, I'll be forever grateful. Life is all about sharing."

"Memsahib's birthday party is next week. I overheard the lieutenant discussing it with her last night."

"What are we supposed to do?"

"I think they invite friends who bring gifts for her," Gertrude guessed.

"We should give her a good gift," Venkat suggested. "We need to decide on it soon."

Nancy approached them, carrying a tray of biscuits and bowls of cream. Lt Croydon followed with glasses, a jug of orange juice – and another bottle.

"What is this for?" Patrick asked, surprised to see them.

"We're going to raise a toast to your new houses!"

"You can drink the juice, while I'll have the whisky! Would you like a taste?" the lieutenant asked Patrick, showing him the glass of whisky, glancing at Gertrude mischievously.

"No, thank you, I prefer the juice!" Patrick replied.

Lt Croydon looked at Gertrude, "It's an occasion, Gertrude."

"If the whisky won't kill him, I will," Gertrude laughed.

Venkat produced a basket of succulent strawberries to accompany the cream – an old English tradition.

"Did you know that Agatha is coming home for a holiday soon?"

"How long will she stay, memsahib?" Patrick asked excitedly.

"Two months."

"Ah, she will be all grown up into a beautiful woman," Gertrude sighed. "She is fond of the lieutenant. Not forgetting all of you as well!"

"She's a delightful girl and she will be thrilled to see everyone." The lieutenant wrapped his arm around Nancy's shoulders and led her away as the stars joined the moon on its nightly trip around the sky. Venkat was satisfied that from the ashes a union has developed, a promise fulfilled and a future bright and at peace. He wished them good night and went into his empty house.

Rosehill Estates

Wealthy well-dressed young men were regular visitors to Rosehill Manor and Victoria, shying away from any long conversations over tea or walks on the beach, always found excuses to shorten their stay. Mrs Harrisford welcomed their visits with the hope that Victoria would enjoy the teachings of British etiquette. She, therefore, encouraged the eligible young men. Victoria was aware of the matchmaking efforts of Mrs Harrisford and accepted her noble intent of encouraging her to adopt a British way of life.

Port Natal

Colonel Alexander Payton stepped onto the pier, amid a shipload of immigrant's intent on being recruited on the rapidly expanding plantations and other commercial enterprises. Passenger Indians sought their fortune in business opportunities that were springing up to cater to the needs of a booming economy. Meandering through the throng, he found the administrative office and submitted his documents.

"Welcome, sir. I'm Graham Barber."

"Thank you."

The colonel waited as his documents and arrival were catalogued.

"All in order, sir."

"How do I get to Rosehill Estates?"

"I'll draw you a map if you don't mind, sir."

"Not at all, thank you."

"You need a horse and a saddle. The army has many. The fort is down the road."

"Thank you once again."

"You are welcome and enjoy your stay, sir."

Leaving the office, Col Payton went directly to the nearby hotel to spend an anxious night awaiting his search the next morning.

Rosehill Estates

The mist hung low over the cane fields at daybreak as workers marched in a single file. As the colonel rode past, they stepped aside allowing the snorting horse a wide berth.

"Good morning. Where can I find Rosehill Manor?"

"Just over that hill, sir," one of them replied, whilst the other pointed.

"Thank you."

An early riser, Mrs Harrisford sat on the porch watching a lone rider take a shortcut through the firebreaks and heading directly towards the manor. She sipped her tea and waited. Jumping off the horse, he straightened his imposing uniform, and removing his cap, he stepped onto the veranda.

"Good morning, madam. I'm Colonel Alexander Payton of the Eastern Command, once stationed in Madras, India."

"Pleased to meet you, sir. I'm Mrs Harrisford. Welcome and come in, please."

He followed her into the living room.

"Could I offer you breakfast?"

"No, thank you. I had breakfast about an hour ago."

Mrs Harrisford shifted nervously in her seat.

"Mrs Harrisford, records show that my wife Sushila and daughter Victoria are currently working on this estate.

"Mrs Payton is employed as a nurse and Victoria is the daughter I wished for. Shall I call her?"

"Please."

"Excuse me for a minute or two."

Victoria stood on the threshold, looking at her father, and the moment felt surreal. Father and daughter then clung to each other, shedding tears of joy and regret.

"It's okay, honey. I'm back."

"After so many years, Father. Why?"

"A soldier's life is not his own, honey," Colonel Payton whispered as he wiped away her tears. Years of waiting and pining suddenly ended in a flood of emotions. Victoria left her father's embrace and the manor. They watched her follow a firebreak and disappear.

"Why? What is wrong with Victoria?"

"Sir, I wish I could explain. She often waited at this spot, longing for your return. Now it has happened she's undoubtedly overwhelmed."

"She has grown into a fine and beautiful young lady."

"That she has. We're just as proud of her as if she were our daughter too."

"Madam, I thank you and Mr Harrisford."

"It's not necessary to thank us. She blesses us with her charm, spirit, intelligence and bubbly character."

"Does my wife work close by?"

Mr Harrisford entered and introduced himself.

"You have a wonderful estate, sir."

"Oh, thank you, Colonel. Colonel, with regards to your wife, we have news that will be painful for you..."

Colonel Payton sat silently for a while, then got up and paced the floor as Mrs Harrisford filled in the details of the past year. She constantly filled in details of Victoria's concerns about him and his efforts, and the promise of uniting the family. He walked over to the porch steps, sat on the last one, and placing his face in his palms, he cursed the military.

"How is Jasper?" Mr Harrisford asked, intending to redirect the conversation.

"He's in college in Berkshire. I'm a huge disappointment to my family, to my daughter. I broke my promise and have no way of mending her heart. As a little girl in difficult times, I promised to take her and her mother home to complete the picture she had painted."

"I've seen a part of the picture. Give her time. She will heal and find a way to overcome her disappointment. She will mend and your commitment and presence in her life will be important."

"Thank you, sir. They are fortunate to have found you."

"Arvin, can you take the carriage and bring back Victoria from her favourite spot? Do you know where it is?

"Yes, sir. I do."

An hour later, an early lunch was served, and Victoria and her father sat in the lounge.

"Father, I'm sorry for being so emotional."

"I've disappointed you. I forgive your mother, as well. You were in my thoughts every moment of every day in all the years that I was away. My promises, your plans and our plans for a reunion with Jasper as a family, now lie in disarray."

"Father, I held it together for so long knowing that the day would come when we would fit the pieces together. However, it's not to be. I cannot fathom how you feel."

"Darling, I will do my best to rebuild our lives."

"Thank you, Father. You are my life."

"And I'm blessed to have you as a daughter."

Victoria broke their embrace when Mr and Mrs Harrisford joined them.

"Madam, sir, I have experienced the greatest joy in finding Victoria. Your kindness in taking care of her is unheard of. I sincerely hope that she could be in your keep for another year or so. My service to the army ends in a year and then I shall return to take her home."

"Taking care of Victoria has been and will be the greatest joy for us all, sir."

"Thank you, madam. Sir, I must take leave now as I have matters to take care of and I would like to pay a visit to my wife. As much as I'm disappointed, my love for her hasn't diminished."

"You are a gentleman in my book, sir." Mr Harrisford wished him well as he shook his hand.

Victoria led her father to the horse. Kissing her on her cheeks and her head, he mounted, promising to return in a few days to see her before he would leave.

As he rode away, Mr and Mrs Harrisford joined Victoria on the porch. Topping a low hill, the colonel waved to them, spun his horse around and disappeared over the top.

"Dear, you shall be my guest in the manor from tonight and as for as many days and nights as you wish."

"Thank you, madam. I love you."

"Oh, we know that, dear."

Nessfield Manor

Venkat welcomed Victoria into his furnished new home.

"Why are you so early, Princess? Come in."

"Aren't you happy to see me?"

"I'm very happy to see you. I was just about to pray."

"Can I join you?"

"Please do. Would you light the lamps while I cut some flowers?"

Removing her shoes, Victoria lit the three lamps and arranged the flowers at the base of each one, the flames reflecting off the polished symbols.

Standing before the lamps they each prayed, consumed by their faith, silent and absorbed. It was the first anniversary of the passing away of his mother.

"Princess, I will go get breakfast for us. Time and again, I stress that you should not come alone. Where is Arvin?"

"When I'm sad, I love to walk to clear my mind."

Venkat arranged the plates and sat opposite her.

"You have more than what we possess," Victoria complimented him.

"Not much to look at but worth a chariot of gold."

"My father came home yesterday."

"He kept his promise. How do you feel?"

"I'm happy and excited, but I also need solutions."

"Does he know about Mother?"

"Yes, he does. He's in a state of shock and blames himself for the break-up of their marriage. He still loves her very much."

"I'm sure he does. The circumstances that led up to this difficult situation is not one single act but many and they are not planned. In most cases, it's just a moment of weakness that changes an entire future."

"I know. I feel responsible for Father's sadness. He expected me to protect the sacred union of our family. He sacrificed a whole lot for us. Life in the military kept him from us."

"How long is he going to be here?"

"A week or so, I think. He wants to visit Mother and take care of a few other details."

"Spend as much time with him. Share your thoughts, be supportive of his decisions and discuss your future about joining him in England."

"I think you're right."

"Am I not always?"

"Don't fool yourself," Victoria giggled.

"I will ask Mrs Croydon if we can drive you back to Rosehill."

Victoria washed the dishes while Venkat talked to Nancy.

"The carriage awaits a princess," Venkat announced on his return.

"Thank you, squire," Victoria curtsied.

Nancy stopped reading her book and asked Venkat if they could talk about a few matters of importance. He agreed and sat on a wooden chair on the patio.

"Madras, you have been with us for many years. Are you happy with the kind of work that you do?"

"At first, I was not, now I'm used to it. It supports me and, most importantly, you have been kind."

"Madras, I know you were uncomfortable with the type of work we employed you to do, so I've found another job for you. Lt Croydon requires a young man to assist him in his office."

"Then I must leave you?"

"Yes, but you will still live here."

"I will speak to Patrick," Venkat replied, thoughtfully.

"Oh!" Nancy collected her thoughts. "I'm inviting you to my birthday party tomorrow. I have already invited Patrick and Gertrude."

"Thank you!" Venkat accepted the invitation.

The lieutenant and Nancy left at dawn the next day to finalise arrangements for the party that was to take place that afternoon, as arranged with Patrick. This allowed Patrick, Venkat and Gertrude the time to move the cumbersome piano from the stable into the living room.

It was not easy as the front door was not wide enough and tilting the piano to gain access needed stronger hands. Patrick, dripping with perspiration, suggested they get help from the neighbour's servants. He walked briskly to the neighbouring estate and returned with two men.

Nessfield Manor

Nancy's birthday celebration was the first for Venkat, Patrick and Gertrude. Preferring to sit outside on the lawn instead of in the noisy living room, the group looked on as the guests arrived in carriages, wagons and on horseback. Victoria ran back and forth with delicious snacks and drinks for the shy trio.

"Uncle, would you like a small glass of gin?"

"No, thank you. I would like to live to be at your party."

Alcohol flowed and music rang out of the mansion. Short speeches were interrupted by cheers and clapping. Nancy called out to Gertrude, Patrick and Venkat to join them. Standing in the doorway, they hesitated.

"Come on in," Nancy encouraged them.

Introducing them, Nancy described their role and their loyalty in ensuring her wellbeing. She touched on the journey to India and explained that although they work for her, she regarded them as part of her family. Nancy walked over to the piano and thanked Patrick, Gertrude and Madras for the lovely gift. The silence was broken by muted applause from the unenthusiastic guests. A groggy man played the piano and guests joined in the singing, cheering as glass after glass added to the merriment. Nancy suggested to Patrick that they stay and enjoy dinner.

"Memsahib, we will have ours later."

"The memsahib is brave – it really shows that not all British people are bad," Gertrude whispered as they left.

Victoria joined Venkat on the lawn.

"Princess, are you enjoying the celebrations?"

"Yes, in contrast to my recent emotional state, I now feel as though I can enjoy myself again."

"How is Mother?"

"Can we visit her next week Sunday? She hasn't seen you in months."

"I would like to, yes."

"We may not have a complete family picture, but she will always be part of our lives."

Rosehill Estates

A week had passed, and every morning Victoria sat waiting and watching the pathway to the manor. One morning, just after sunrise, Victoria awoke to find her father sitting at the breakfast table with Mr and Mrs Harrisford. Victoria gave her father a hug and went to ready herself for breakfast.

"Mr and Mrs Harrisford, I'm leaving for India tomorrow. I have received confirmation that my services to the Crown ends in thirteen months and only then can I take Victoria home to England. I should be back in fifteen months, or a short while after."

"That should be about it," Mr Harrisford agreed.

"Sir and madam, would it be possible for Victoria to stay on in your beautiful house for the next fifteen months? I shall pay the amount you deem fit as boarding fee."

"Colonel, there is no need for payment. We are fond of her and love her as our own," Mrs Harrisford answered, quite surprised by the suggestion.

"I have with me this letter which I shall entrust to you with details of my possessions – both financial and my property back home – and my wishes as to its execution. Should I not return in eighteen months, as there are, unfortunately, always a slip between the cup and the lip, would you discuss the contents with Victoria?"

"We will do our best," Mr Harrisford replied.

"We shall pray that this won't be necessary," Mrs Harrisford replied as she shut the safe door.

Victoria spent the morning with her father. In the few hours available to them they rode on the sandy coastline, raced through the firebreaks and sat at her favourite retreat beneath the drooping branches of a willow.

Many of the issues that burdened her mind were laid to rest and she was hopeful that her shattered dreams might be mended.

"Darling, my love for you and Jasper is the purpose of my existence, and I love your mother as much as I did when we first met. I know she is heartbroken that we can't be a family. I wish you would not blame her. Sad as I am, I wish her well. It was not her fault; it was a consequence of a situation over which we had very little control."

"Father, I still love her, but Mother should have waited for your return. A dream never dies, sir."

"Will you wait for me for fifteen months?"

"Even when I reach 100, I will be waiting for you."

"I should be about 150 years old by then."

Having decided it was time to leave, Colonel Payton pulled Victoria onto the horse, rode with her for a hundred yards, spun around and rode back to the manor. He kissed her and gently lowered her to the ground. Jumping off, he thanked the Harrisfords. Then he rode off. Victoria waved until her father was out of sight.

Rosehill Estates

Mrs Harrisford answered the door.

"Good morning, madam. You must be Mrs Harrisford."

"Yes, and you are?

"I'm Venkat. Victoria invited me to join her to visit her mother."

"She went riding with her friend. She'll be back soon."

"Would it be all right with you if I wait here?"

"Yes, and would you like tea?"

"Yes, thank you, madam."

Arvin set the tray on the table, wished Venkat well and went back into the house.

Mrs Harrisford unexpectedly joined Venkat outside.

"How is Mrs Croydon?"

"Very well, thank you, madam."

"Venkat is it? Victoria has told me a lot about you."

"I'm surprised."

"Do you know much about her?"

"Just her wishes and dreams, madam."

"Are you going to be with her for the rest of her life?"

"Forgive me, madam. It is not a habit of mine to share my inner thoughts and feelings with those whom I do not know. However, if you keep our conversation confidential, then I will oblige you with all that you need to know because Victoria is precious to us both. As far as my future with Victoria. It shall not extend beyond the day she leaves to pursue her dream in Britain."

"Candid young man! I thought you are fond of her."

"Yes, in a special way, but I would be selfish if I pursued what Victoria hinted at what would be an ideal future for us both. My allegiance to her is temporary, which she is not aware of. I'm providing her with the stability she needs to overcome the difficulties she has gone through. When she is well enough and old enough to examine the permanence of the choices she makes, she will find a union that shall give her happiness, fulfilment and the life she deserves."

"Here I thought you an illiterate young man bent on taking advantage of a beautiful, intelligent and educated girl."

"Victoria has openly declared her admiration for you and Mr Harrisford; as being the kindest people she has ever met; therefore, I regard both of you with the utmost respect. It's not my habit to hurt anyone or their feelings. My comments are made as I see or feel it."

"Just what I admire, young man," Mrs Harrisford agreed

"A broad assumption is that all Indians wearing oversized turbans, semi-naked, jumping from tree to tree, tossing coconuts are without common sense or intellectual thought. Unfortunately, if one doesn't have a grasp of English, then, without doubt, one is classified as being illiterate. Victoria is determined to complete her studies so that she can return to India to reverse the perceptions of narrow-minded British nationals. She knows more about India's past than I do."

"I believe millions of your kind are dying in prolonged famines that forced you to come here?"

"Yes, madam. Famine is an avoidable tragedy. Millions, madam. Indian nationals; men, women and children succumb to the catastrophe, orchestrated in the name of king and country, by your kind, not dissimilar to the vermin that perpetuated the Black Death that swamped Europe a few hundred years ago."

"I had no idea of these atrocities," Mrs Harrisford accepted after much deliberation.

"Difficult to imagine, even more painful to experience, but it does occur. I think you will not understand the reasons behind such acts of genocide."

"I am sorry."

"We all have a gift, madam, whether one is a priest or pagan, prince or pauper, and we cherish it."

"What is it, pray tell?"

"Life itself," Venkat replied, as Mrs Harrisford sat completely at a loss for words.

"Do … do you carry hatred for the British?"

"Hate is repulsive and rarely exists in us as people. Hate is detrimental to the human mind because it dwarfs future actions that could, if vented, destroy relationships. In its place we develop plans that could yield success if nurtured correctly. Harbouring hate is like me drinking poison to kill those who I feel created injustice. A mind saturated with hate has no room for other emotions. Love for India and its people drive me; it is an endearing and ancient culture, spanning thousands of years, willing to adapt and foolish enough to be subservient. The British have given India much in the years that they have been there, which we are thankful for, but all things have a beginning and an end. Destroyed to be reborn."

"I'm sorry you feel the way you do," Mrs Harrisford was truthful in her reply.

"Madam, a great divide stands between us, yet Victoria sees that we're the same, born with the same breath, hope, dreams and ambitions. In life, without knowing the union of opposites, one cannot be objective. How does one know what darkness is without light: good or evil, happiness or sadness? There must be an understanding of the elements that provide the balance to secure extreme knowledge. For that reason alone, I shall provide Victoria with the environment she needs to attain her goals. You have been supportive of her rediscovery as well, which I applaud."

"Can I send Arvin to inform her of your arrival?"

"No, thank you, madam. I'll wait."

"I will be off then. I have much to chew on!"

"Thank you for your hospitality," Venkat replied as Mrs Harrisford got up to leave the room.

In the balmy heat of the day, Venkat swished away the buzzing insects that hoped to dine on the drops of perspiration accumulated around his collar. Clouds were blowing from the west – an ominous sign of an impending storm.

Victoria passed the reins to a waiting stable-hand, raced to meet Venkat and hugged him excitedly.

"How long have you been waiting?"

"Two hours."

"Have you met Mrs Harrisford?"

"She's the best."

"Yes, she is. I will clean up and we can leave to visit Mother."

"Rain is imminent."

"We will chance it," Victoria replied.

Ogilvy Home - Rosehill Estates

A tropical storm raged, tossing huge waves against the rocks. Tall plumes of water shot up into the air and then crashed onto jagged rocks. In between cane fields, drenched, heads covered with long coats, Venkat and Victoria slipped and wobbled along the muddy firebreaks. Two hours later, they reached the cottage. Sushila opened the door, invited them in and embraced them both at the same time.

She urged them to get rid of their wet clothes and found them each a fresh set to change into. Mr Ogilvy's shirt and pants hung loosely over Venkat's frame.

In the ensuing excitement, Sushila made coffee, stacked cakes on a plate and called out to Victoria.

After calm was restored, and Venkat had the chance to catch up with Sushila's news, Victoria and her mother sat alone in the dining area. Venkat sat outside, appreciating the calm after the storm. The storm abated as the wind changed direction and the aftermath of the freak storm became clear. The outer fringes of mature cane lay flattened and firebreaks were now tiny rivulets, pulling in large chunks of fully-grown cane. Birds once more left their roost and preened themselves as the sun reappeared from behind retreating clouds.

"Sorry for having left you on your own," Victoria interrupted Venkat's thoughts.

"Not at all. I was enjoying the peace and quiet."

"Mother, Victoria and I will need to leave soon as it's a long walk. We promise to visit you as many times as possible."

"I'm holding you to your promise. I love you both very much."

Victoria embraced her mother, holding on to her for a while.

"Come here, son," she embraced them together. "The clothes are too big for you," she giggled.

"I will give them to Patrick."

When the two left, Sushila stood alone waving to them.

Rosehill Estates

The fifteen-month wait for her father was by no means boring. Victoria divided her time equally between Rosehill Manor and the Croydons. Besides spending time with Venkat, Victoria taught the labourers – both men and women – English as well as about the obligations and rights of their indenture contract. Nancy supported her valiant bid to encourage more to join, but labourers were restricted in using their daylight hours for any activity other than contractual mandate. Nonetheless, together with Guru Sundrum, she contributed to removing many doubts and made clear the available options and their choices on the expiry of their indenture (girmit).

Many anecdotes were told about Victoria's lessons and of the British girl's intentions to educate labourers in improving the knowledge and the language that were once furthest from their minds. Those who tried to converse in English during classes caused much laughter and fun, completely disrupting classes. It was a pleasure for Victoria as it took her back to her childhood days. She also found comfort that those whom she taught found her to be no different than themselves. They danced, sang and enjoyed every moment of their interaction.

As the months passed, Victoria and Mrs Harrisford spent more time together – during afternoon tea, visits into town and long picnics on the beach. Conversations, as always, were focussed around their wish that Victoria followed through with her plans.

It was no different a month before her expected departure to England with her father.

"Victoria, have you written to Jasper?"

"I did, madam, and he replied."

"Have you selected a college yet?"

"My father will do all that once he is in England or he might have contacted my grandparents."

"Venkat and you are inseparable. How are you going to cope without him?"

"I will miss him very much and I'm certain he will miss me too. He has a great insight into the aspects of my future, of which even I am unaware."

"I am sure of it. He surprised me when we met. He has an uncanny ability to shred sentiments that we as British thought ideal for colonialism."

"British as I am, I hope Mother India gains her freedom so they can rebuild the glory they once owned."

Victoria slept late the next day. Arvin made breakfast and called her out of bed. Taking the tray to the porch, she tucked in freshly baked scones, doused with jam and washed them down with fresh milk. Breakfast done, Victoria walked to the stables and saddled a horse. She was about to mount when Venkat spoke.

"Hello, Princess."

Turning around surprised, she took a few steps and kissed him on his cheeks. Embarrassed, Venkat looked around.

"Missed me?"

"Not much."

Victoria looked at Venkat with mock indignation. "Be truthful now!"

"Have I ever given you an indication that I do not miss you?"

"No, not yet. Let's visit Mother. Is your weekend free?"

"Yes. Let's go on Saturday," Venkat suggested.

Would you like to ride there?"

"Gladly, in the life hereafter," Venkat grinned.

Ogilvy Home

Victoria carried Mala Anne as her mother prepared a snack.

"Beautiful is how I describe her – an image of her big sister," Venkat complimented Victoria.

"Am I?"

"Ask the world."

"You make me blush," Victoria slapped Venkat's shoulder.

When the day ended and Victoria suggested it was time to leave, Mr Ogilvy intervened. "Stay over tonight. Your mother will be most pleased," he pleaded politely. "I will ride out to Rosehill and tell them about your stay."

"Mother, what do you think?"

"I have no words. It has been a long time since we spent a night together."

"I will, as long as Mala Anne and I share a bed."

"Agreed."

"Venkat, are you okay with staying over?"

"Yes. I'm comfortable here."

Port Natal

The day of Victoria's voyage to England finally arrived. Colonel Payton and his 'family' stood in a small group to bid each other farewell. The hours ticked over, and the group was left with only minutes. Mr Ogilvy, with Mala Anne in his arms, stood next to Sushila. He handed her to Victoria, who held Mala Anne close and promised to take her to India someday. Colonel Payton and Mr Ogilvy shook hands and wished each other the very best.

"Take care of our ladies."

"I will, sir. You can be sure of that."

"You are a good man. Thank you."

Giving Mala Anne to her mother, Victoria walked over to Patrick and Gertrude who both held her for a while. Gertrude, not without crying, promised that she would carry the memories of Victoria till her last breath.

Sobbing, Nancy wiped away Victoria's tears. She turned away to face Lt Croydon, who held her close, then Nancy said, "We will miss you."

Turning around to her mother, Victoria exclaimed, "Mother, saying goodbye is worse than I ever imagined!"

"My darling, I've disappointed you and took away the chance of reuniting the family. I have no way of taking away the pain you feel. However, know that I love you more than ever. You were my strength through the troubles we endured. I hope someday you will forgive me. You also have another mother waiting for you in Southampton who also will be there to brighten your life."

"Mother, there is nothing to forgive. I'm looking forward to a bright future – fulfilling the plans we made and those that Mr and Mrs Harrisford have for me. You will always be my mother and my inspiration."

Sushila wiped away Victoria's tears and then her own.

Finally, Victoria held Venkat by his hands and searched for words.

"Princess, I've dreaded the dawn of today, and if I had known that this moment will hurt so much, I would have hidden in a cane field till this day was over."

"That would be an easy way out for you, I guess."

"Not an easy way out. In moments like these, I'm at a loss for words. It is indeed one of the saddest days of my life … but it also gives me great pleasure to see that the universe has granted you some of the wishes you prayed for."

"You will be alone!"

"I have Mala Anne and Mother to spoil me."

"Mother, promise me you will take care of him!"

"I will, I promise. He is my son, as well."

"Princess, you have brought me from the depths of ignorance and bridged the chasm that separates us."

"When my studies are over, I will come back here and take you home… Your eyes mirror what is in your heart. I've waited years for you to tell me the truth and even now you resist."

"I am one person. You have a dream for millions. I regret that you are leaving and will miss you. I shall not walk in the shadows of my losses but will live in the brightness of promises made and your successes. You live in all things I cherish." Venkat said as he held her close.

Venkat pushed back the strands of hair that covered her eyes and kissed her on her forehead. She bowed, touched his feet, got up and kissed him once more.

"These moments will come to pass, but it will live in my heart for the rest of my life," she sobbed.

"Princess, I am once again at wit's end to find answers at this moment of separation, and truthfully, there shall be no other to fill the emptiness in my heart, and it would take a lifetime and still understanding of your feelings will elude me. More importantly, the value of our commitments is different, and it was near impossible to cross the divide, which I feel would have been not in your best interest."

"I have waited for a very long time to hear you say that, or even a hint," Victoria said, now satisfied that Venkat miraculously revealed his true feelings. Victoria turned around and followed her father onto the gangway and joined the passengers along the white rails on the top deck.

Colonel Payton put his arms around his daughter's shoulder. The ship's horn blew, the engines growled, and the harbour hands released the ropes. The ship moved slowly and then picked up speed as it headed for the harbour mouth. Victoria waved until the ship turned into the open ocean and followed the coastline heading for the Red Sea and then the Gulf of Suez. Tall columns of smoke were the only visible signs of her departure, until it eventually blended in with the grey clouds, taking away even that final sign of her. Gertrude joined Nancy in the carriage as Lt Croydon kicked it into a trot. Patrick and Madras followed in the wagon.

"Uncle, another chapter of our lives is closed," Venkat said.

Nessfield Manor

Since Victoria's departure, Venkat spent most of his afternoons in his little cottage, reading the books that she left behind. He did confess to Patrick that it would be a long time, if ever, before the void left by Victoria's departure could be filled.

"Young man, we spoke of her feelings for you many times."

"Well, someday I may find out about what you have been talking about. For now, we have families to care for."

"I think you must pay Victoria's mother a visit. It has been a while. She would love to see you again."

"Thanks, Uncle. I will."

Ogilvy Home

Two months went by and Venkat finally paid a visit to Sushila. Mala Anne was a beautiful baby, and as Sushila handed her to Venkat, she cried and reached out for her mother.

"It has been a very long time," Sushila complained.

"How is Victoria?"

"Well, you will know if you read your letters."

"I don't think I should."

"Why not?"

"Ma, there will be questions that I wouldn't be able to answer."

"She's doing well but misses you a lot. Her father – with the help of the Harrisfords – enrolled her at Girton College in Cambridge."

"College studies were her ambition."

"How is Mrs Croydon?"

"She is doing fine. Are you still working, Ma?"

"I cannot really work. Taking care of Mala Anne is important and makes up most of my day. I crochet, sew and knit when she's in bed and I help on the estate when I'm needed. I've altered some of Mr Ogilvy's shirts to fit you."

"Oh, thank you."

"Can we talk about you?"

"There's not much to tell. I may work at the fort with Lt Croydon."

"What about Nancy?"

"She suggested it. I will still live there."

After lunch, Sushila and Venkat spent a little while chatting and reminiscing about their trip to Port Natal. Mala Anne woke and crawled over to the living room.

"Son, even in my wildest dreams I never imagined to be living here. Out of the uncertainty that Victoria and I experienced there is one outcome that overshadows all other problems we went through. In many ways I have disappointed Victoria by being with Mr Ogilvy. She will understand someday. Victoria today is a girl reborn. Gone are the emotional problems that haunted her for years. Through your friendship she outgrew her troubled childhood. You helped in ways that I was not able to."

"Ma, I did very little."

"I believe you did much more than you think. You brought back her happiness, her spirit and the love for the people with whom she couldn't engage as a child."

Venkat accepted one cotton bag filled with shirts, letters and another with cakes and biscuits. Picking up Mala Anne, he gave her a kiss.

Sushila kissed him as well. "Son, this is your home away from home. Visit me as many times as you like. I promised Victoria I will take care of you."

Nessfield Manor

Venkat was working in the flower beds the next morning when Patrick drew alongside him with the wagon.

"Let's go see Guru Sundrum. We have an important meeting with him."

"Will memsahib allow us to go?"

"Yes, it was she who suggested it."

"I'll wash and put on a clean shirt." Venkat was excited and on edge as this visit was shrouded in mystery.

"What is this meeting about? Please tell me," Venkat implored.

"I cannot give you details now, but Guru Sundrum and I received a letter from Ayepakkum. I'm sure it will be a pleasant surprise." Patrick lied.

"Now keep still or I'll tie your bones to the seat," Patrick scolded.

He tugged at the reins and stopped a short distance away from the market.

"Boy, please wait here."

Under the bright Saturday morning sun, Venkat watched the crowds meander through the narrow passages of the market. Ladies in brightly coloured saris, baskets laden with fresh vegetables and fruits, emerged from the nearby streets. Pigeons dodged sweaty men as they scuttled across their feeding ground. The men wheeled trolleys and barrows – some empty, others laden with wet sacks filled with crops of beans, carrots, cabbages and herbs. Patrick, Guru and Rathna emerged from the crowd and headed for the wagon.

"Hello, my son," Guru greeted Venkat.

Jumping off the wagon excitedly, he embraced the guru.

"How… how are you?" Venkat stammered.

"Well. Do you remember this person?"

"Yes! Uncle Rathna from Tindivanum."

"Let us look for shade. We have a very important matter to discuss."

Patrick led the way to a shady spot. He poured four glasses of juice and opened a tin of biscuits.

"Do you know why we are here?" Sundrum questioned Venkat.

"No."

"Patrick and I have been discussing your present situation with Uncle Rathna – your age and eligibility, and I think it's time you accept marriage as your next step in life," Sundrum suggested calmly.

Venkat was surprised at the suggestion. Nervously, he replied, "I'm unsure of how to answer you."

"We all take steps we are uncertain about. We are your elders and have watched you grow as a person. It's time to start your own family. Nagamah, Uncle Rathna's daughter, will be an ideal wife and a good mother," Guru Sundrum added.

"I will gladly approve such a marriage," Rathna confirmed.

"I will write to my family about it and give you an answer as soon as my father blesses this unexpected arrangement."

"Good, we will wait till then," they accepted Venkat's suggestion.

They discussed other issues and then parted company.

"Uncle, I'm afraid of the added responsibilities that marriage would require. Will I be able to be a husband, a father?"

"Don't worry; you will cope," Patrick assured him.

CHAPTER 17

Six months had passed since the meeting that initiated the idea of marriage. As expected, it also took firm root in Ayepakkum. A letter had arrived from Venkat's father, blessing both the proposal and the subsequent marriage. It also spoke of their excitement and the wish that he could attend the auspicious event.

As the months progressed, Venkat also grew to consider his options and the idea of marriage, knowing little of its implication with just knowledge of family bonds as experienced living with parents. He planned to discuss it with Nancy. He procrastinated until, one morning, as he rehearsed his request, she overheard him.

"Do you have something to ask me?" Nancy questioned.

"No, yes … yes, memsahib. Memsahib, Uncle Patrick and my guru have decided that it's time I marry," he calmly began his well-practised announcement.

"That's wonderful! Have you decided on a bride yet?"

"My guru and Uncle Patrick decided. She's the daughter of an immigrant who works for Major Gailey," he replied as he swept the living room floor.

"Let us sit, then," Nancy suggested. "Have you seen her or spoken to her?"

"No, I received the approval from my family a month ago. The astrological charts predict that our marriage will be blessed with happiness and many children. I was a bit afraid of how you would react to this news," Venkat expressed, at last, the feeling that had prevented him from approaching Nancy.

"I'm excited. Patrick did mention that he promised your father that he would find you a bride. You haven't met her, yet you would marry her?"

"It's customary in our culture for the elders to select a bride for their sons."

"Will there be love?" Nancy pondered.

"Love I cannot explain. Someday I may learn about the love between a man and a woman that so many of you talk about. Madam, I will be her husband and a good father to my children." Venkat shifted uneasily.

"Madras, I will gladly accept whoever you marry as part of this family. Did you consider what Victoria will say about this?"

"Her leaving has left an emptiness in my life. I have denied her the pleasure of knowing. It was impossible to share my thoughts when she was here. I was bound by my own rigidity and was unable to break down the shackles that separated us into groups. We are worlds apart, memsahib, and traditions guide us, which I must uphold."

"Do you miss her?"

"Very much. She has left in me images, thoughts and ideas, indelible for a few lifetimes."

"Why did you not tell her how you felt?"

"I did guise my feelings. Memsahib, the choices I made did not include a person like Victoria and I will cherish the memory of our time spent together."

"If Victoria was not right for you, how do you know that this new girl you're willing to marry is right for you?"

"We are both with little to our name and a future unknown. There's a chance that we'll build our relationship and provide our children with a future brighter than what we had. It's a changing world. Memsahib, the vestiges of my past is as distant as the promise I behold for the future."

"Will you be able to understand then, the love between a man and a woman?"

"Memsahib, life is a mystery governed by the cosmos and perhaps I would. However, though it pains me, I must accept my father's wishes and maybe Mother's spiritual wants, as well."

"Are you going to tell Victoria about your plans, or have you discussed your plans with Mrs Ogilvy?"

"Yes, I must. I will."

"Madras if you don't talk to Mrs Ogilvy about it, she won't forgive you. Victoria must know as well. I'm proud of you. You've grown into a remarkable person. I wish you well in all that lies before you."

"Thank you, memsahib," Venkat said. Getting up, he bowed and continued with the sweeping.

Ogilvy Home

Venkat sat opposite Sushila and her husband and waited for a response after his lengthy monologue.

"Son, I fully understand our culture and its position on marriage. It's sometimes hard to accept it, but it's a family choice. I actually don't know how to answer you," Sushila responded.

"I'm afraid, confused and concerned about how my life will change. Victoria was a huge part of my life, and now I'll exclude her even more."

"Do you miss her?"

"Yes, I do. I'm most alone when I recall the friendship we shared and the promise I couldn't keep. Now the idea of a marriage is a new yoke I carry."

"Young man, love and marriage you cannot explain. It's like a river: the water flows downstream, not knowing its destination, over rocks, down waterfalls and finally, it enters the sea," Mr Ogilvy tried to help.

"Rather a simple, outdated and backward explanation, Mr Ogilvy," his wife remarked.

"It could be the tipple... and you're welcome, dear," Mr Ogilvy belched.

"I need Victoria to know and I need her understanding. She's a big part of my life and to deny her the knowledge of the intended plan could hurt her feelings."

"I will write to her," Sushila promised.

"I have written her a letter which explains everything we talked about. I hope she understands."

"I will include it with my letter to her," Sushila suggested.

"Thank you. I will proceed only after I receive Victoria's response."

"Son, she will reply, but what happens if the answer is not to your liking?"

"Then I will wait for her to reconsider, for as long as it takes."

The Fort - Durban

Venkat followed Lt Croydon nervously as he entered the offices at the fort. He felt just as uncomfortable when he first entered Nancy's house. It was as though he was a new exhibit placed on a pedestal to be examined from head to toe by soldiers.

"He's a man, not an object to gawk at!" Lt Croydon shouted as he introduced Venkat to all the staff at the fort. Although he felt totally out of place, Venkat accepted the new challenge and outwardly displayed a calm demeanour.

"I shall not tolerate any insults or derogatory remarks in this establishment," Lt Croydon instructed.

"That's rather new and might be difficult to keep, sir," an officer joked.

"Give Madras a tour and outline his tasks," the lieutenant instructed.

The hysteria of the news of Venkat's proposed marriage subsided as all hinged on the reply from Victoria.

Over the next few months or so the stalemate continued as news from England failed to arrive. So Venkat remained true to his word and went about his new tasks with his usual gusto. He was wedged between the wishes of his father and the unease he felt about the contents of a letter he expected from Victoria. Venkat knew that he wouldn't go against his father's wishes, but he needed some sort of acceptance from Victoria. Mindful of the fact that Victoria might have had views of love and marriage contrary to his own, he had no option but to wait.

Agatha loved her stepfather, Lt Croydon, dearly and in return, he loved her as his own. The loss of her father had been traumatic and at the time of his death, she was unable to express her love for him fully. The lieutenant easily fulfilled the role of father and accompanied her and Nancy to England to find her a suitable boarding school, paying all the costs and providing her with everything she needed.

He wrote to her every chance he could, and Agatha replied to every letter.

Emily Nessfield accepted the relationship. Her only objection was to changing Agatha's surname. After a prolonged period of resisting, she finally relented and she, too, acknowledged the loving bond that existed between the lieutenant and his stepdaughter. Emily eventually married a retired British railway engineer and settled, as fate would have it, in the picturesque North Indian hillside village of Shimla.

More and more Indians arrived into the colony. Durban was also used as a stopover point for the thousands who were making their way into the interior to find employment in areas around Ladysmith, Dundee, Newcastle and the mining towns around Johannesburg.

The rich diamond fields helped produce numerous entrepreneurs who embarked on arduous journeys seeking new areas where opportunities existed. Educational institutions were being established to accommodate a growing population of children. The indentured Indians, through support from some sectors of the municipality, built state-aided schools. Large businesses were mushrooming and Britain was expanding their ambitions. David Livingstone, who had set about opening Africa to the world, and men like Lord Jameson and Cecil John Rhodes stretched the boundaries of the Empire northwards.

The ship from Southampton had just docked when Lt Croydon and Venkat reached the quayside. The carriage had been decorated with floral braids – Gertrude's handiwork – befitting the occasion. They waited at the foot of the gangway, wilting in the intense heat and humidity of the day. Agatha slowly walked down the steps looking at the crowds, searching for her mother. Excitedly, she ran to the lieutenant to hug him, then she hugged Venkat who collected her bags from a member of the crew. The three walked to the carriage.

"Where is Mother?"

"At home waiting for you," Venkat answered as the lieutenant climbed onto the driver's seat. "I can't believe you're so grown up! How was the voyage?"

"Long and cold. I cannot wait to get back home!"

The carriage had hardly pulled up outside the main house when a jubilant Agatha jumped off and ran to her mother. They stood clinging to each other while Venkat unloaded the bags.

"I have to leave you now as I must return the carriage – I'll be back soon," the lieutenant told Nancy and turning the carriage, he drove off. Agatha and Nancy waved as Gertrude joined them.

"You are so pretty!" Gertrude cuddled Agatha warmly and helped her into the house. "Now, what would you like to drink?"

"I missed your tea," Agatha said, thanking Gertrude.

"Only my tea?" Gertrude joked.

"I missed you and I love you. Sorry."

"I accept," Gertrude smiled.

Mother and daughter sat together on the patio and enjoyed the cool breeze blowing in from the ocean. They were still there when the lieutenant rode into the yard. Patrick accepted the reins and led the horse into the stable. He scooped fresh feed into the box and went home. Agatha walked into the kitchen and continued her conversation with Gertrude who was ready to tip a tray of freshly baked biscuits into a metal pan.

"Do you like England?"

"Not much – it's wet, grey and always cold," she answered, pinching a biscuit. "I missed all of you."

"We missed you, too – very much."

Answering the knock, Venkat opened the door. Mr and Mrs Ogilvy and Mala Anne stood on the steps. Surprised, he invited them in. Stepping out and picking up Mala Anne, Venkat followed them into the house. Mala Anne didn't cry.

"Can I offer you anything?" Venkat asked, recovering from his speechlessness. "Tea, juice or fruit?"

"No, thank you; perhaps a bit later. You have a cosy place here, Venkat."

"Thank you, we built it ourselves. Uncle Patrick's is the one next door. Mrs Croydon helped us a lot." Venkat was a bundle of nerves and it showed.

"You seem nervous."

"Yes, sir, I am."

"We received a letter from Victoria. You can read it when you're ready," Sushila informed him. "Son, have you thought about your father's wishes for you to marry?"

"Yes, Ma, I thought about it, but I was waiting for Victoria's response."

"Why?"

"Victoria and I shared much in overcoming the difficulties we went through. She is my strength and a mentor. She knew more about dealing with matters affecting my life than I ever did. I made promises which I knew I could never keep because she is a 'princess'. She had ambition and knew what she wanted in life and I was just floating along on a tide, with so many of our kind.

"Do you miss her?"

"Yes, very much. I'm excited and happy that she is where it suits her, and sad that I must embark on a journey that I don't really know much about."

Gertrude and Nancy arrived with lunch. Sushila helped to set the table. The group enjoyed a sumptuous lunch followed by ice cream and fresh strawberries from the garden – English hospitality at its best.

Venkat served tea and biscuits a bit later and Sushila helped to clean up. A pleasant day was about to conclude and Venkat was more nervous than ever when Sushila handed him the letter. "Son, know that I'm your mother here, so keep me informed."

"Thanks, Ma."

Venkat carried Mala Anne to the carriage and she waved back as they rode out through the gates.

Opening the letter, Venkat read it many times and finally placing it at the base of the lamp, he prayed.

A few days into her holiday, Agatha came bouncing around the building, closely followed by Nancy.

"Hello!" Nancy greeted them and pulled up a chair.

"My daughter is eager to ask you something herself."

"I want to say goodbye to my father," Agatha whispered.

The request surprised them all and they sat silently, waiting for someone to provide an appropriate response.

"Honey, why?" Nancy asked.

"I love him, Mother. I love him and I want to say goodbye," Agatha repeated.

"What should we do?" Nancy asked.

"I think we should take her to the burial ground," Venkat suggested.

"I'm sorry. I really don't know what to do."

"It's okay," Patrick comforted Nancy.

"I thought she had accepted the loss," Nancy blew her nose into her handkerchief.

"She's a different girl now and the trip may help her to find what she seeks," Venkat offered his opinion.

They decided that they would visit the cemetery as soon as arrangements could be made.

"What about our responsibilities at the fort, memsahib?"

"I'll sort that out with the lieutenant."

They stood in a small group looking at the graves. The ultimate sacrifice the young men made had been forgotten and with the passing of time, memories of the battle that claimed so many lives had been all but erased. The mounds of rocks were the only testament of their bravery. Patrick and Venkat led the way.

"The flowers we planted should help us," Patrick wished. A few minutes later, they located the grave. The stones that once covered the grave lay scattered around, but between the tall grass grew small plants with yellow flowers. Lt Croydon – who was eager to accompany them – Nancy, and Agatha stared down at the grave. Patrick walked to the carriage, returning with a sickle and a couple of spades.

Bush fires had burnt the wooden cross and only small, charred pieces remained. While Patrick cleaned up, Agatha knelt and picked up a leopard tooth.

"Mother, look!"

"Yes, I know. I remember it."

It took them about an hour to clean up and repack the displaced stones. They planted the wrought-iron cross that Patrick had made and when they had finished, they picked up their tools and sat beneath the shade of some trees. Nancy and the lieutenant joined them, leaving Agatha alone at the grave.

Agatha knelt beside her father's grave and she raised her hands in prayer. Eventually, she got up and wiped away the tears, dusted her knees and walked away from the grave.

"This time, Father told me he will always be my father. He smiled and said that he loves me," Agatha told her mother.

Agatha climbed into the carriage next to her mother and hugged her as the lieutenant joined them. Patrick and Madras sat at the driver's seat. Patrick urged the lead horses into a trot, and they began their return.

The ride to Pietermaritzburg Coach station took a shorter time than their first trip and was much more comfortable.

A storm of great intensity blew in from the ocean and the moon quickly disappeared behind the clouds. Streaks of lightning illuminated the night sky and the pale undersides of the leaves shone white as the wind caught them. The rumbling of the thunder drummed up the support of the crashing waves. Mountainous waves raced up the beach, churning up the sand. The clouds released their load in incessant sheets.

The next morning, as the first rays of the sun broke the horizon with golden beams, humanity gradually shook off the effects of the storm and prepared for the challenges of the new day.

Venkat got up very early to assess the damage before work. Patrick accompanied him around the house and to their relief, they found the damage to be minimal. The pair agreed that it could wait for the weekend to be fixed.

The following months were marked by feverish activity. Guru Sundrum, Singaram, Sushila and Patrick made several visits to meet Mr and Mrs Pillay to finalise all the details for the upcoming wedding. Venkat accompanied them on their last trip and caught only a glimpse of his future wife, as he was too shy to lift his head when Nagamah served them tea and biscuits.

Nagamah and her three brothers, Mariemuthoo, Sagatheva, Vasantheva and their parents, Rathna and Radha, waited in anticipation for the great occasion. Nagamah became the butt of her brothers' many jokes and Rathna was kept busy pacifying her.

Months of planning and excitement quite miraculously dissipated with the conclusion of the wedding. The shy Venkat and his bride bowed down and were blessed by Patrick and Gertrude who acted as Venkat's parents. Sushila, who was responsible for much of the planning and preparation of the wedding, was the last to leave the temple, satisfied that her promise to Victoria was achieved.

The wedding entourage walked the short distance from the temple to the cottage. A reception party consisting of Sundrum's wife and his friends awaited their arrival so they could perform one last ritual.

The bride, young and bashful, was given a brass vessel filled to the brim with water which she had to carry into the house on her shoulder without spilling, signifying the belief that their lives would always be filled with prosperity and good health.

Venkat adjusted to married life and the couple spent most evenings with Patrick and Gertrude enjoying old tales and good food. When alone, Patrick tried to coax information from Venkat about married life and its perks – regrettably without much luck.

"Deepavali is only a week away. We should celebrate the festival with all our friends," Venkat suggested to his wife and Patrick.

"Oh, we must!"

"What is Deepavali?" Lt Croydon asked when Venkat invited them to the celebrations.

"It's a celebration of the victory of good over evil and light over the shadow of darkness and it's symbolic of the victory of Lord Rama over Ravanna. Deepavali actually means rows of light: millions of lamps placed by villagers light up the path that Lord Rama took on his way to Ayodhya," Venkat explained.

"Does it have anything to do with the sign over the school entrance?"

"The balance between light and darkness, and good and evil – I am sure it has," Nancy said.

Lt Croydon nodded and accepted the invitation.

Agatha was packing her bags for her long voyage back to school in England when Venkat came in to hand Nancy a package from the lieutenant. She thanked him, but as he was about to step out, Agatha called him back.

"I'm leaving in three days."

"I know."

"Will you come to say goodbye?" she asked.

"I'll get permission from the lieutenant."

"Maddy, my mother and I have no better friends than you, Patrick and Gertrude. All of you have changed my life, and I have no way of repaying you."

"You changed your own life because you had faith," Venkat told her. "You are an intelligent girl. Remember that life holds important lessons; learn from these lessons, and you will have thanked us all. I cannot explain it in words, but I can tell you a short story that applies even today …

"Agatha, many years ago, I found a little bird. It had fallen from the nest and injured its wing. I fed it and nursed it for a while and kept it in a bamboo cage because it would not have survived in the wild. When it was freed, it stayed within the unlocked cage for many days. Then one morning, it was gone. You too have that freedom, but you must follow your dreams and always have faith in god,"

"I will, Maddy, always," Agatha thanked him and stepped back into her room to complete her packing.

Before breakfast, Venkat and his wife sat deliberating their loneliness. There was a knock at the door, and to their surprise, Guru Sundrum stood there smiling.

"Guru, how nice!" Venkat welcomed him in. Nagamah bowed, touched his feet and brought her hands together as she rose.

Venkat led Guru Sundrum to the living room.

As the two were alone, the guru ventured, "It has been a while. Are you enjoying married life?"

"Yes, I think so," Venkat replied.

"Guru, I am disappointed that my father has asked me not to send home money. He says they are comfortable, and I have a family now."

"Well, it's his wish and you must respect it."

"Guru, how do I know if it's the truth or not."

"Son, write to him and explain your concerns and consider your choices when he replies."

"I think I should return home."

"Your life is yours and now Nagamah's as well," the guru confirmed.

"Not knowing about them is painful."

"Young man, that is commendable. I shall not prescribe the road you take, but write the letter, wait for the reply and then decide."

Nagamah apologised for the interruption and invited the guru for breakfast. He accepted after a little persuasion but urged Nagamah to join them.

"Remember, marriage is a union of two people with their own views and perceptions. You will fight, you will cry and you will laugh; all these are part of life. You must know who we are. Uphold our traditions and teachings, for in them live the fruits of a good life," Guru spoke as he sipped tea.

"We will follow our traditions," Nagamah promised.

Patrick knocked and waited at the door. Nagamah welcomed him in and he was delighted to see the guru.

"I'm glad to see you, Patrick. I'm just here to counsel the newlyweds and I think you arrived at the right time as well," the guru said. He pulled a tray towards him and cut the last pancake into four pieces.

"Life is divided into four important teachings," he said, pushing one piece to the edge of the tray.

"God and his teachings are our first object in life. Second is our mother – to many, closer to us than god. Third is Mother Nature, and the fourth is respect."

Four pieces of the pancake sat on the four corners of the tray.

"What would this world be without them?" Silence prevailed. "I want you all to think about this, and when we meet the next time, you will provide me with answers," he instructed.

"Now can I eat Mother Nature? She is the biggest piece!" Patrick joked, and when one leg of the stool collapsed, he fell, and his slightly oversized tummy bounced. Guru and Venkat hurriedly picked him up.

"You have felt the fury of Mother Nature," Sundrum chastised Patrick, stifling a laugh.

"Patrick, I am glad to say that during my stay here, I have researched the African culture, its customs and traditions, and was amazed how close both our traditional practices are and will be proud to take that back to India, someday."

"I am surprised."

"Don't be, it has been a great pleasure to be given the opportunity of knowing you and Gertrude."

The day for Agatha to leave arrived and it brought with it mixed emotions. As much as Nancy would miss her, she was excited about the improvements that Agatha had made academically. In just a few years she would be eligible for college. But most importantly, she had changed ever since the trip to the memorial site where her father was buried. The visit had unveiled a new Agatha and she seemed to dance in an aura of happiness. Nancy believed that her daughter had at last accepted the loss of her father.

Patrick had the carriage ready and they waited for Agatha, Nancy and Gertrude.

"The lieutenant will meet us at the harbour," Patrick said as he went into the house to fetch the luggage. Agatha came out with a neatly wrapped box and approached Venkat.

"I want to give this to you and my aunt Nagamah."

"What is it?" Venkat enquired.

"Let's go to your house."

Nagamah stood at the entrance.

"I have a gift in this box, and it must only be opened when your first baby is born," Agatha insisted.

Venkat gestured to his wife in a manner indicating that he knew nothing about it.

"Thank you. I will honour your wish," Nagamah promised.

Agatha then stepped up to her, held her hands and promised that she would see them again during the next holiday.

The ship bound for Southampton slowly eased out of the harbour and the passengers waved their farewells. On the pier, people stood silently and watched as it passed the entrance, rounded the headland and faced the open sea. Nancy, composed but saddened by the departure, started towards the carriage followed by the others. Patrick guided the horses away from the harbour and urged them into a trot. He pulled the brim of his hat lower, shielding his face from the rain. The lieutenant rode beside the carriage for a short distance and then peeled off towards the fort.

The months following Agatha's departure were a period of great attrition. The Anglo Boer War was intensifying, and thousands of British soldiers sailed into Durban. Lt Croydon was kept very busy coordinating military tasks. Nancy was not pleased with the recent developments and feared that her husband could be called out to serve in the front lines. She knew she was being selfish – duty to the Crown superseded personal commitment, and should the lieutenant be called up, she would have no option but to endure an agonising wait for his return.

News from the front lines told of heavy losses suffered by the British. Reinforcements poured in and marched straight into the trenches.

Bloody battles raged between the British and the Boer forces. Some of the notable confrontations occurred at Mafeking, Kimberley, Johannesburg, Pretoria, Ladysmith and lesser-known areas in Natal. Hit and run 'guerrilla' tactics employed by the Boer commando devastated British garrisons.

The treaty ending the war ushered in a period of reconstruction and the consolidation of peace. It was June and the dryness of winter was closing in. It was also a period when industrialisation in Europe was drastically affecting the colony. Major inventions like the automobile were slowly replacing the horsedrawn carriages. Street lamps lit up many streets and electricallydriven trams were now a common sight. Durban was indeed gripped in a frenzy of progress.

Venkat and Nagamah were expecting their first child, thus creating much excitement as Patrick and Gertrude eagerly waited to become 'grandparents'. Some weeks before, Patrick had constructed a cot and was busy polishing it when Venkat visited him.

"You look nervous!" Patrick observed.

"I am very!"

"Why?"

"I don't know."

"You don't have to be. We are here and you have other friends as well," Gertrude reassured him.

"I'm thankful to have you; you are my family," Madras replied with sincerity.

The day was Monday, 13 June. In the dullness of winter, from behind the fallen trees, Nancy plucked a beautiful rose, a rare find. She knocked on the front door and waited. Nagamah opened the door and invited her in. Nancy gave her the rose.

"Your baby is due soon …"

"Yes, very soon," Nagamah said as she positioned herself on a chair.

"Are you afraid?"

"Yes, a little… a lot," she whispered and winced. Nancy jumped from her chair and led Nagamah to the sofa.

"Are your contractions beginning?" Nancy asked, concerned.

"I… think so," she winced again.

Nancy rushed out and shouted to Gertrude to help her.

"The baby is coming," she shouted excitedly to Gertrude, who reached into a drawer, grabbed fresh towels and raced into the kitchen.

"We need lots of hot water, quickly," Gertrude took charge.

Nancy tucked the towels under her arm and carried a kettle filled with hot water. Gertrude marched ahead with a baby blanket and two empty pots.

"We will help you," Nancy comforted Nagamah.

Gertrude filled the pots, placed them on the stove, dropped coal oil on the wood and blew onto the tiny flame.

They guided the expectant mother to the bed, adding more pillows against the headboard. Gertrude wiped Nagamah's forehead as she leaned back onto them. Wide-eyed, Nancy dabbed the perspiration from her own face and neck.

On seeing the feverish activity, Patrick added to the excitement.

"Venkat is at work," Nancy told Patrick.

"I will get him."

Patrick rode to the fort and broke the news to Venkat, who stood rooted for a few seconds, then turned on his heels and raced to the wagon.

"Have you told them that you are leaving?"

"Oh, no," Venkat replied, then he jumped off the wagon and raced into the office. He raced back again, climbed onto the wagon and hurriedly urged the horses on, to the amusement of a smiling Patrick. Venkat and Patrick spent two worried hours outside the house, pacing and engaging in idle banter until Gertrude, the midwife, ably assisted by Nancy, raised a cry from the new-born baby.

Gertrude wrapped the baby in a white towel and handed her to an exhausted, but proud mother. Nagamah, who sat propped up against the headboard, ran a hand gently over the wrinkled little forehead.

"Can her father and uncle see her now?" she asked.

"You two can go in now," Gertrude told Venkat and Patrick, as she stepped out to dump the soiled towels into a pit, to be incinerated later. They tiptoed into the room and approached the bed, took a quick peep and left the room. Mother and daughter were asleep.

"She's tiny," Venkat whispered as he left the house.

"Most babies are small, I think."

"Gertrude, I will go home and make some soup for Nagamah to drink when she wakes up."

"Thanks, madam," Gertrude said.

The two men spent the next few hours as if hitched together, making frequent trips to the main house to collect soup, a shawl and a blanket or return items borrowed.

It was late afternoon when Singaram and a few friends arrived. Singaram referred to an astrological chart. "We will call her 'Annamah'. She will be a mother to many, and to not only her own children."

The next morning Venkat carried the baby tucked in a blanket and visited Patrick. "You carry the hopes and dreams of many, my baby."

Annamah yawned, her tiny fingers folding as a proud father caressed her palm, now fully aware of what married life truly was about.

"She's so small, but she's the future of our country."

"Yes, she is," Gertrude agreed with Patrick.

Stepping back into the house, Venkat passed the baby to his wife who pointed to the box that had been sitting on the table. Venkat unwrapped the covering, opened the box and placed the stone bird on the table. He read the attached note:

"I am who I am, for the stars that shone in the brightest of days
That dulled the moon and the sun, soon to be lost
Not forever I pray, as the steps I took and that I take
I shall cherish the touch, the heart, the love, blossoms of friendship
As I meander the seasons of life, I will recall
The stars that shone in the brightest of days."

—Agatha

CHAPTER 18

Threat of War

Years later, war loomed large in Europe, and the world would be brought together to fight on a scale unprecedented in its history. Millions would lose their lives and millions more would be maimed by it. It was inevitable, an indication of man's brutal lust for power and dominance.

Lt Croydon was appointed to head a reconnaissance unit based in Kings Lynn, Norfolk. He accepted the posting; the experience he gained in the Zulu wars and the training he had received as a cadet at Sandhurst stood him in good stead. The melee caused by his appointment and the speed with which the arrangements were made, left very little time for the close-knit household to feel the effects of the impending separation.

Life changed even for Venkat and Patrick. They stood for one last time on the pier and watched the ship bound for Southampton blow her horn as she pulled away. Onboard were members of their family: Lt Croydon, his wife Nancy and their children Frederick and Daphne. They waved until the ship sailed beyond the warehouses and out into the open ocean.

Patrick, Venkat and Gertrude also had an ocean to cross. The sudden departure of the Croydons was a cavity not easy to fill. Theirs had been a friendship that crossed cultures and personal beliefs. Many would have seen it as taboo at that time, yet it thrived in that new world which was otherwise filled with racial dislike, opportunism and exploitation. Although it might have been regarded as unimportant by some, it proved that despite man's bigotry, there would be occasions when independent actions could subdue cynical rhetoric.

A day before they shipped out, when the dust settled and as the moon rose above the calm ocean, memories of the past had flooded in. Nancy held Gertrude close and sobbed. Patrick, Venkat and the lieutenant sat silently on the patio.

"I cannot express my feelings, my dear friends, so I don't know where and how to start, but you know in your hearts how much I will miss you all," the lieutenant choked, turning away, concealing his emotions.

"We shall forever remember the time we shared," Patrick spoke as they stood and embraced. Venkat, not wanting to show his true emotions, slipped out and spent a few minutes alone. Coming back to the patio, he sat next to the lieutenant and thanked him for being an employer, friend and mentor.

"The main house had been sold. The contents are for you to share. A title of ownership for your houses shall be finalised by the barrister I've appointed," the lieutenant confirmed.

"To say farewell to you and the memsahib is far more saddening than anything I ever expected," Venkat addressed the lieutenant.

"Is the move permanent?" Patrick questioned.

"For a soldier, life in a brutal war is short, and my coming back is not certain. We shall return if I'm spared. It will also be better for Nancy to be close to Agatha than to be thousands of miles away from her in these uncertain times."

The next morning, as the sun broke, members of the Croydon household sat for the last time as a family. A solemn breakfast ensued, emotions swayed as if on a pendulum.

Venkat approached Nancy, dismayed because the moment of parting was at hand. "Memsahib, I cannot find words to describe my feelings. You were responsible for all that is good in my family. Our stories will be told and retold as a memory of a shared life. I have learnt new lessons and your understanding of my culture far exceeds my own. Memsahib, you and Victoria taught me much more about India than I knew. The stories you told me hold lessons that no books will impart. You have overcome difficulties just as we did. Remember, always that the power of god will keep you protected."

"Venkat, I cannot say goodbye to those I love so very much. I will live my life knowing that you have made all our lives here better. You were not only my servant but a friend when I needed one the most."

"Talking to wise and knowledgeable people has been a revelation of the depth of your culture," Nancy commented.

"Memsahib, you undertook journeys, firstly to discover your emotional and physical strengths and to find closure to a tragic occurrence. Secondly, to India to uncover the power of faith and furthermore to understand its people, their traditions and religious belief systems. The anecdotes of both trips will be told and retold as an inspiration to others. Let us not bury the lessons learnt."

"Thank you, Madras."

"You are special and, memsahib, I have one last favour to request of you?"

"Madras, I shall not say no to anything you request, at this moment."

Venkat handed her a box.

"I make a promise that Victoria receives your gift."

The stone bird once again took flight.

This union fostered in the worst of times was on the brink of taking a turn. The friendship of master and servants, with an understanding of each other's commitment, expectations and desires, would change by midday. Yet there remained in each one of them a hope that when the smoke of the guns had cleared, and men had accepted the finality of defeat – when peace ruled supreme – there would be a chance that they could be reunited. Until then, the inevitable separation was another twist in the journey of life.

Some years later, in a modest home in the London suburb of Walworth, Agatha Moorcroft lit a candle and stood next to the mantelpiece, praying for an end to the war. In the next room, Nancy sang a lullaby to her grandson, James Patrick Maddy Moorcroft.

A South African Legacy

Life for Indian communities between 1920 and the 1960s was an enigma. Mass forced removal and resettlement, deceptive agreements, limited educational infrastructure, restrictive job opportunities and suppressive laws – even for indigenous locals – were the catalyst that would unite the very people separated by the ethnic uprising of 1949.

In the 1940s, the Pegging Acts and the Asiatic Land Tenure and Indian Representation Act, 1946 were passed. These acts gave the government the right to remove and destroy shacks and small self-made shelters, with the reputed intention of improving sanitary conditions. It was a tragic event that took years for those affected by its ferocity, to heal.

The Indians and Africans were separated and each projected as dangerous. At the same time, they were re-settled within viewing distance of each other, so that they could constantly be reminded of the strange and different ways both lived. The appointment of an Indian overseer over African mill hands, and the use of African police to suppress Indian strikers, were all calculated to keep the two peoples violently divided. The stereotypes were fabricated, in the first instance, for the peace of mind of the whites themselves, to relieve them of Christian guilt for the humanity they degraded and the inhumanity they perpetuated.

A growing neighbourliness was put to the test when African neighbours shielded Indians during the violence of 1949. In that time Venkat would lose his dear friend Patrick Cele, but it also brought together the two families who would go on to live the legacy dreamt by two men who withstood the realities of a changing world.

It was a time of racial discord. Mind-sets changed, some in delight, others forced by the rules that prevailed. Bonds nurtured over time strained and snapped. Emotions ran high and people knelt in prayer for an insight into the tragic situation where equality of the human soul suddenly vanished. In its place, the supremacy of one race was enshrined in law. Governance carried out by ruthless instruments separated communities, friends, relations and neighbours, giving credence to their firm belief. However, the greatest threat to social normality was the tentacles of racial intolerance that reached deep down into the human spirit, denying freedom of choice, fundamental for self-realisation.

Apartheid was born, and the roots run deep.

Reflections on a Golden pond

"I stood next to the pond as the last crimson glow of the setting sun fell on the water. As I knelt and dipped the bucket into the pond, the golden surface broke into small ripples, and a long shadow fell next to mine. I could not get up, and in that few moments, I relived the life I shared with your grandmother. She stood next to me, and when I stretched my hand to touch the shadow, she left me. I pulled the bucket out of the water, walked over to her grave and washed the headstone. The next day was the anniversary of the last day we shared together. At the last moment, it was as if the winds had blown away the clouds and the sun shone once more, as did her smile. She was buried in a place she loved, but for me, she still lives in my heart."

We sat in the living room, I think for the last time, mesmerised and saddened as our grandfather, Venkat Konar, recalled his past.

This sudden change in the way he spoke made me uneasy as his usual humour faded into the background. Although we knew he harboured a deep sense of loss, he rarely displayed his feelings. That vacuum was filled by the love his children and grandchildren blessed him with. My grandfather had an inimitable ability to sense our thoughts.

"Yes, my children love me, and they have shown me how much they miss their mother. She loved the fleeting cherry blossom." He pulled on his pipe as he pointed to two frames.

Two hand-painted frames hung on the living room wall. One had two red roses and the other had three – two red and one yellow – both with the inscription: 'What is a home without a mother?'.

Just below one of the frames, on a wooden bookcase, a snow globe reflected the light of the lamp. Within the glass ball, Santa Clause in a golden sleigh was ascending into the skies above Buckingham Palace.

January 1949 - Mariannhill Village, twenty miles west of Durban - during the Zulu uprising in Durban.

A mother stood steadfast at one end of a long passage. Hiding behind her were her five very young daughters. At the entrance a gang of barbaric men stood menacingly, armed with crude homemade weapons. A brick flew across the passage, striking her on the side of her forehead. Bleeding, she stood firm. In her arms was her threemonthold son. She cried and begged for mercy; her daughters screamed in fear. Her son slept, oblivious to the danger. He was my brother.

Gunshots rang out nearby and the men scrambled out of the house. My mother knelt on the wooden floor and prayed. They were safe.

Further down the road, a savage attack on a family was taking place. A young mother lay on the ground, her head split open by an already bloodcovered machete. The man stood over her. His colleagues grabbed her sevenyear-old daughter and fled into the bushes and her younger daughter knelt next to her mother and hugged her, crying, trying to wake her up. The little four-yearold girl wiped her tears, then moved her mother's bloodsoaked hair from her face and kissed her. Getting up, she wobbled into the house.

Unfortunately, both Africans and Indians were not to be blamed for the two days of carnage. The issue was that the great war just ended a few years earlier. The war had consumed both economic and financial resources, and the aftermath was the recession that followed, where the cost of consumer goods escalated five times that of pre-war prices. Indians, being in the forefront of trading with the African population, were now seen as the exploiters. The life for Africans at that time was inhumane, living under prohibitive laws engulfed by poverty and neglect.

Even at the height of the brutality, the police stood transfixed at the brutality of the attack, yet they did not intervene, and many white men with darkened faces joined in the mayhem. The question remained for many years whether it was a deliberate action by police not to protect the Indians, allowing women and girls to be raped and then butchered. Due to the sudden surge of the attack, the menfolk were trapped in the city, leaving their families vulnerable to face the savagery. When calm was restored, both sides and even whites sustained casualties. For their part, our ancestors, scattered by the surprise attack, re-grouped, although being severely outnumbered, they retaliated.

When the barbaric packs fanned out, wave after wave, from the epicentre, opportunistic elements, transported by vehicles owned by both international and local businesses, fuelled the spread of the violence. The animosity that bubbled in a seething cauldron, which was subdued for decades, suddenly erupted, firstly to vent their pent-up fury and secondly to loot businesses. Joining the Africans was opportunistic as mob violence provided a shield from possible recognition. Darkened faces, arms and legs, dressed alike, they carried out horrific destruction of businesses and brutal assault on Indians, sparing not even women and children.

As in the words of my grandfather, Venkat Konar, "They may have washed off the blackness, but the blackness of their heart shall be indelible. However, there are many who would help us restore peace."

Only in the face of pressure from outside countries did the army and the police act. Even then, the police themselves, in safety camps molested the females. Later, it came to light that many Zulu households protected their Indian neighbours, and these were the seeds that united the two groups in later years.

August or September 1969, 14:45, on a train from Durban Central to Cato Ridge

Sitting opposite us on the train was a youngish woman, her head covered with a flowerpatterned hood. Her face had three scars of tiny vertical cuts, about two inches long and about an inch apart on each side of her face, the type which traditional Zulus mark their faces and arms with. She sat for a while, examining my fellow students munching on snacks that my mother bought. She then reached out and held my mother's hand.

"I miss being who I really am," she said, tears aplenty.

The lady covered her eyes with her hands and then wiped her hand across her face, as if to wash away the marks that scarred her face with her tears.

My mother took her hands, eyes wet.

She told us about her abduction and the death of her mother in January 1949. We went to another compartment to leave her alone with my mother.

"For twenty years of my life, my mind was imprisoned in a body that succumbed to the will of those who changed my life. I remember very little, only that I couldn't run away because my wrists and legs were bound with wire. When I was older, I was embarrassed to leave as I was already tainted and marked. So, I chose to stay and await the end of my life."

"We heard about the tragic story and that your brother and other men from the village searched far and wide for you. Many feared the worst. By god's grace, you have survived."

"I think my name was Kasturi before they gave me another name."

"Maybe someday I will be free to be who I really am," were her last words as we jumped off the train.

The real reason for the anarchy that swept Durban and surrounding towns and villages shall forever be hidden by those who perpetrated the onslaught. The fury of the 1949 riots, where one group aimed to decimate another, was not an act thought and carried out by bands of renegades, but rather a plan hatched many decades before, and at last stoked by racial dislike of those who governed. It may have created a chasm between the Indians and Zulus, but in the ensuing years, a bond grew between them to ensure that both were free of the oppression of apartheid.

King Edward V111 Hospital - Durban

I knelt beside my mother and held her hand as she slept, peaceful and silent, strands of moist grey hair spread across the pillow. Doctor Yanandan Perumal told me she was resting, and I should come back the next day. I gently placed her hand by her side and pulled the sheet over it, kissed her and walked away. Three years earlier, I had cradled my father's head in one arm as he drank water from a glass. I kissed his forehead, and as his head touched the pillow, I wiped away tears that rolled down his face and told him that we loved him. He looked at me for a few moments, his eyes red and tearful, and reaching out, he touched my face. A thousand thoughts raced through my mind. He closed his eyes and fell asleep, seemingly content.

As I stepped out through the double doors of the King Edward VIII Hospital in Durban, I realised that I had not told my mother that we loved her. I turned around to go back in, but the guard refused to let me. He stood there deaf to my pleas, bound by rules, with a total lack of independent thought or empathy. It was early autumn and the rainy season was just about to end, yet a torrent lasted most of the night. Drenched, I sat in my car and prayed.

Parents are god-like, carrying the weight of their responsibilities, unwavering in their tasks. Deep in their private worlds, they have their own dreams, wishes and difficulties, but we may know little of them. Imbued with a mysterious ability to overcome adversity, to us, they are beacons of light amidst the ebb and flow of life's challenges.

My mother passed away that night, and in her passing, our last pillar – a bastion against the fragilities of our existence – vanished forever. We were now adrift, cast upon an ocean, reliant on nature's plan to steer us through the days that lay ahead.

The priest chanted hymns from the scriptures, closed the book and said, "We are here today to say our goodbyes to Annamah, our mother, our sister and a divine soul. We will cherish her in our memories, bless her in our prayers and must live as she expects us to live."

In our search for the gifts of life, we need to look no further than our parents. In them we find the love that has nurtured us into who we are. Measure them by their commitment and not by the frailties of material endowments. When the sun sets, bless them and demonstrate your feelings or else it could be too late, for life itself is just a fleeting moment.

To Our Parents

There are no words that I can put together to portray the gratitude I have for our parents. At a time when life swayed between turmoil and tranquillity in a land of torment and trepidation, they stood firm. I pray that I will once more bow, touch their feet and wipe away the tears of a joyous reunion.

"Light up, then, the lamp of faith in your heart…
It will lead you safely through the mists of doubt and the black darkness of despair; along the narrow, thorny ways of sickness and sorrow and over treacherous places of temptation and uncertainty."

– *James Allen*

DORASAMY MOODLEY: SON OF MURUGAPPA NAIK MOODLEY, ROSEHILL ESTATES

ANNAMAH MOODLEY: DAUGHTER OF VENKAT KONAR, NESSFIELD MANOR

When generations pass on, they leave behind a torch that others may carry with pride. In the flame burn a legacy of commitment, dedication and the strength of spirituality. As time marches on, lives are moulded and shaped by a new order where traditions, lifestyles and spirituality swing on a pendulum, but let us preserve the memories of those who etched the tapestry of our lives.

My indebtedness goes out to my sisters Logie, Ambigay, Dolly, Nalini and Kogie; and brothers Poobalan and Ganasen for their commitment and dedication to family and the values that preserve cultural and religious practices.

Last, but no means a small measure, my sincere gratitude to my Cousin, Dr Sivapragasen Pillay and to my friend T.S. Vandayar.

Other Details

- Most of Venkat Konar's descendants reside in and around Durban and Johannesburg. Many thirdgeneration descendants now reside in the USA, Canada, Great Britain, Australia and New Zealand.
- Patrick Cele's descendants live in small towns, Kwa Ndenghezi, Dassenhoek, about twenty miles west of Durban.
- Guru Sundrum and Mrs Thulasingam returned to India and settled in Tangore.
- Lt Croydon survived WW1 and visited South Africa in the late 1930s.
- Nancy Croydon visited India just before Independence to visit relatives.
- Agatha Moorcroft established shelters for children affected by WW1.

- Chandrakanth Patel spent a few years in India, in Surat, and later moved with his family to settle in Durban, relocating to Johannesburg. Two of his grandchildren (Mihir and Chetan) live in Johannesburg.
- Mrs Sushila Ogilvy and her husband returned to England after WW1. Victoria, Jasper and Mala Anne reunited.
- Victoria Payton returned to India after completing her studies and worked tirelessly to achieve her dreams of a free motherland. She remained single. Lt Payton joined her a few years later and settled in Uhagamadalam (Ooty), a beautiful hill station located in the Madras Presidency.

- The emphasis in Britain was placed on writing about post-independence nationalist myth, and the contributions by Indians slipped by the wayside. In its contributions to world order and chaos that reined during the world wars, India in her fight to preserve her own sovereignty and of other nations, sent 1.3 million and 2.3 million soldiers, respectively, on foreign campaigns in all theatres of WW1 and WW2.
- 163,187 soldiers perished in both wars, not including the thousands who lost their lives in other support services. “Indian soldiers were the bravest of the brave. It was an honour to command them,” says Major Tom Conway (retd), 98, one of the last surviving British officers who had commanded Indian soldiers.
- Field Marshal Claude Auchinleck, Commander-in-Chief of the British Indian Army from 1942, asserted that the British “Couldn’t have come through both wars if they hadn’t had the Indian Army”.
- Yet, back home, at the height of the war, in India, millions were dying of famine and associated diseases. Rations were re-directed to soldiers in Europe and the Pacific by ‘Sir’ Winston Churchill. His resentment of Indians was made public, even by a quote: “The famine was their own fault for breeding like rabbits.”
- Business Today – New Delhi November 19, 2018. It has been calculated that an equivalent of $45 trillion dollars was siphoned by Britain during 173 years between 1765 and 1938. Colonialism may have enriched, even the Royal Family under whose banner exploitation was deemed legal.

References

1. Roman Trade with India – Wikipedia (Google)
2. Girmit, History, Memory, Brig. V. Lal
3. Girmit, History, Memory, Brig. V. Lal (Refers – Tinker)
4. KZN History – Google
5. Ancestry24 – Learning Centre – Indian Indentured Migrants.
6. Joseph Baynes Pioneer, RO Pears – Shutter & Shooter 1983
7. History – Mankind and His Story, Odhams Press Ltd (London), p.261
8. The Scottish Soldier and Empire 1854–1902, Edward M Spears, Edinburgh University Press 2006, ISBN 10–7486–2354, p.41
9. Zulu War, Ian Knight, Osprey 2004
10. Fields of Battle, Peter Doyle, Matthew R Bennet, Kluwer Academic Publications 2002, ISBN 1–4020–0433–8
11. History of the Zulu Wars and its Origin, FE Colenso – London
12. Battle of Isandlwana – Wikipedia
13. The Struggle to be South African – The O'Malley Archives
14. Madushree Mukerjee's – Churchill's Secret War: The British Empire and the Ravaging of India During World War II – Ingram Publishers US ISBN 0465024815 ISBN13 9780465024810
15. The historian Robert Shell has estimated that between 1652 and 1808, when the slave trade was abolished, an estimated total 63 000 slaves were imported to the Cape, from the African continent (26.4%), Indian sub-continent (25.9%), Madagascar (25.1%) and Indonesia (22.7%). Thus, the Cape Malay ancestry is a combination of African and Asian descent.

-END-

CPSIA information can be obtained
at www.ICGtesting.com
Printed in the USA
LVHW031624260821
696192LV00004B/45

9 781648 057281